THE TWO DAYS OF DARKNESS

CONNOR BOYACK

ILLUSTRATIONS BY ELIJAH STANFIELD

Copyright © 2023 The Tuttle Twins Holding Co.

All rights reserved. No part of this publication may be reproduced, distributed or transmitted in any form or by any means, including photocopying, recording, or other electronic or mechanical methods, without the prior written permission of the publisher.

Libertas Press
2183 W Main Street, A102
Lehi, UT 84043

The Tuttle Twins and the Days of Darkness

Edited by Chris Jones

ISBN-13 979-8-88688-015-1 (paperback)

10 9 8 7 6 5 4 3 2

For bulk orders, send inquires to info@libertas.org.

The Tuttle twins, Ethan and Emily, sat at their kitchen table and tried to decide how worried they should be.

The power had gone out before. This wasn't something new to them. But it had never gone out over the whole city. And it had never gone out when there was no rain, no hail, no snow, not even a breath of wind. At 3:17 p.m. Central Standard Time on June 16, the power simply... stopped.

"Are you hungry?" Ethan asked.

Emily nodded. "A little."

The truth was, she should have been ravenous. It was getting close to 6:30 and she hadn't had anything to eat since lunch. But it was hard to muster an appetite under the abnormal circumstances.

"We can have cereal," Ethan said, after realizing for the second time that afternoon that they had no stove or microwave to cook a dinner with. "That's the easiest, anyway. And there's enough milk for both of us." He rummaged in the cabinet and came up with two bags of bulk cereal. "Loopy Fruit or Shredded Wheat?"

Emily shrugged. "Whichever there is more of. I'll probably eat a few bowls."

"That would be the Shredded Wheat."

Ethan got a pair of bowls from the cupboard, two spoons from the drawer, and the bag of cereal, and set them on the kitchen table by the flashlights they had prepared for the night... just in case the power issue wasn't resolved soon. Then he went back for the milk. He opened the fridge and the light did not come on.

"Can't get used to that," he said. The light had always come on. It was one of those things, like the rising of the sun or the Spoonerville Tigers making the playoffs. You could always count on it. The darkness of the open fridge wasn't just strange, but eerie... spooky, even. But not as spooky as the temperature of the milk.

"I don't think this milk will last much longer. It's barely cool," Ethan added, unscrewing the cap from the milk and setting it on the table. Emily sat there with her hands folded, fingers laced together, and tried to ignore the sinking feeling in the pit of her stomach. But food was food. "You don't eat because you're hungry, you eat to keep from getting hungry," Dad always said, so after a moment, Emily picked up a spoon and shoveled some cereal into her mouth. Even with the less than cold milk, it worked to a certain extent—at least her nerves ratcheted down. Carbs make calm.

Despite the circumstances inside the house, the weather outside was beautiful, a light breeze under a few wispy clouds, the sky a deepening navy blue. Birds flitted back and forth from tree to tree, chirping and squabbling over bits of fruit and the odd stray bug. The Tuttles' bees did their droning and making of honey. It all looked perfectly peaceful. Normal. Just another summer evening, filled with comfortable smells and sounds wafting in through the screen of the open sliding door that overlooked the backyard. Emily was sure that she should be as content as a cat with cream.

But.

What possible appeal was Portland, Oregon when Spoonerville was at its most beautiful? Emily wondered. Nonetheless, her parents had gone, though they'd be back soon, just another day. The twins had been left alone before and were used to it—kind of liked it, even. It was nice to be a little bit more independent. There was a little piece of Emily that loved the respect and confidence their parents showed by trusting them to take care of themselves for a whole week.

That was when everything was normal. Like now, Emily told herself. This is normal. The power's gone out before. It's only going to be a few hours, and then the power will come back on, and we will remember why we love having electricity.

But still, it would have been better had Mom and Dad been out in the garden instead of eating wild marionberries next to the Oregon freeway (that was the text message report they received earlier that day) or a farmer's market with free honey samples (that was three that afternoon, right before power cut out). Now... nothing. No texts came through. There wasn't any evidence they were sending, either. It didn't stop Ethan from tapping his screen every thirty seconds, checking to see if *Hey, Dad, the power went out all over the city. Kinda freaky.* had finally gone out over the cell network. It had not. The phone showed zero bars.

And that was *not* normal.

Ethan ate his cereal and shoved the thought away. "What do you want to do the rest of the evening?" he said between bites.

"Read a book, maybe. Go for a walk?"

"I thought we might ride our bikes a bit. It's a great night."

"Okay. I do want to read some, though. I'm at the critical point in my book."

Ethan polished off the last crumbs in his bowl and went to swish it out in the sink. He pulled up the lever to the faucet, and water gushed out, then stuttered, then slowed to a trickle.

"What on earth?" he fretted. "Everything's gone wonky. I'll be glad when the power comes back on and everything goes back to normal."

They rode out, down the driveway, onto the blacktop, and up the street in the direction of the high ground in Spoonerville. They didn't think much of it—there were hardly any roads left in town they hadn't ridden over dozens of times. Immediately, though, there were differences. People were out in front of nearly every house, with clusters of people chatting or standing around, but all of them—*all* of them—were holding their phones out in front of them as if doing so would call up a signal.

"Nobody has service," Emily said.

"Just like us. How can all the cell towers be down at the same time?" Ethan said, crooking his arm for a right turn.

Last summer, a huge semi-trailer had gone out of control and slammed into a cell tower on the outskirts of town. Two or three different cell carriers lost their signal that day, and it was a week before it had been restored to normal. But someone always had service. Apparently, not today.

Their tires bit into the road as they stood up to pump themselves up the hill. To Ethan it looked as if the traffic was less than it should have been. Admittedly, he didn't know what normal traffic looked like at 7 p.m. on a weekday. But what he did know was that no one was smiling. The faces in the cars looked out with apprehension.

"They're all scared," Emily said, noticing the same thing.

One man drove distractedly, fiddling with his radio. His windows were down. A thin hiss blared from his speakers. He punched a button. Hiss. Another. Hiss. Finally, he pulled over to the side of the road, his face creased with worry. Over and over, he punched buttons on the dash, and over and over, he got nothing but static.

"The radio stations?" Emily worried, and now there was an edge to her voice.

"Something is wrong with his radio," Ethan said, and they swept on by.

The coming night was beautiful, as pretty as an early summer evening could be. It was particularly quiet, and a cooling breeze swept gently over them. Instead of calming them, the peace of the evening worked against the reality of the power outage, as if they were seeing double or hearing a tune played off-key. They pumped their pedals a little faster and roared up the hill to the church by the baseball field.

To the right of the church was a path that led into a little wilderness, a place they'd hiked many times. The path was smooth enough that they could ride for a ways, though they had to slow down. There in the woods was abnormally quiet too. It was as if the birds themselves were holding their breath.

A few hundred yards down the trail, a steep rocky section stopped them from riding any further, but as they'd hiked it dozens of times, it posed no obstacle. They left their bikes in the brush and ran, first jogging upward, then in an all-out sprint as the terrain leveled at the top, heading for a place that would show them that everything was going to be okay.

Emily reached the spot first and stopped dead.

Ethan arrived a moment later and stood as still as his twin.

The lookout was a certain point where the path took a sharp turn to the right and ran along the crest of a large hill overlooking the river below. It gave one of the best views of Spoonerville, and across the river, the city of Malantown, laid out almost like a map. Pretty enough during the day, it was also spectacular at night, when the dock lights reflected off the water and the grid of the town illuminated in streetlights.

But that wouldn't be the case tonight. Not a single streetlight or building had illuminated from the cities on either side of the river, and it was almost 8 p.m.. There was still a glow from the pink and orange sky, but the sun had finally tucked behind the distant hills. The only signs of a living civilization were the headlights of the cars as they aimlessly and cautiously ran back and forth along the streets, searching for the same thing as the twins—hope.

"Well," Ethan said, after what seemed an age, "looks like the power is out over there, too."

"We'd better get down from here," Emily gasped, realizing the folly of their adventure through the woods. "We won't have any way to light our way home."

Above them, the stars began to come out, unconcerned and unaware. By the time they made it to the church, it was pitch black. They had made it out of the woods just in time.

It was a slow ride back home in the dark. Almost everyone had retreated to their homes, which would be completely unremarkable, except that none of those homes had lights. They could, however, see flashlight

beams going back and forth, crisscrossing over the walls through the windows. Here and there, a candle flame flickered within the deep recesses of the houses' interiors. And always, always, the deep and unnerving quiet. The twins didn't talk much, leaving the sounds of their bike chains and rolling rubber tires as sound effects fitting for a horror film.

That is, until they reached their own street. Here, somewhat against the rising anxiety and alarm, a chorus of noise hit them like a wall. A flock of gas engines howled out their shuddery song from behind half a dozen houses on their street. Generators. Apparently, their neighborhood class on emergency preparedness had a significant impact.

The noise coaxed a smile out of Emily. "I like the quiet," she said, "but it's kind of nice to hear the noise of civilization."

"I never realized how noisy civilization was until it all went silent," Ethan said. But he was smiling too. On this street, some lights glowed in the houses. Not many; no one wanted to waste their precious generator power on lights. Instead, they saw the soft blue glow of computer screens and even the flickering scenes of DVD players. There was still no internet. Their cell phones still had no service. But it was a little bit of normalcy, and it helped to settle their stomachs.

"We have a generator, too," Ethan said. "We could fire it up if you wanted."

Emily thought for a moment, pedaling slowly down the street. "I don't think so," she finally said. "My phone still has a decent amount of battery, in case Mom and Dad call, and without the internet, I don't really want to use my computer much tonight, anyway. Maybe we should just go to bed."

It sounded like a good idea.

But as they passed Fred's house, he came strolling out to the street. They braked to a stop in front of him. He flashed his characteristic bright smile, which seemed to take on even greater wattage in the darker-than-normal night.

"You two go up to the lookout?" he said.

Ethan nodded. "No lights. Malantown is out, too."

"It's not just Spoonerville and Malantown. I just got off the ham radio with a guy I know in Pittsburgh, and their power is out, too. He has contacts all over the East Coast, and he hasn't come upon anyone yet that still has regular power. Apparently, the grid in Raleigh is still partly functional, but they're having rolling brownouts and he says his contact there doesn't expect the lights to stay on after tonight."

Emily looked up. The stars were plentiful—more than she could ever remember seeing. Even the broad band of the Milky Way showed up in the still summer air. "I don't see the Northern Lights," she said. "If this was a solar flare or a coronal mass ejection we'd be seeing them, wouldn't we?"

The Tuttle Twins and the Days of Darkness

"Ah, you've been studying astronomy. We're pretty far south to see solar events like that," Fred said, "though maybe we would in an extreme case. But I get the feeling that's not what this is."

"It's definitely not an attack from an electromagnetic pulse weapon," Ethan said. "Cars are still working, and your radio, and the generators, and our phones." He held his phone up. It had 26% battery left. There was still no service. "Those would all have been knocked out by an EMP weapon. So this has to be something else."

"Maybe it's just a... drill?" Emily said with hope—but not belief—in her voice.

Fred grinned but shook his head decidedly. "Not that, no. And I think Ethan's right about the EMP. This doesn't have those signs. There are other things that could do it, but I don't know anyone who's sure about what's happening."

Ethan hated to ask, but he couldn't help himself. "Our folks are out of town," he said. "They're in Oregon. Do you, by some chance, have any radio contacts in Oregon we could talk to?"

He had tried to keep the worry out of his voice, but he could still hear it, and he knew Fred heard it, too. But he didn't show it. He acted like it was the most natural request ever made.

"Could be," he said, stroking his chin. "I'd have to go through my contact log book. Tell you what. You two go home, get changed into whatever you're going to wear to bed and come on back. It might take us a while to raise someone, you know. We might want to stick together tonight, anyway."

Ethan smiled gratefully, and the twins said they'd be back in a minute.

When they were stowing their bikes in the shed, Emily said, "Having Fred next door is great, but talking to him only made me more sure of something."

"What's that?" Ethan said, sliding the shed door closed and clicking the padlock shut.

"This isn't just a power outage."

"Sure it is. What else could it be?"

Emily shrugged. "I don't know. But it's not what everyone is saying, it's what they're *not* saying that's freaking me out. Everyone acts like this will all be over tomorrow. But what if it's not?"

"It will be," Ethan said, and this time he kept his voice confident. "Besides, we're with Fred. What could happen?"

Continue on page 13.

Fred's ham radio setup was familiar to the twins from several sessions they'd had with their neighbor, talking to people across the US and even in Europe and Australia. But that had been fun. This was… not fun. This was something serious. And as hard as Fred tried to keep the news from sounding terrible, the same bad-to-awful reports were coming in from everywhere. There wasn't any denying it. This blackout was far, far more than a downed power line.

"CQ, this is NX7JCS in Spoonerville. Can you read us? Over."

Ethan sat in a wooden chair to the right of the old oak table Fred used as a platform for his set. He and Emily sat hunched over, staring at the readouts of the radio, each with a set of headphones pressed to one ear. A push-button microphone in battleship gray stood in front of Fred. He hit the broad, flat transmit key again. "CQ, CQ, this is NX7JCS in Spoonerville. Who's out there?"

Static. Emily reached out and delicately twisted a large black button, moving the needle a fraction of an inch across a large number field. There was a garbled noise, and then a voice resolved itself.

"NX7JCS Spoonerville, this is AG3UUK Alpha Golf Three Ugly Ugly Kilo in Spokane come back."

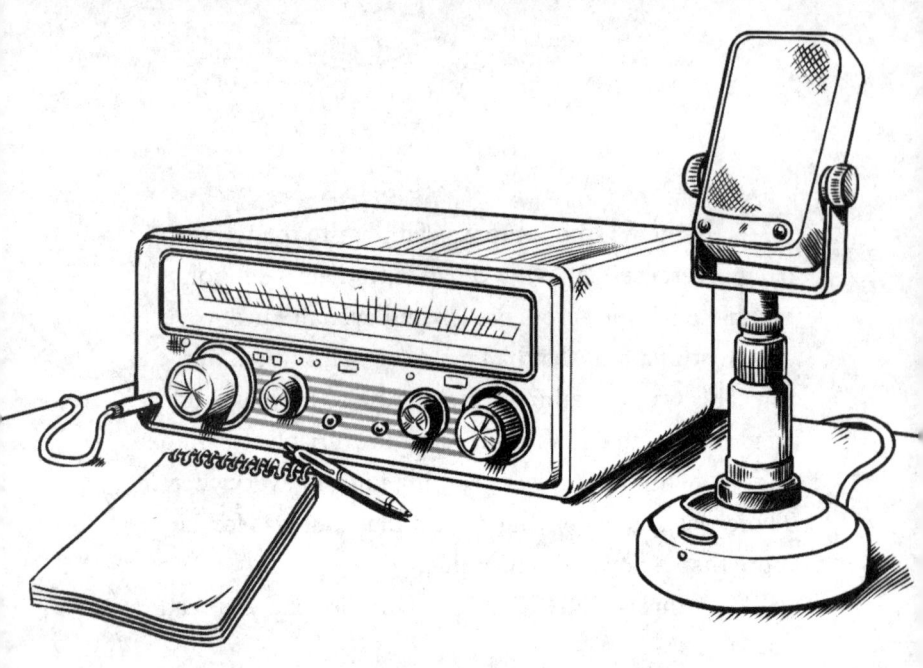

They all leaned in toward the set, although there was no reason to. It seemed like the right thing to do.

Fred said, "Spokane, we read you five by five. Looking for news about the situation there. Over."

The set crackled, and the voice, a young male by the sound of it, said, "Spokane power is out through the city. No response from the grid or from the cell network. Internet is down, too. What are things like in Spoonerville? Over."

"Pretty much the same. We're on generator power, with no grid lighting to any residence or business. We haven't had cell reception since… " Fred looked at Ethan.

"3:17 p.m.," he said.

"Since fifteen seventeen hours. Commercial radio is down, or uncommunicative. Over."

"That's about as bad as it could be, Spoonerville. I'm getting the same report from all over the Northwest and down into the Rockies. Denver, Kansas City, Bismarck, Helena, all of them are down. It sounds like the grid has failed right across the US. Over."

Tapping the send button, Fred asked, "Any word from anyone on how that happened? Was it a solar flare or a massive cascade failure? Over."

"Folks are speculating that it was an EMP that blew the regional stations in Seattle, which caused domino failures right across the Pacific Northwest, but if you're seeing the same thing there, that theory is out the window. I haven't spoken to anyone that knows anything. Over."

Fred wiped his forehead, giving his head a shake. "You're the first we've talked to. We're trying to reach Portland. Any info on them? Over."

"No info on Portland or Seattle. Sea-Tac airport is dark. There were a few airplanes landing at Spokane Airport a few hours ago but nothing since then. If you want, I can give you the band ID for Portland ham operators I know. Over."

Fred told the man that he would love to have those, and Emily took down the information. "Thank you,

Spokane, and God bless. We'll be back tomorrow night at twenty hundred hours if you're around. Over."

"I hope you and I have better news then, Spoonerville. Spokane out."

Emily was already dialing the frequency of the first Portland ham operator almost before the mic squeal had died from Spokane.

"I can't believe it," Ethan said. "They don't have power either. No one has power. How can that be? The power grid doesn't just fail by itself."

Emily's fiddling had returned nothing but static so far. She said, "We've known for years that our power infrastructure was weak and vulnerable to all sorts of shocks or attacks. It could be something like that."

"Not a good idea to speculate," Fred said. "We'll just get ourselves worked up and learn nothing. Go with the facts as we get them, and don't make up theories just because we don't know for sure what the truth is. It's okay not to know."

"CQ, CQ, this is NX7JCS Spoonerville for Portland, anyone in the Portland, Oregon area. Come back." Emily let go of the transmit button, and they waited. The static was light, the airwaves mostly clear, but no voice answered. Emily tried again. No response.

"That one isn't online," she said. "I'll try the next one."

But that one, too, gave no response, nor the third. Emily cycled back to the first one and tried again.

"It's not too surprising that we can't raise them," Fred said. "It's two hours earlier there. The sun is just going down, and there will be a lot of interference. Plus, if they're in a power outage as well, they might not have generator power."

"Speaking of which," Ethan said, "how long can you run your generator?"

"With no lights and just drawing power for cell phone charging and the radio here? A pretty long time. Days, at least. I have a large fuel drum in the back."

That sounded good to Ethan. Days of some power, some access to electronics, even if they didn't work very well or connect to the internet. He wondered how long their own generator would last and resolved to find out as soon as he got home.

He didn't remember falling asleep listening to Emily tirelessly repeat her CQs out into the black, but the next thing he knew, he was turning over on one of Fred's huge couches and finding a more comfortable position. A small lantern gave out a dim yellowish light at night. The radio was dark, and Emily's sleeping form was on the deep shag rug next to the couch. Ethan couldn't tell if she was asleep or not, but when he shifted position, she said, "Ethan? You awake?"

He grunted, trying to stay sleepy, but she wouldn't let him. "I can't sleep thinking about Mom and Dad."

Annoyed, Ethan said, "I'm sure they'll be fine. They're grown-ups. Have you ever seen anything that Mom or Dad couldn't handle? Much less together?"

"No, but this might not be like anything else. This isn't a Rotary fundraiser or a busted church window, you know."

"It might be," Ethan said, rolling over to try to get comfortable.

"It's not and you know it," Emily said. Ethan heard her shift, and her voice got clearer; she'd turned toward him. "We talked to that guy in Spokane. That's almost the whole country away. He had the same problems there that we do. If his power is out, and it's out in St. Louis and Denver and everywhere we talk to, that's not something simple. That's a major problem. It might be too much for them to solve."

Now Ethan was wide awake and not too happy about it. He sat up. "Look, we're okay. We have Fred and the house and plenty of food and we're going to be fine. Mom and Dad will be home in a couple of days and we'll sort everything out together."

He thought he'd settled the argument when Emily didn't say anything for a minute or two, but then he heard her breathing in and out really fast. She only did that when she was scared and about to cry.

"What, Em? What's wrong?"

"You don't get it, do you? They're not going to be home in a couple of days."

"What? You're crazy. Of course they will. Their flight lands the day after tomorrow at 4:07 in the afternoon."

"No, Ethan. There isn't going to be a flight. Remember what Spokane said? At first, there were airplanes coming in to the airport on a regular schedule, but for a while now there hadn't been anything. That's because without power the airport radar doesn't work."

"They have backup generators. They have to."

"I'm sure they do. But how long can those last? Airports take up a lot of power, with lighting and security and all sorts of things. They can't run those things off generators. It takes too much power. They have to ground the planes or they'll crash."

Ethan had not thought of this.

"I'm sure some flights will still happen," she said, "but there's no reason a passenger flight from Portland to Malantown will be one of them. If the grid is down everywhere, then the transportation network is down, too. Mom and Dad aren't getting on a flight unless the power comes back."

"They'll… I don't know, take a bus or something."

"You think they'll be able to find a bus? With everyone in the country trying to get someplace?"

It simply hadn't occurred to Ethan that his parents were stuck on the other end of the country. He tried to process this and couldn't. People went where they wanted to go. That was how things worked. If you couldn't fly, you drove. But there wouldn't be rental cars available. All the rentals required electronic verifications, and without power, those were impossible. For that matter, how did someone buy a plane ticket without power? All of that was handled on the internet. And there was no internet.

The more he thought about it, the less he liked it. *How did anything get done without power?*

"I see what you mean," she said after a while. "It might be a long time before Mom and Dad make it back here."

"We have to pray very, very hard for the power to come back on. If it doesn't, this is going to get very bad."

It was a long time before Ethan could get back to sleep that night.

Things were not better in the morning.

The power had not come back on during the night. It was warm, being early summer, so nobody was freezing to death because their heaters hadn't come on. It probably wouldn't get so hot today that people would die of heatstroke, but Emily started thinking about air conditioning when Fred's house smelled a little stuffy. Fred had opened the doors and windows to let the breeze blow through and pulled out a propane camp stove to cook breakfast in the driveway.

The twins thought they'd probably better go back home for some fresh clothes and a shower, but they'd come back for breakfast if Fred was cooking.

"Have to use this up," he said, carrying a carton of eggs and two packages of bacon. "It won't keep, and I can't run the generator to power a freezer and a fridge."

"Oh," Ethan said. "Yeah. We might need to make a contribution to the meal."

The power was out at home still, as it was everywhere, and Emily risked a quick look into the kitchen freezer. When she cracked the door open, drips fell onto the floor, although most things were still frozen fairly solid. The ice cream was softening. She couldn't face eating it. She held it up for Ethan, and he made a face.

"Not for breakfast," he said.

"Then probably not at all," she said. "It's not going to get any harder."

"Maybe after a shower," Ethan said, and then he thought about it. "Will we have hot water?"

"The water heater is gas-powered. It should work."

And it did, but again the water flow was sketchy, and the pipes burped. Ethan passed Emily as she headed for the bathroom. "I wouldn't take all day in there," he said. "Something's funny with the water."

They mentioned it to Fred when they came back over, bearing orange juice and a gallon of milk that still smelled borderline decent.

"Hmmm," he said, turning bacon. "Could be that the water treatment plants still have some power, but they won't have it for long. Our water supply is pumped uphill from the river. Without power those pumps won't work. We might not have water for long. You should go home and fill up every bucket you have. Fill the tubs, too."

"We have water storage," Emily said.

"How many gallons?"

"Two hundred, I think. We can check."

"That would be a good idea. In fact, after we have breakfast, we should make a list of everything we have and in what quantities. If it won't keep, we should cook it. And we need to know what resources we have."

Emily slumped into a lawn chair and looked up and down the street. People came and went like bees working a flowerbed, checking their cell phones, filling up generators, firing up their cars, and heading… somewhere.

"My phone battery is low," Ethan said, watching a car roll slowly by. "I'd use the backup charger, but I don't want to deplete it in case we need it later."

"So what are you going to do?" Emily said.

"I'm going to use the car."

"You don't have your license yet."

Ethan smiled at her. "I'm not going to drive it. I'm not even going to start it. I'm just going to tick the key over and engage the systems. The phone will charge off the car battery."

"And if it gets low, you can always start the car and recharge it. Smart."

But then something occurred to Ethan. "How much gas do we have?"

"In the car? I don't know. Half a tank, maybe."

"Do we have more gas somewhere?"

"Only the two-gallon jug that we use to refill the lawnmower. Why?"

Ethan pointed to Fred's generator. "Those use gas. Ours uses gas. What if we run out?"

"No gas, no generator; no generator, no power. I see where you're going." She got up. "Hey Fred! How are you fixed for gasoline?"

He scraped some eggs to the side of the grill and salted and peppered them. "I have a 50-gallon drum in the garage. That should be enough for a while."

"We're thinking we need to get our car filled up and probably all our spare gas cans, too. Dad was great at getting the preparedness taken care of, but that's one thing we don't have."

Fred scratched his balding head. "Good idea. Unless…"

"Unless what?" Ethan said, drifting over.

"Most gas stations run on electricity—the pumps are electric. No electricity, no credit card system, so most people won't be able to fill up unless they have cash," Fred said, his brow creasing.

"And will the pumps even work?" Emily said.

Fred shook his head. "I don't know. Probably not. They're all on the grid. You won't even be able to pay inside because they won't have power there, either." He scooped eggs onto a plate and handed it to Ethan. He didn't wait to start wolfing them down.

For a minute, they stood there, trying to think of options. "We do have some cash for emergencies," Emily said. "But that's no good if the pumps don't work."

Then Fred's face burst into a big smile. "Oh, I have an idea! Here, kids, pound this chow, then go get your containers and meet me back here in ten minutes. I have a solution to our problem."

The twins knew it was no good trying to get him to say any more, so they did as directed.

Fred was waiting in his driveway in their dad's old beat-up Ford, dubbed Esmerelda by the twins. "Get in," he said, jerking his thumb toward the truck's bed.

The twins hesitated. Riding in the back of the truck could be dangerous. They did it sometimes, but only when they were going to be delivering things and jumping in and out.

Fred saw their hesitation. "Don't worry. We're not going far, and I won't be going fast. Remember, there aren't any traffic lights, so we'll have to be careful. You can ride in the cab if you want, but it's a pretty day."

It was that—the sun was up and beating down warmly, and the air was filled with the scent of flowers. Emily ran her fingers along the rusted edge of the pickup bed and decided it was far too nice a day to be cooped up inside the cab. She tossed her two-gallon gas jug into the bed and climbed in after it.

Ethan was right behind her with his two gallon-sized cans.

"Is that all you have?" Fred said.

"Yeah," Ethan said. "We have other containers, but they're not good for carrying gas."

Fred opened the door of the pickup, jogged into the garage, and came back with a big 5-gallon jug. "Here." He tossed it into the bed, climbed into the driver's seat, and backed out into the street.

As they cruised slowly through Spoonerville, it became obvious that not everyone was as calm about things as they were. At one intersection there had been an accident, and a shouting match had broken out between the two drivers. No police had come.

"They probably don't know about it," Ethan said. "No one can call them."

Fred leaned his head out the window. "I can," he said and held up the handset of his citizen's band radio. Ethan heard him call in, and after a moment, a voice answered. There was some back and forth. Then Fred said, "They're coming, but I don't know how long it will take them to get here. They're very busy at the moment."

"Good thing you have that radio," Ethan said.

"I have it for just such an occasion," Fred said. "I was hoping it would just be another hobby. Now, though, this is about all that's working. Communication is so important, but we're very dependent on cell phones and the internet. And as you see, that's a problem when the power goes out."

"So a CB radio is like… a ham radio for short distances?" Emily mused.

Fred turned left so slowly Ethan thought he could have run alongside without getting winded. But they were leaving the houses behind and entering a commercial district. The offices were all dark, of course, as were the stores, but some stores were open, and the workers pulled racks of clothing out onto the sidewalk. Business as… well, not quite *usual*, but at least they were trying to keep their doors open. *Wide* open at the moment. One shop had set up an old-fashioned cash register, the kind that didn't need power.

Toward the end of the street, tucked back behind a strip mall, was a gas station Ethan recognized from fishing trips—they sold cheap worms. The sign read "Hardy's Garage and Bait," with a dingy cartoonish set of letters. The garage itself was a brick-and-cinder block one-story with two bays on the side, both closed, and a large tinted window almost completely covered by posters advertising cigarettes and beer.

There was a single bank of three pumps out front, the very old kind that Ethan knew had been upgraded everywhere else long ago. Six cars waited in line to use them. A stocky fellow with an impressive beard and a bulge in his overall pocket took money as the cars came in.

The Tuttle Twins and the Days of Darkness

"Wow, these guys are a lot more popular than I remember from the last time we were here," Emily said.

"You'll see why very shortly," Fred said, pulling the beat-up truck into line.

All the cars had extra gas cans they were filling up. The pumps seemed to be working just fine, to Emily's surprise.

"That's right," Fred said, climbing out of the truck. "These pumps are old, but they are also mechanical. They don't require electricity to operate. I hoped they wouldn't have sold out of gas before we got here, and it looks like they haven't."

He walked back to the bed and patted Ethan on the arm. "You think you can nurse this bad boy up to the pumps if Emily and I go inside for a minute?"

Ethan's eyes went wide. "I, uh, sure. Yeah, I think I can do that."

"He doesn't have a license," Emily said.

"Good thing he's only driving on private property, then," Fred said. The truck was half off the street into the parking lot of the station.

Ethan vaulted out of the truck and clambered into the cab. He started the truck and put it in gear. He let it roll a car length forward as the line advanced. A huge smile lit up his face.

"Yep, he's got it. Come on, Emily. I want to talk to Ezzy."

A bell jingled as they entered the shop. No one came out. Emily took in the decor. The windows facing the street might have had advertising on them, but inside, those same windows were practically blacked out with newspapers taped to the glass. Most of them were yellowed with advanced age, and Emily could see why—they were events of fifty, even a hundred years ago. "Oahu Bombed," one of them said. "JFK Shot in Dallas," said another. "6.5 Earthquake Shakes San Francisco." Bits of each article were circled in red, and some of the red circles were connected by lines to other parts of the article or even to other sheets. The effect was like a huge connect-the-dots picture that took up the entire wall. But if there was an actual picture there, Emily couldn't see it.

"Ezzy!" Fred called out.

Through the slivers of glass windows that were not covered in newsprint, Emily could see that the bays were both occupied by older-model pickup trucks, lifted off the floor on huge hydraulic platforms. A bearded man in filthy overalls stood under one of them, his wrench turning on something in the undercarriage.

"Ezzy!" Fred called again. "A fellow in Spokane told me a solar flare blacked out the town."

The interior of the shop was divided in two by a floor-to-ceiling wall painted bright red into which was set a battered door with a scarred, brass doorknob. From somewhere behind the door came a voice. "That's ridiculous! Your Spokane spook knows less than yesterday's newborn."

The door sucked inward, and there stood a tall, thin woman with a long, sharp face on which was fixed an eloquent expression of disgust. "And you can quote me."

"Why not?" Fred said, but Emily knew his vocal tones well and knew he was just asking to be annoying. Why, she did not know.

The woman—Ezzy, Emily supposed—whipped a cell phone out of her pocket and waved it like a hatchet. "Know what this is doing?"

"I have no idea. Dialing the bank?"

"It's playing solitaire. It *could* be dialing the bank, but it wouldn't get anywhere doing it. Because the *grid* is down, but not the *electronics*. There was no flare, or everything would be on fire. There was no EMP, or all our electronics would be fried." She stalked past them and whipped open the front door, held it, and pointed at the pumps. A Honda Accord was pulling in. "That car wouldn't roll anywhere except downhill. It's too new. The computer bits would have been torched like a bad defensive back. But there it is, working fine—as long as there's gasoline. No. This is not an EMP, and it's no solar flare."

"What, then? Grid overload?"

Emily was very interested in what this woman would say. She wasn't like anyone else she'd met.

"Grid overload! Pah!" Ezzy spat out the door and pulled it back shut. "In June? It hasn't even been that hot. Nobody's running AC right now. The load on the grid is nothing. Nothing!"

Fred folded his arms and waited, a tiny smile on his face. He was playing her like a harp, Emily thought. But then she wondered—did Ezzy want to be played? Was this some kind of dance they had done before? Adults—Fred especially—seemed to have this whole social structure going on above the level where most kids could see it.

Sure enough, Ezzy stalked over to the wall, to one of the newspapers, and stabbed her finger at it so hard

Emily thought the glass might break. "Right here, man. This is where it is. This is what's going on."

The type on that part of the paper was so small Emily couldn't read it from where she was. Fred certainly couldn't, either, but he made no move to get closer. Ezzy opened her mouth to say something, but the front door opened before she could.

"Ezzy, here, take this," the bearded man wearing overalls said, holding out a wad of cash thick enough to block up a car. "I don't wanna have too much on me."

She rifled through it. "If this isn't the end of everything, we're gonna do okay."

He smiled, showing gleaming white teeth against his deep tan and thick, black beard. "If it *is* the end of everything, we're gonna do even better."

"Except no internet."

"Internet ain't everything." A honk sounded from outside. "We're down to about half on the reservoir. Any chance of resupply?"

Ezzy cackled like a mother hen. "Same chance as you shaving that beard."

His smile got even bigger. "I better raise my prices, then."

Another honk. He turned to go. Ezzy said, pointing to Fred, "Not for these folks, though. Blue beater truck."

He nodded and went out. Ezzy turned back to the paper, put her outraged face on again, and stuck her finger on the circled red article. "In 2019, just before the

'Covid' panic, there was an attack on the grid. Atlanta. Massive, multi-day attack. Caused some brownouts—"

Fred put up a hand. "What kind of attack?"

"Cyber," she said, smiling like someone enjoying a really fine meal. "Russians, most likely. Could've been India or more likely Pakistan, but that's a difficult spoof. My people tell me probably Russia and Belarus."

"But it didn't work," Emily said before she could help herself. "We beat it back."

"Did we? Who's to say it didn't work? Who's to say the attack was the point? What if they hit our outer defenses, kept them occupied while they slipped something in behind them?"

"A trojan horse?" Fred said.

Ezzy shrugged. "It's what I'd do. Hammer the visible defense, probe, feint, dodge and dink, and keep the cyber-jockeys busy while you do the real work in the dark. Then you set it to go off down the road later when everyone's asleep at the switch."

Emily tried to imagine someone doing that. "But… why? And how do they get to all the systems at the same time?"

"Not that many systems," Ezzy said, "and all of them interlinked. You'd need twenty, maybe twenty-five of the big ones. Gotta do Texas all by itself—they're not connected to anyone. Takes a long time, you bet, but it could be done."

"Why?" Emily asked again. "Why would anyone do that?"

Ezzy slowly extended her arms—they were impossibly long and thin like straws—and began to spin slowly like Fraulein Maria on the mountaintop. "Look around you! Some people just want to watch the world burn."

"But—"

"Thank you for the gas and the conversation, Ezzy," Fred said, laying a hand on Emily's shoulder. "I think we're up now. Is anyone going to have gasoline tomorrow?"

She lowered her arms, and Emily thought her face was a little disappointed. "No. Leastways not around here. There are bigger tanks, of course. Refinery's over the hills to Teeterborough, but they're all fancy electrified now and maybe can't unscramble. It's a spaghetti fight out there, that's for sure." She went back to her door and opened it. "Y'all take care. I'd hate to have to come to your funeral, Fred."

"You wouldn't come any more than I would, Ezzy."

She cackled again. "Got that right. Bigger fish to fry... *much* bigger fish to fry... " she muttered as she slowly shut the door and disappeared.

Emily stood there a moment like she wasn't sure which direction the earth was spinning.

"Come on," Fred said. "Ethan's filling the last can."

Back out in the open, Emily said, "But Fred, she doesn't make any sense. A cyber attack? On the whole

US grid at once? What for? People just want to *watch* the world burn. But the one thing you *can't* do if you turn off all the cameras is *watch*."

Fred laughed. "That's Ezzy. Everything's a deep conspiracy, it's all tied together, and if any part of her theory doesn't make sense one day, she'll just toss it out and stick something else in its place. Still… she's astonishingly bright, and if she's a little paranoid and I think some of her theories are a little wild, that doesn't mean she's wrong. Not about everything, anyway. Plus, her theory does explain some things."

Ethan finished topping off the last can. He stowed it in the back of the truck. The man in beard and overalls was acquiring another large bundle of cash. Ethan said, "Someone's going to try to take that money from him, I bet." The line was now at least fifteen cars long and getting longer every minute. Short beeps on the horns were getting longer and more annoyed.

"Could be," Fred said. "But I know Hardy. Whoever tries to rob this place would have to be pretty desperate." Fred pointed to the bulge on the side of the man's overalls. Emily had thought that bulge was money, but now she could tell it was more likely a gun. "Hardy's a good shot."

They climbed back in and headed home. They passed the clothing store with its racks of bright-colored shirts and slacks, all set out in the open. No one was stopping, despite the cheerful waving of the store employees. "Not a day for clothes shopping," Ethan said.

When they got home, Fred insisted on taking the Tuttles' van back to Hardy's to fill it up, too, and brought along a pair of five-gallon buckets from his garage. "With what Ezzy's saying, this might be the last gas we can get for a while."

Ethan and Emily went home and took stock of the food situation. "It's a good thing we went to the grocery store right before the blackout," Ethan said. "But I wish we hadn't bought so much milk."

"We couldn't know," Emily said. "Come over here, and get ready."

"Ready for what?"

"Ready to flash-inventory everything in the freezer. You get the bottom two shelves, and I'll get the top two." She grabbed the freezer handle and took a deep breath. "Ready? I don't want this thing to be open more than a couple seconds."

Ethan licked his lips and nodded. "Ready."

Emily whipped the door open and held it, eyes scanning. Ethan crouched and did the same to the bottom part of the freezer. There was already some significant melting.

One, two, three, four, and Emily slammed the door shut.

"What do you have?" she said.

Ethan closed his eyes. "Two one-pound packages of hamburger, a flat of pork chops, two packs of chicken breasts, dry yeast… a box of popsicles… and two lumps wrapped in white butcher paper, and I have no idea what they are."

Emily plucked a pad of note paper from the kitchen counter and scribbled. "I have the remains of the ice cream, the melting ice, two jars of freezer jam, and the deer steaks and roast from last year's hunt."

"Most of mine is melting pretty fast."

"Mine too," Emily said. "This afternoon we're going to have to fire up the barbecue, unless a miracle happens. Cooked food keeps a lot longer than raw."

"We can't eat all of it ourselves," Ethan said. "Should we invite the neighbors?"

"If we do the grilling in the front yard, I don't think we'll have to ask."

They took a walk around the house. For maybe the first time, Emily noticed how many things were plugged in. Every socket in the house was home to some cord or other. Alarm clocks, computers, lamps, the wi-fi router, charging stations, mixers, washers and dryers, radios… was their whole life electrified? And Mom and Dad had several times made the point that they should try not to get reliant on things that wouldn't work if the power went out.

Bees, she thought. *And the plants in the garden. They don't care. They don't even know. But everything and everyone else... It's like the magic trick where the illusionist whips the tablecloth from under the plates and glasses and candelabras, and they all stay right where they are. But if he gets the trick wrong, everything comes sliding off and smashes.*

She wondered which kind of trick this was and felt immediately she didn't want to know.

The neighborhood barbecue was a big success, if you counted the number of people they fed and the festive atmosphere. Nor were they the only ones that provided goods. Once they fired up the big Camp Chef they'd moved to the driveway, people gathered from all over the street. The Andersons brought bags of chips, which Ethan thought was a bit silly since those would keep, but the Phams carried down six tubs of ice cream they'd been hoarding—still frozen and good—and others iced down drinks in wheelbarrows full of melting cubes.

And everyone brought meat. "Can't bear to see it go to waste," Ed McGill said. "It's already starting to thaw. Only a day or so and the whole pile would have to be thrown out. This is better."

In the end, they needed another couple of grills, so the McGills rolled theirs down two doors and parked it in the middle of the street. "Let them try to arrest me," he said, laughing. "Always wanted to try this."

The whole party chattered away like a flock of seagulls as if they had no cares in the world. Gaggles of children ran by playing tag and ninjas. Sometime in the middle of it, Fred gathered the kids and taught them how to play Kick the Can. Shrieking, joyful kids bolted back and forth, and by the time the sun began to get low, the entire street was out there, sitting in lawn chairs, nibbling on meat and talking about, well, the blackout. But not with fear, more in astonished curiosity. People told jokes. Everyone laughed like it was the biggest party the neighborhood had ever seen.

"Gallows humor," Ethan said to Emily as she passed him with a tray of meat.

She shook her head. "Most of them don't think it's going to last very long. They're saying another day or so at most."

"Who's telling them that? Where did they get that info?"

Emily shrugged. "Common knowledge. Everyone seems to just know."

"You know what we learned about common knowledge. When everyone knows something is so, it's time to start betting the other way."

"Do you *want* to bet against that?"

Ethan dragged his phone out of his pocket. He had 6% battery left. "Not on your life."

Most families took home big piles of meat in plastic containers and baggies. Fred acted as food inspector, reminding them that the meat would only keep for a week or so at most. "After that, it will make you sick. If you can smell something off, don't eat it."

Ali Jabbar was one of the last to go, wheeling a rusty barrow down the middle of the street while Emily and a half-dozen kids picked up bits of trash. "Thanks for a great party," he said. "You guys heard from your folks?"

"Not a word, Mr. Jabbar," Emily said. "Cell networks are out."

"Use a carrier pigeon!" he said brightly. "My father used to raise homing pigeons. Maybe I'll have to start."

It's still a kind of joke to you, isn't it? Emily thought. *I hope you have a lot of wheat and beans stored up in your basement for when the meat runs out.* Then she thought it might be a good idea to check on her own storage before she got snooty about other people's.

"I hope it doesn't come to that. Have a nice evening," she said.

Mostly, the twins wanted to get back to the ham radio with Fred and start trying to reach Oregon. Maybe tonight they'd get some news.

Fred, though, was deep in conversation with a woman Emily had met a couple of times from up the street, Amihan Legaspi. A short, dark-skinned woman with a smile that flashed out like distant lightning, she often jogged past the Tuttles while they were out working in the yard. She always seemed to choose the hottest part of the day to take her runs, her toned arms and legs flashing brown in the beating sun.

"You're headed for the radio, right?" Fred said. Emily nodded. He said, "I'm going to talk with Amihan here for a bit. Go ahead—you know how it works."

Emily waved to Amihan and went inside. Ethan was already heating up the radio and looking through the book of call signs for the ones they wanted.

"I'm going to try Portland right off," Emily said. "Someone up there must be on the radio."

And someone was—they got a hit with the first frequency they tried. A conversation was already going on. After a minute, Ethan reached for the mic to broadcast, but Emily dropped a hand on his arm. "Not yet," she said. "They're talking. It's rude to cut in unless we have something to add."

"You're worried about being rude? We're trying to find our parents!"

"Yes, I'm worried about being rude. It's not like Mom and Dad will be sitting next to this lady. If everyone starts cutting in all the time, no one will be able to use the radio at all. It's rudeness that ruins things. Being polite helps things run smoothly, and we can use some smoothness right now."

Ethan sat back in his chair and tried to be patient. It wasn't easy.

The conversation was informative, at least. Not surprisingly, Portland did not have power. The other voice—coming from Bismarck, ND, apparently—was also out. The grid was down all across the US. No planes were in the air except for those flown by the Air Force and the Navy. No trains were running, although there was some talk of being able to get some rail traffic back up in the next few days. But the biggest thing was that rioting had begun in the bigger cities, according to Bismarck.

Did Portland count as a bigger city? Ethan did not know. And Emily wouldn't ask.

Finally, she keyed the mic and said, "WT5BBY Portland, this is NX7JCS November X-ray Seven Juliet Charlie Sierra in Spoonerville. When you have a second. K?"

"Hey, NX7JCS in Spoonerville, five by nine, I heard from TU1RGT Spokane that you were asking about what's going on here. Your parents are in town?"

"Yes, sir. We were wondering when they'd be able to get out of Portland and return home to us."

The radio crackled and went still for what seemed a long time, though it was probably only a few seconds. Then a new voice said, "Break channel, this is DR4VAH in Meridian for NX7JCS, and I think I can answer Spoonerville's question. Or at least give an idea what the answer might be."

Emily and Ethan exchanged a look. Emily scribbled the call sign while Ethan reached out and hit the transmit key. "That would be great, DR4VAH Meridian. Anything you can tell us would be wonderful."

And another new voice said, "Emily? Ethan? Is that you?"

Mom.

"Mom!" Ethan screamed, forgetting the transmit key. But Emily whacked it, and both of them were babbling at the same time—how are you, how did you get to Meridian, what's going on, when are you coming home, and especially oh, great Heavens, how we missed hearing your voice. Etiquette or no, politeness or no, it took a little while for them to calm down and realize that they were never going to get any answers if they didn't let up on the transmit key and listen for a minute.

Finally, they did, and the set crackled just as Fred came into the room. "We took a bus from Portland—the only one we could get on—and made it to Meridian before the bus ran out of fuel and we couldn't find more. So right now, we're stuck here unless someone has a way for us to get closer to you."

The twins' faces fell, but Dad was saying, "You aren't to worry about us or about our getting home. We're coming if we have to walk the whole way. You hear me?"

"We hear you, Dad. But don't walk. There has to be a way to get back here."

"I'm not entirely sure there is," said Mom this time. "If we had fuel or a chain of places that might be open with fuel to sell or trade, then maybe. Probably. But I don't think we can count on that, and what happens if we get stuck in the middle of nowhere?"

"That's better than being two thousand miles away and not even coming closer," Ethan said, knowing she couldn't hear him.

Emily slugged him in the arm. "No, it isn't. At least we know where they are and that they're safe. They'll get to us as soon as they can."

"...we'll take it one leg at a time. Right now, at least, we're not going to be able to get a car. We couldn't be sure we'd be able to return it, at least not in the near future."

"What's going on there, Mom and Dad?"

"Portland was not good," Dad said, and Ethan could hear him choosing his words carefully. "We thought it was best to get out while we could. Lots of other people were doing that, too. The buses were all full. The airport was a madhouse, with everyone arriving there and nobody being able to depart. The airlines tried their best, but what could they do? Shuttles could gas up at the airport, so they could send people to local hotels, but so many of those hotels run electronic keys. They couldn't even open the rooms for people to stay in. Frustrated people do bad things. We thought a smaller town would be a safer bet."

"And was it? What's it like in Meridian?" Emily hunched over the radio with her muscles so tight she didn't know if she'd ever be able to relax again.

"Meridian is fine. People are friendly here. We got off at the bus depot and didn't have anywhere to go until this van pulls up and a man and his son get out. Theron and Adam Harmon. They just had the feeling people would be stranded and might need help. So we're at the Harmons' small farm right now."

"We're doing okay too," Emily said. "We just had a big neighborhood barbecue to cook up all the thawing meat. We have some gas for a generator—Fred took us down to Hardy's Garage."

"What about groceries? Have you gone to the store yet?"

"No, we haven't." Emily cast a worried glance at Fred. "We should probably do that soon, though."

Portland spoke up again. "You'll want to get water. That's the most important thing."

"Water? Why water?" Emily said. "It comes out of the tap. Easy as pie."

"That's going to stop. Probably tomorrow, or the day after that, where you are."

Now it was Fred's turn to reach from behind them and key the mic. "DR4VAH is that because the backup power systems will run out of juice?"

"Affirmative, NX7JCS. US pump systems in water treatment facilities are rated for three days of backup, and that's about used up. When that goes down, watch for the end of all things."

Emily took Ethan's hand and wouldn't let go. No showers. No refilling the water pitchers. *No using the toilet.* Maybe there was something worse than that, but she was having trouble coming up with it.

"We'll be filling tubs and buckets all night," Fred said.

"Ethan and Emily, you two and Fred need to decide what you're going to do. Spoonerville is pretty safe, but Malantown won't be, and there will be people coming over the bridge any time now."

"We saw fires over there last night," Ethan said. "When the water goes down they won't be able to put them out."

"You know what we've discussed about emergency situations," Mom said. "You're prepared."

"We'd have liked to have a lot more fuel in storage, though," Emily said.

"Ah. Yeah, I meant to get that 50-gallon steel drum and never got around to it."

"We're going to make the best of it. Fred is here, and the neighborhood is all working together, or at least they were at the party tonight."

"We're about to shut down the generator for the night. Don't know how long it will last, but we should be on at least another few nights, if you want to hit us back."

"We'll definitely do that," Fred said. "Don't worry, I'll take good care of the kids."

"We know you will," Mom said, and there was a catch in her voice. "We'll get to you. Somehow. Eighty-eight, NX7JCS Spoonerville."

The last thing Emily wanted to do was get off the radio. For a few minutes, it was like Mom and Dad were back with them. Now they were saying goodbye, and who knew when they would talk again? Who knew *if* they would talk again? But the radio was silent, and she couldn't risk them turning off without hearing a goodbye.

"Eighty-eight, DR4VAH Meridian. We love you."

And then there was nothing. The three of them sat in the basement and stared at the radio, trying not to think about what was to come.

Continue on page 47.

"Prioritize containers that you can carry," Fred said, "just in case."

The water did not last the night. The twins filled every container they had all the way to the top, and around 1 a.m., just as they were scouring the garage for anything else they could fill, the kitchen tap gave a gurgle, belched twice, gushed one last pint of water, and gave up.

"Well, that's that," Emily said. She went to the bathroom and looked at the toilet. "We'll be able to flush one more time."

"No, we won't, not if we want to be smart about it. There's a lot of water in the tank. We'll want it."

"So, what? We go out to the garden and squat down?"

"Yep!" Ethan said, a bright smile on his face. "Just like scout camp!"

Emily grabbed a fluffy white roll from the bathroom cabinet. "This one is mine. My last vestige of civilization."

Ethan opened the garage door, letting in the powerful smell of gasoline from all the filled containers they had stored there. "I'm not sure that TP is compostable. We should look that up online. Oh, wait."

The roll of TP was soft. Emily rubbed it against her face. "I hope Fred got more of this last night at the store."

The three of them agreed that Fred would go down after their radio session and try to get as much as he could into the pickup. The twins must have been asleep when he came back because they hadn't heard his truck come down the street.

Ethan said, "I'll go and get our part of the groceries. How much cash do we have left?"

"Around $500. That isn't going to last very long."

"Better than nothing. I'll be back in a second. You want to inventory our food storage?"

"Already on it," Emily said, taking the clipboard off the kitchen wall. They wouldn't need to be leaving messages to each other for a while, that was for sure.

Ethan went out the front door into the sharply-slanting sunshine of the early morning. Birds chattered in the trees, and the sun was warm on his skin. It smelled of roses, and the bees zipped back and forth almost like an aerial highway between their hive and the rosebushes across the street. The hum was comforting. The bees had no idea the power was out, and they couldn't have cared less. No matter what, they went on doing their thing. The sun rose and set, the breezes blew, grass grew, trees put out leaves, all of it happened without any help from the grid. Ethan felt a pull toward that kind of life—unbothered by anything but the weather. How would it be?

And in the next breath, he didn't want to find out. He wanted his phone to work. He wanted to be able to watch movies on his computer. He wanted to call his parents at any time, for any reason. He wanted to text his friends.

The bee life did not seem quite so appealing after that.

Fred's garage was closed, the truck hidden inside. Ethan knocked on the front door. He waited, not really looking through the pebbled windows on either side of the big front door, but after a moment, he noticed that there was no shadow moving, no response to his knock. Fred must still be in bed.

At 8:22 a.m.? Fred?

Impossible. He was probably around back, working in his garden. Ethan went around the garage and through the side yard gate into the backyard. The trees swayed slightly in the indifferent breeze, and the newly planted tomatoes waved at him with their yellow blossoms. But Fred wasn't there.

Heart beating just a bit faster now, Ethan went up the concrete steps to the back door and knocked. He waited, listening for the thud of footsteps or for Fred to call out for him to come in. He heard nothing.

A dog barked in the distance. Ethan knocked again. Waited again.

No response, again.

On impulse, he reached out and twisted the handle of the door. It turned. It wasn't locked.

Fred always locked his doors—home or not—unless he was working in the yard.

Seriously alarmed now, Ethan pushed the door open. "Fred? Are you here? It's Ethan."

The kitchen was dark. The oven was off, and all the lights were out. *Duh, of course it is.* Feeling a little sheepish, he stepped into the kitchen and called louder, "Fred? I came to get our part of the groceries."

That was when he heard it. A sound like a person breathing through a mask, maybe lightly snoring. It was coming from down the hall toward the bedroom.

"Fred! Hey, I'm getting worried here. Where are you?"

The Darth Vader rasp kept going. Ethan couldn't imagine what it could be—no way Fred could sleep through all the racket Ethan was making. And suddenly, he didn't want to go down that hallway, either. What if it wasn't Fred at all? What if it was someone—or some-*thing* else?

Keeping his steps quick and quiet, he tiptoed across the kitchen to the garage door and gently opened it a crack. Dark. Curse all this darkness! He stuck his head through.

It smelled of oil and earth. With the light from the crack where the rolling door met the concrete imperfectly, Ethan could see that the truck was there. Good. So Fred had come home last night.

But then what happened?

There was only one way to find out.

Before that, though, Ethan saw the shovel hanging up on the tool rack mounted to the near wall. He stepped into the garage and plucked it from its hanger. Gripping it with two hands, he went back into the house. It made him feel braver.

Down the hall, one step at a time. Now he was nervous to call out—what if that told the bad guy where he was? The thick carpet swallowed the sound of his shoes, but it didn't do anything to muffle the sound at the end of the hall, nor Ethan's quick, shallow breathing.

Fred's bedroom door was ajar, just a couple of inches. But it was light in there, or at least not pitch dark. The sound was louder here, and it was definitely coming from the bedroom.

Holding the shovel by the blade, Ethan pushed the bedroom door open wider.

The sound increased. Now Ethan was sure it was someone breathing. It wasn't pitch black, maybe, but it was a long way from bright in there. Ethan couldn't make out much. It smelled sour, like dried sweat and old socks.

There was nothing for it. Pulling the shovel back, he got a two-handed grip on the worn-smooth wood shaft and took a deep breath. *Go quick, don't give them time to react.*

He leaped through the doorway and nearly fell over the clothes hamper, lying on its side in the middle of the floor. Catching himself just in time, he let out a yell of fright and surprise.

There was someone in the room lying on the bed, face-down.

"Fred," Ethan breathed.

Then he tossed the shovel down and shook his friend by the shoulder. "Fred. Wake up!" He was fully clothed, wearing the same thing he'd been wearing the night before, sleeping on top of the covers as if he'd flopped down there, like a fallen tree.

Ethan's shaking didn't rouse him. He snored on—but it wasn't quite a snore. There was a note in it that spoke of trouble breathing. Was he sick?

Ethan flipped the light switch. Nothing happened. Rolling his eyes, he went to the blinds and tugged the dangling string, raising them. Light flooded into the room, and he could see that Fred was filthy. Dirt was ground into his shirt as if he'd lain on a garden bed. One shoe was off, and the sock underneath was muddy.

Then he saw Fred's face.

The right side was swollen, angry, and red, and his nose was nearly double its normal size.

"Fred!" Ethan shook him again, now with enough force to set the bed rocking. "Fred! What happened? Wake up!"

For a moment, he thought Fred wouldn't respond, and he might have to go get help—though who would he get? It wasn't like he could call 911—but then Fred rolled onto his back and groaned a deep, painful groan that made Ethan's teeth ache.

There was blood on his sleeve when he raised his arm to shade his eyes.

"Where am I?" he croaked.

"In your bedroom. It's Ethan. What happened to you?"

Fred groaned again. Ethan had never heard anyone make a noise like that, and he didn't want to hear it again. But Fred pushed himself up to more or less a sitting position, and like that, he didn't look quite so bad. He leaned over and put his head in his hands. His hair was matted as if someone had poured syrup on it.

"Is that my shovel?" Fred said.

Ethan laughed. If Fred could make jokes, even lame ones, there was hope. "Yeah. I heard you snoring and thought it might be burglars."

"Not yet. But I wouldn't be surprised to see some later today—or tonight."

"What? What *happened*?"

There was crime in Spoonerville, like everywhere, but not much compared to most places, especially in this neighborhood. People were safe here.

Weren't they?

"I went to get… the groceries," Fred said, slowly, like he was paying in pain for every word, "and I got… I got… I don't remember if I got them. I think I did. I

remember going out the door, and then I was... someone put me in the truck and... is the truck here?"

"In the garage."

Fred nodded as if his head weighed a thousand pounds. "Good. I must have driven home. I don't remember what happened after that."

Or much of what happened before, apparently. "Where are the groceries?" Ethan said, kneeling down so he could look up into Fred's face.

Fred shrugged, then winced. "I don't remember."

He tried to stand up, but he was wobblier than a one-legged stool. "Whoa," Ethan said, grabbing him around the waist, and steadying him. Fred's breath was acidic, like vomit. "Are you sure you want to try standing up?"

"Have to... have to go to the... " Fred pointed to the master bath.

"Just a minute, then," Ethan said, his face falling even further. "I don't think you can flush."

"There's a bucket."

"Oh. That will do okay then."

Ethan helped Fred to a seat on the side of the tub. "I'll be right back," he said. "I'll go check the truck for the groceries while you do what you have to do."

He went down the hall and back into the garage. He wanted to open it to get more light in, but suddenly he felt very vulnerable and wanted to keep the rolling door between himself and the rest of the world. There was enough light to be able to see that the truck bed was empty. And not just empty of groceries—the toolbox Fred kept there was missing as well.

The cab was unlocked. The dome light came on, and Ethan sucked in a breath of hope before he remembered that this light wasn't on the grid. But there might as well have been no light for all the good it did. The cab was empty, too. No food, no toilet paper, nothing.

He shut the door and went back inside. Instead of going to Fred's bedroom, though, he bolted out the front door and across the lawn, up his own steps, and into the house. He knew where the first-aid kit was.

"Emily! Come quick! Fred's been hurt!"

Emily dashed into the kitchen, skidding on her socks. "What happened? Fred's hurt?"

"Bad. I think he was mugged last night when he went for groceries. Do we have any ice?"

Emily closed her eyes and shook her head. "There's nothing cold left… wait. The first-aid kit!"

"There won't be ice in there," Ethan said, wrenching open a closet and taking a red box off the wall.

"No, but there are chemical packs. Some of them make heat, and some make cold. I'm coming with you."

"Not in your socks."

She made a face. "Honestly, what a thing to worry about," she muttered and stripped her socks off. "There. Happy?"

For an answer, Ethan turned and jogged out of the front door carrying the medical supplies. For the first time in his life, he wondered if he should lock the door behind him.

But he didn't, and Emily was halfway across the lawn, feet flying. Ethan followed.

Fred had closed the bathroom door, which Ethan was glad of. Still, the twins pounded on the door and called for Fred until he—somewhat testily—called out that he was okay, he was just taking his time, and they could wait for him in the kitchen.

"Sit down in there," Ethan said. "If you fall, we'll have to kick the door in."

There was a squeaking and a thud but no outcry, and Ethan took that for Fred sitting down safely.

In the kitchen, Ethan filled Emily in on what he knew. "Sounds like he was hit on the head when he came out of the grocery store," Emily said. "If he's having that much trouble remembering, he's probably got a concussion. That's not good."

"His face is pretty swollen, and I think that was blood on his hair. There was more on his sleeve."

"It sure would be great to take a shower about now."

Ethan put his head on the table and covered it with his arms. "This is not good, Em. None of this is good."

A few minutes later, Fred came unsteadily into the kitchen, but he was walking, and he looked a little better. "Washed a bit in the sink. Wet rag," he said.

Emily cracked the instant ice pack and felt it go cold in her hand. She gave it to him, and he put it to the side of his face with a sigh.

And then they sat there for a long time.

"What do we do?" Ethan finally said.

"We're not out of food," Emily said and waved her hand toward their house. "There's two huge bags of rice and beans in our storage. We have wheat and a manual grinder, and until the yeast gives out, we can make bread—and sourdough at some point without yeast. We have some water—about a hundred gallons, I think."

"That's enough for fifty days for the two of us," Ethan said. "Sorry."

Fred groaned a bit and twiddled his fingers at Ethan. "No, I've got more than that. Maybe… two hundred? Not sure… "

"And there's a lot more in storage I didn't have time to get to because, well, you know."

"I'm glad you found me," Fred said. He looked blearily around the kitchen. "I need an aspirin."

"You need a hospital. But I don't think you'd get much attention there," Ethan said, getting up and going to the cabinets. He opened every one three times before he found the acetaminophen, ibuprofen, and, finally, some aspirin tucked in the back behind some powdered garlic. He put three of each into his hand and held them out to Fred.

"It's a lot," Fred said.

"It's less than what they'd give you in the ER."

Fred nodded at that and took them. Emily handed him a glass of water dipped from the bucket on the counter.

He tipped them back and drained the glass. She handed him another one. He shook his head. "Need to… conserve… "

"You need to be well. We're kids. This is serious. We need you. Drink."

He didn't argue, and one side of his mouth turned up. "Need you too."

Fred went back to bed. The twins didn't want to leave him alone, so while he slept, they got a pad of paper and some pens and started writing.

"We've been acting like this is just going to blow over," Emily said, "but it isn't, and it's time we started acting like it. We prepared for this. We're ready."

"We're *not* ready, and we should realize that," Ethan replied, standing up and pacing. "We don't have enough water for more than a month, realistically. A little more if it rains. Are we going to have power back in a month?"

Emily shrugged.

"Right. We have to assume we won't. So what do we do? Stay here?"

"Or what? Where would we go?"

Ethan scratched his head. "Come on, Tuttle. Think. When we ran simulations of this, what did we do?"

Emily scribbled on the pad for a minute. "Communication. First thing is to inventory assets. We know a little about what we have, but we need to know more. We need all of it. Then we need to make contact with other people and see what they have. We don't work together, we're dead, like literally dead."

As if to underscore this, the floor rumbled, and a second later, a massive *crump* sounded from outside. The twins ran to the back window, but there were too many trees on Fred's fence line. They couldn't see anything.

"Come on," Emily said, sprinting outside.

They ran pell-mell to the top of the street and looked down toward Spoonerville. Except for a lot of flashing red and blue lights, everything looked normal.

"No," Emily said. "There." She pointed toward Malantown.

They didn't have a good view of the town—there were too many houses in the way—but a thick black column of smoke was rising from across the river.

"What on earth?" Ethan said.

Just then, a police car rolled slowly around the corner and stopped a few yards away. The policewoman inside was on her radio but not talking. Her windows were down, and they could hear bits and pieces of shouted communication—*explosion* and *refinery* and *emergency*.

They walked slowly over to the passenger side. The officer's eyes were closed for a moment. Then they saw her take a deep breath and let it out slowly. She opened her eyes and saw them.

"What are you two doing?" she said.

"Standing on the street looking at a big cloud of smoke," Ethan said. "Do you know what that was?"

The officer's mouth tightened into a hard line. "Not important for you. Stay off the streets."

Emily reached out a hand, palm up. "Please," she said. "Our parents are stranded out of town. Our friend was beaten and robbed yesterday at the grocery store. We just need some word about what's going on. We're scared."

Ethan nearly glared at her when she said this but thought it would be better to go with it.

The officer glanced away, then shifted her shoulders a bit and said, "The grocery store situation should be fixed. If you need food and you have cash, you can go there. We're rationing the food, but you'll be able to get some. Water, too. We have supplies in town. There's a center at the high school where families are gathering. You can go there. You *should* go there."

"We have some food and water," Ethan said, pitching his voice a bit higher than normal. "We don't want to leave home in case our parents call."

"Hah," the officer said, laughing without humor. "If only. Look, you kids should get with the rest of the people in Spoonerville. It's for your safety."

"Do we have to go?" Emily said. "We want to stay with our friend."

"He should go, too."

"Is that an order?" Ethan said, back to his normal voice. Neutral, but older. Game time was over.

The officer stared at them as if they'd suddenly grown six inches and sprouted horns. "No," she finally said, "It's not an order. It's a friendly suggestion. Spoonerville isn't like Malantown, not yet anyway, but it could get that way fast. And if it does, we're only going to be able to protect the people who aren't being stupid."

"Thank you, officer," Emily said, "but for now we'll stay put."

She shrugged as if it was no concern of hers and put the car into gear. "Suit yourself," she said.

"And officer?" Emily said.

"Yeah?"

"Thank you. I know this is pretty much the worst and you feel like you have to solve all the problems in the city at once. Just know we're grateful you're trying to help."

If the last stare was puzzled, this time it was dumbfounded. She swallowed. "You stay safe now," she said, and the car rolled down the street, lights flashing.

The twins stood and watched until the car turned the corner at the end of the block and disappeared.

Emily sniffed. The air smelled oily. She rubbed her fingers together. Could she feel something? She wasn't sure. Her mouth was dry, sandpapery. When was the last time she'd had a drink?

"They're going to order us all into camps," Ethan said, eyes still down toward where the policewoman had gone.

"That's the government playbook. Page five, section three."

"Do we want to be here when they do?"

Neither of them spoke for a moment. A dog on the next block was going nuts. The street was deserted. Other than that, it was a beautiful day.

"A pint is a pound the world around," Emily said.

"What?"

"Water," Emily said, glancing over. "It's awfully heavy."

They sat around the radio, locked on to their accustomed frequency—the one their parents would surely try to find them on—and tried to decide what to do.

Emily had completed the inventory, including Fred's extra water supplies, and she believed that between his emergency storage and their own, they could probably live pretty comfortably for about three months. They would smell bad. They would smell *awful*. But they could probably make it. After that, the water would run out, depending on the rain. There was obviously the river, and Fred knew where there was a well, but they couldn't count on being able to access it. Would criminals be waiting there to prey on us like crocodiles at a watering hole?

Without water, they'd be in trouble. Quickly.

"At that point, the government would likely step in and control the natural water sources and distribution," Emily said.

"I'd be surprised if that order isn't already in motion," Fred said. "But we'd be lucky to make it long enough to see the last of our water supply." His face looked worse, though he said it felt better. The red was now streaked with black and yellow, and the swelling had returned. They didn't have any more cold compresses.

"Why wouldn't we make it that long? Do you need medical attention?" Ethan asked, arching an eyebrow.

"Well, that's not quite what I was thinking of. But maybe. I'm thinking more of our need for physical protection… defense." Fred shifted in his seat as if he couldn't get comfortable. "Those guys at the grocery store won't stay there. They'll get chased off by the police for now, but what's to stop them from going to other places where there's food to steal. Like people's houses."

Emily picked up her clipboard. "We have rifles and a thousand rounds of ammunition. You probably have more."

"I do," Fred said. "But are you certain you could shoot someone?"

It was hard to imagine, that was for sure. "If they tried to hurt my sister," Ethan said, "I bet I could."

"Still. Let's not go down that road until we have to. There are other alternatives."

"Like going down to the government shelter?" Emily said. "I don't think so."

"You just said we had three months at the most. There's a good chance we wouldn't make it that long. A government shelter might not be ideal, but it would be safe. There would be food, and there would be water. It's a long way from the worst option."

Fred let that sink in for a moment. The radio crackled, and for a moment, they thought someone might connect. But the crackling stopped without any voice saying anything. They sat back in their chairs, disappointed.

"That isn't the only other option, though," Fred said. "I was talking to Miss Legaspi from up the street, and she's part of a group that might be able to help us."

"What sort of group?" Ethan said.

"A... kind of prepper group, I guess," Fred said. "They've spent the last couple of years getting disaster preparedness gear together, and they've got an impressive store of equipment and supplies stashed in a place not too far away. Out of town, though. In the woods."

"How do we know we can trust her?" Emily said.

"I've known her for a while. She's retired Army, an ultra-marathoner, and knows her stuff. I suspect the rest of her group would be similar."

Emily blew out a breath. "We'd have to leave here." It wasn't a question.

"Yes, we would."

"And what do they want with a couple of teenagers?" Ethan said. He got up to pace the room.

"You have skills. I vouched for you. You're smart, and you have resources. You can shoot, and you have food, and you're good in a crisis. Those are all valuable things. Plus," Fred said, shrugging, "I told them we were a package deal."

The twins grinned at each other. Fred was a good friend.

"We do have a decision to make, though," Fred said. "If we're going to go, we need to go soon. Their group is not going to wait around for the police to start rounding people up. She said they've been listening to the police scanner and at most we have another couple of days."

"But… they can't make us leave, right?" Emily said.

"No, but they can make it pretty uncomfortable. And once the police evacuate everyone that will go, that will make the bad guys bolder to move against everyone that's left."

"Or their empty houses, yeah," Emily said, rubbing her eyes. They burned. She knew she needed a shower.

"There is one more option we haven't talked about," Ethan said. He stopped pacing for a moment and ran his hand through his hair. "Going to Gnarled Oaks."

"To Grandma's?" Emily said. She hadn't even thought about it. But what an idea! If there was anywhere they'd be safe, it was there. And the river ran right through the backyard—all the fresh water they could want!

"It's an option… " Fred said. "How far is it?"

"We stop for gas once in the middle of the trip, but we have to fill up the tank again when we get there. 650, 700 miles, I think?"

"You don't know?" Fred said. "You guys go there almost every summer."

Ethan got a sheepish look on his face and spread his hands. "The GPS tells us. That's all I know."

"Do you have paper maps?"

"Uh, those weren't in the inventory," Emily said. "I mean, why would they be? There are so many things we didn't think about."

Fred blew out a breath. He looked very old all of a sudden. "Ezzy will have maps, and you have a full tank plus 15 gallons to refill. You could make it. You can take pictures of the maps on your phones—that will still work, as long as you charge them in the car. It isn't a bad option for you two."

Emily swiveled in her chair. "But… you'd come, too, right? I mean, we wouldn't split up."

Fred shook his head. "As much as I'm sure your family would welcome me, I think my best bet would be Miss Legaspi's group if you decide to make a run for the Little Pink House."

"We're not even quite legal to drive!" Emily said.

"Oh, I'm pretty sure the police have other things on their mind than checking your licenses. You drive well. I've ridden with you. You won't have a lot of traffic to deal with, I don't think."

There they were. Three options. Four, if you counted hunkering down in the house and going nowhere. Emily didn't think Fred would go for that one. Was there anything else they could talk about that would give them a better idea of which option to pursue?

"Comms?" Emily said, running a hand over the mic. "This isn't portable."

"No," Fred said. "I put the CB in your dad's truck, and Miss Legaspi says her people all have BaoFeng radios. I can take the shortwave, too—it's not heavy. They'll have generators."

"We have to be able to talk to Mom and Dad. They have to know where we are." As if to reinforce that thought, Emily reached out and fiddled with the band dial. The radio squealed and went silent again. She drew her hand back and sighed.

"If we go to the government shelter, we're leaving all that behind." Ethan rested his head on the wall as if it hurt him to think.

"We try for Grandma's, there's no guarantee we'll make it. There's a lot of unknown trouble between here and there," Emily said. She wanted to lie down, go to sleep, and wake up in a year or so.

"We go with the mutual assistance group, we know almost no one, we're part of an unfamiliar community, living heaven knows where," Fred said. His voice was rough, and he coughed once he'd finished speaking.

"And if we stay here," Ethan said, coming over to sit on the floor between Emily and Fred, "we get to renew acquaintances with whoever it was that sucker-punched Fred."

They sat quietly for a few moments while the radio hummed and crackled. Emily could smell her brother—and Fred—and probably herself. Right now, she was all for taking whatever option meant she could have a bath pretty soon.

"Well hey!" Ethan said, pasting a big smile on his face, "At least we've got some swell options!"

If you think the twins should try to ride it out at home, go to page 154.

If you think the twins should make a run for Grandma's house, go to page 417.

If you think the twins and Fred should join Miss Legaspi's group, go to page 341.

If you think the twins and Fred should take refuge in the government shelter, go to page 136.

"This is a terrible idea, one of the worst in the history of terrible ideas," Ethan said.

"But you'll come anyway," Emily said, reaching for his hand.

He let her take it. But then he said, "No. I won't."

Emily sat bolt upright, heart racing. "What? Of course you will. We've never done anything without each other."

She couldn't see him in the dark, but she could imagine him shaking his head. "I can't, Em. It's suicidal. Worse, you're going to make it harder for Mom and Dad."

"I am not. I know how to help them—"

"You said that." He wasn't really making much of an attempt to keep his voice down. There was a smell of new sweat in the tent, and Emily wasn't sure if it was his or hers.

"And you don't believe me."

She heard him sit up, and he put his hand on her knee. "That's not it. I believe that you believe you're going to pull this off. What I don't believe is that you can. The odds are too long. And then what? Mom and Dad make it to the Little Pink House, and you're not there. You won't *ever* be there. Think, Em. *Think*. What if the power wasn't out? What if we were in the backyard right now, and you proposed walking and hitchhiking from here to *Cheyenne, Nebraska*? What would Mom say?"

They both knew the answer to that.

"And what would you say if I was the one that proposed it? You'd tell me I was crazy. And you'd be right. So instead, your proposal is to do the entire thing on foot, with a backpack of food, no water, and hundreds of thousands of terrified, desperate people out there that would rob you, or worse, and leave you in a ditch at the first available opportunity—"

"There are good people out there, too."

"Of course there are, and aren't you lucky they come labeled with a big blinking sign to tell you which ones to trust. You're a teenage girl. I don't think you'd make it through *Malantown* right now, let alone all the way to Cheyenne. I know I wouldn't. No. Absolutely not. And if you try to go, I'll try to stop you."

Emily reached out, picked up his hand, and dropped it back in his lap. "Fine. I won't go. But if we never see Mom and Dad again, I'll blame you."

Heart hammering, she crawled back to her side of the tent and rolled into her bag. He wouldn't go to sleep for a long time, she was sure. He might not go to sleep right away for quite a few nights now that she'd shown her hand. But one day, he wouldn't be watching. And she'd sneak away.

Oh, she was still going to go. No doubt about it.

She was good, he had to give her that.

Maybe for the first time in their lives, there was a division between them, a hard, unbreachable wall that kept them apart. Ethan certainly couldn't remember any such thing happening before.

On the surface, everything was fine. Emily did her work on the Farm and in the radio shack with the same exactness and the same commitment as before. She didn't skip work, didn't pretend to be sick. When it was her turn to put the hours in, she did it without complaint.

But there was something missing. She rarely smiled. There was no joy in her efforts. Where before, even the hardest work was leavened with joking around, now it was like she had become a robot, going through the motions but never letting any of the life around her touch her. It made Ethan sad. But it also made him watchful because he knew her. And she could no more live like that for long than she could sprout wings and fly.

There were other signs. Because they shared a tent, it was nearly impossible for her to get up in the middle of the night without waking him up. At least once a night, each of them would get up to go to the latrine to pee, and Ethan was rarely so soundly asleep that he didn't hear her when she went. But she was gone longer, now, he was sure of it. Not too much longer. Not anything like twice as long. But longer. There was nothing he could accuse her of, but he knew.

Also, she had volunteered for kitchen duty. Of all the jobs in camp, this was one of the least favorite because of the heat. Cooking in a lightly ventilated room in the middle of summer was nobody's idea of a good time, yet Emily had signed up for scullery maid even during times she could have been rotated off. He asked her about it. "I'm trying to be helpful," she said. "Since we're going to live here for the rest of our lives."

There was a bitter edge to everything she said. The words were the same, or nearly, but the undertone was wrong. It wasn't Emily.

Two weeks went by. Three. She did nothing to call attention to her sadness. She made no overt attempt to keep her plan in motion. But Ethan knew she was going to go.

He just hoped he was there to stop it.

Emily knew Ethan was watching her. Sometimes, before she told him her plan, he'd sleep through her bathroom trips at night—now, he never did. Before he'd gone off to play in the woods with some of the other kids in camp and left her to work, or to nap, or whatever she wanted, but now he stayed close enough to her to be glued on.

She knew why. She wasn't stupid. He didn't want her to go, and he knew she was still planning to.

Well, nobody ever called him stupid.

The kitchen was the way out. Ethan couldn't watch her in the kitchen hut, couldn't see her build a cache of food and utensils, then stash it in the woods when she was throwing scraps onto the compost pile. His radio shifts were also useful—it was the one time she knew beyond doubt where he was and that he could not follow her. She made sure that her extra kitchen duty shifts corresponded to his radio time, and then she would beg off for half an hour in the middle. She was extra help, after all. They didn't need her.

The trick was leaving. Her pack was in the tent. If she took it with her to the latrine in the middle of the night, that would be altogether too obvious. Neither could she take the pack and hide it during the day—it wasn't like there were a lot of personal possessions in the tent where something like that could go unnoticed. And she couldn't really disappear during the day. There were a lot of people in camp, and they knew her. There were rules for hiking, too, and one did not go off into the woods by oneself. Someone would see.

When she was as ready as she could get, she watched for her chance.

It turned out not to be as difficult as she imagined. She realized one night that Ethan always woke up when she went to the latrine in the middle of the night. He would often go at the same time. So from that night on, she simply made sure she had thoroughly gone before she went to bed. She slept all night where she would normally have had to get up.

But Ethan used the latrine very early in the morning, a couple of hours before they had to get up. That was her window. All she had to do was wait until Ethan was forced to go. Then she would have a few minutes—three at the most—to get out of the MAG.

That wouldn't be enough, of course, because as soon as he returned, he would see that she was gone and raise the alarm. But she had a plan for that.

It took a week to be completely ready. Then, when Ethan had become accustomed to the fact that Emily didn't pee at night, she made her move. When he left the tent, she counted to ten, then pushed her head out of the tent. He was nowhere to be seen. Heart thudding, she arranged her sleeping bag and slipped into the night.

One minute gone. She stopped at the kitchen, let herself in the back, and retrieved the backpack she had hidden there, fully stocked with water purification tablets and as much freeze-dried food as she thought she could carry. Back out into the night.

Two minutes gone. Last preparations. Emily took the lighter from the backpack and flicked it into flame. She lit the four cans of Sterno fuel she'd placed in a strategic spot, one at a time. Then she took a deep breath, forced away the regret she felt at deceiving her twin brother, and marched into the forest, heading north. Within ten steps, she was effectively totally invisible.

Ethan always hurried to the latrine and hurried even more coming back. He wasn't especially worried tonight; it was curious that Emily hadn't needed to pee for the last week, but maybe she was just drinking less or sleeping more deeply. Either of those things would be good, so although he hurried there and hurried back, he hadn't pushed it.

Before he reached the tent, though, he knew something was wrong. A reddish flicker lit up the back of the kitchen shed. Everyone's worst nightmare—the kitchen was on fire!

Ethan shouted, "Fire!" at the top of his lungs and broke into a run toward the kitchen. But even in this moment of potential disaster, he didn't forget his first priority—keeping an eye on his sister. So even as the camp began to stir and raise the alarm, he still swerved in his path to reach his own tent and throw back the flap. He stuck his head inside.

Emily's backpack was still there. The pillow was lumped over her head.

Sighing with relief, Ethan sprinted for the kitchen.

Emily heard the alarm break out just as she reached the bottom of the hill and started west. She didn't run—that was far too dangerous in the dark, in the thick brush and deep leaves of the forest floor. Her hands shook, and her breath came in gasps—she was as terrified as she'd ever been. She had no way to know if the alarm was because of her diversion at the kitchen or if her absence had been discovered. All she could do was keep going. Quickly. Far more quickly than she had planned.

Her boots sank into the spongy floor, pushing her onward and away from the MAG. The shouting died away behind her. Had she done it?

Ethan and three other campers extinguished the fire without too much trouble. Greasy rags had caught fire on some cans of discarded Sterno—sloppy, and he'd have to point it out to Amihan in the morning, but for now, the crisis was averted, and the kitchen was saved.

Most of the camp had been roused by Ethan's shout and grumpily took themselves back to bed once they found they were too late for any excitement. All of them agreed that Ethan had done the right thing, and they hoped everyone could still get a couple hours of sleep before the sun rose.

Emily hadn't come, Ethan noticed, but neither had Fred and a few other campers. So she was sleeping especially soundly. That was probably a good sign. Maybe she was getting back to normal.

"Hey, Em!" he said, slipping into the tent and sitting on his sleeping bag to unlace his boots. "You missed it. The kitchen was on fire."

She really was sleeping awfully deeply. He reached over to shake her, just to be sure she was still alive.

His second scream was far less well-received—until the camp found out what he was screaming about.

Maybe they didn't search for long. Maybe they thought she'd gone in a different direction. Whatever the reason, none of the searchers came anywhere near where Emily was hiding.

She had walked as far as she thought she could for the night, then curled up under the cover of a dead oak tree. She hadn't meant to fall asleep, but when she awoke, it was a full day, the sun halfway to the zenith. There was a taste of mold and dirt in her mouth. She spat, disgusted. But something else remained. Betrayal, perhaps. Whatever it was, it was bitter, and she could not get rid of it.

Ten minutes later, she was moving again. She purified some water she found in a small creek burbling by, drinking as deeply of the foul, chemical liquid as she could make herself. The tablets might kill off any harmful organisms, but they took bad-tasting water and made it so thickly awful it nearly choked her.

She knew she needed to drink, so she got it down eventually. She had a couple of mouthfuls of freeze-dried strawberries—surprisingly good, though afterward she needed more water—threw her pack on her back and marched off, heading northwest by the compass. There was a road in that direction she wanted to try. It should take her almost fifty miles north until it met an east-west state route that she could take back to the main highway that would get her into Nebraska. Judging by the sky and the feel of the light breeze, it would be a hot day, maybe with a thundershower that afternoon. She wanted to be under some shelter when it hit.

Perhaps she should have thought about where she would find shelter—and who might object when she did.

But she was too busy putting miles on the road. Her parents were out there. She was going to find them. All thoughts of failure vanished with her confident stride in the midday sun.

The work on the Farm and in the woods of the MAG had toughened her, and she felt quite strong as she marched along the road. There were even a couple of people out traveling the tarmac as well. She saw them coming from quite a ways on the long straight road. Men, both of them, with beards and dirty clothing. They looked like they might have been on the road for a while. She stayed far to the right, all the way on the gravel shoulder, and they marched along like metronomes, packs on their backs, faces tanned deep brown by the sun, hugging the other side.

They each nodded to her as they went by. And then they were gone.

Clouds gathered in the afternoon, dark and lowering, and she was grateful for the shade. The road went through a town so small it had only one blinking four-way yellow traffic light. Emily slowed, thinking to go around it, but, in the end, she thought it wasn't worth the extra time. It seemed like a small risk worth taking.

There were people in the town. No lights, no cars, but people occasionally on the street in clots like leaves collecting in slack water. They eyed her without suspicion but without friendliness, either. She asked one man for water, and he said she could have a drink from his well. It was two blocks east.

Emily thanked him and followed him to his house, where his wife gave her a slice of bread, and their daughter, a lass about six, asked if she was tired. Emily said no. It was just one more lie, after all.

No rain fell, and Emily left the town and headed out again. She slept in a dry ditch next to the road and was up before the sun, moving again, a little water sloshing in her canteen from the well the day before.

She was making good time when the motorbikes appeared.

They came from the state highway—she saw them long before they made the turn to come her way, but there was no way to get out of sight. This part of the country was flat farmland as far as the eye could see. She stood out like a lamppost on a dark street.

Emily hitched her pack up a little higher and kept walking. Confidence was her best defense, though she fingered the pocketknife at her hip and drew the blade, just in case.

They stopped in a semicircle around her, blocking the road before and behind, leaving her a space no more than six feet across. She could have run down the shallow depression and tried to climb the woodpost fence into the alfalfa field, but they would catch her before she could make it.

All of them wore helmets and goggles, obscuring their faces. They cut their engines and stood there straddling the machines, saying nothing.

Emily tried to remain quiet. She was sweating hard under the hot sun, and the beat of the radiating heat from the pavement came up through the soles of her boots.

Finally, she couldn't stay silent. "Let me pass, please."

They said nothing. The one right in front of her shifted himself a couple of inches and settled again. They clearly weren't going to move.

She trudged down into the ditch, went around the semicircle's edge, and back up onto the road. She walked away in the same direction she'd been traveling.

Behind her, the bikes started up.

She ran.

Five steps along, some loose gravel slid out from under her boot, and she fell sideways into the ditch, her ankle throbbing. Gravel bit into her right arm, and the pack came loose.

Something dropped over her head, a sack of some kind, and she screamed until a wad of cottony material was shoved into her mouth. She couldn't breathe.

Emily thrashed and kicked and tried to bite for as long as she had air. And then she blacked out.

When she came to, she was lying on her left side in some sort of shed. It was late afternoon, judging by the sun peeking through the slats of the shed wall. Her hands were tied behind her. The whole place smelled of machine oil and something else, something rusty and metallic. It might have been an old tractor, might have been blood.

Her ankle had swollen, and just moving it almost made her cry out in pain. The cotton gag was gone, but no one had washed the grit off her. Her right side felt like it had been raked with a cheese grater.

And she wasn't alone in the shed.

Two other women—girls, really, not much younger than Emily—sat against the wall to Emily's left. Their hands were bound, too, but in front of them. Grime coated their faces, and their clothing hadn't been washed in some time.

"Where am I?" Emily said to them.

They just stared at her. Emily had never seen eyes so dead.

"My name's Emily," she tried again. "I'm trying to find my parents. Where am I? Who are those bikers?"

One of the girls flinched when she said "bikers." Other than that, they might have been carved from teak wood.

Emily tried to lever herself into a sitting position, which was surprisingly difficult. As yet, she wasn't afraid. This was just a setback, a mistake. She'd get out, find her pack, and get back on the road again. Maybe she could steal one of the motorbikes. That would make her trip that much quicker.

From quite nearby, there was a flash of lightning and a crack of thunder just a half-second later. Wind buffeted the shed, which didn't sound too structurally sound. One of the boards to Emily's right rattled, loose.

Another boom sounded almost right above them, and the rain broke through and sheeted down like Noah and the Ark.

The roof of the shed was not made to repel this much water. It dripped straight down in streams from half a dozen holes overhead—one of them right over Emily's back. She was soaked almost before she could move. Wind rocked the structure, and the two girls huddled like scared rabbits.

Emily worm-crawled over to them. The noise from outside was ferocious, and the dirt floor of the shed was rapidly turning to mush.

"Help me," Emily said when she was almost touching the nearer girl's knee. "I need to know where I am."

The girl turned her eyes to Emily, still with no life in them. "You're dead," she said. "We all are."

"We have to get out of here," Emily said, searching the girl's face for some sign of hope.

"We can't. They'll catch us. And then they'll beat us, and we'll be right back to… " She stopped abruptly as if the thing she was about to say was so horrible she couldn't finish.

A gust rocked the shed, and Emily felt the walls sway. Water sheeted in through the far wall, blown through the narrow gaps in the wood.

Now that Emily was close enough, she could see that the girls' clothing was worn and tattered—barely held together by threads. Their feet were bare, crusted in mud. What Emily had taken for dirt on their faces was at least partly bruises.

The wind moaned through the rickety shed, and the loose board abruptly gave way, tearing loose and flinging itself halfway across the floor. There was a gap there, now, and Emily thought it was wide enough to wriggle through. The pouring rain outside made it dark as pitch except when the incessant lightning flashed. She could see they were in a field. Bare for a hundred yards. But then a cornfield, wide and deep and as endless as the sea, stood on the other side of a dirt road. If she could make it there, she might have a chance to hide.

If *they* could make it there. She wasn't leaving without these girls.

"Come on," she said. "Untie me." She rolled over so her hands were close to them.

But no fingers touched the rope. Neither of them so much as moved.

Emily rolled back over. "Come on! Don't give up! We have a chance to get out of here."

Like puppets, they both shook their heads.

The ferocity of the storm wouldn't last. While it did, there was a chance—no one would come out in a storm like this—but if it slackened, died, all chance of escape would go with it.

The closer girl shook herself as if she were coming out of a dream. Something like humanity rose in her eyes. "Go," she said and nodded to the gap in the wall. She tugged on the ropes on Emily's wrists, and in a moment, they loosened enough for Emily to slide her chafed wrists out of them. She was free.

She tried to stand up, and her leg gave way. She fell against the side of the shed with a cry that was drowned by a deafening crack of thunder. The peak of the storm. She had no time.

One last try. She held out her hand to the girls, touched their arms, and tried to get them to move. But whatever humanity had stirred them a moment before had gone again, and they sat there, dripping, as still as death.

Emily crawled to the gap in the wall and out into the storm.

The wind lashed her loose hair into her face, and water sheeted down so thickly she could hardly breathe. She tried to stand, but even if she had both good legs, she'd have had trouble keeping her feet against the gale. She hopped. The wind tossed her to the ground like a broken doll.

So Emily crawled. In the dark and the mud, over thistles and gravel and horse dung, as fast as she could, while the wind howled, then blew, then gusted, and threatened to die. The thunder receded, passing to the east. The stench of herself almost made her retch, but the clean rain kept falling, washing her filth away.

As the last of the storm blew itself out, Emily made it to the cornfield and crawled in, trying desperately not to make a hole that would show where she had gone.

The skin on her hands had been torn by the gravel and brambles, but she forced herself onward. Ten feet. Twenty. Fifty. The sun had returned, the last of its rays slanting overhead. Couldn't be much daylight left. Nightfall would be even better cover than the cornfield. She dragged herself another ten feet.

Despite the heat of the late summer day, she began to shiver. Her sodden, filthy clothes dragged at her.

Then she heard the shouting. They had discovered her absence.

Then screaming. Two voices. Pleading without hope.

The voices were cut off by the slamming of a door, and it was quiet again.

Her pounding heart, the adrenaline coursing through her, her terror of being discovered, none of it mattered. Her body gave out, and she lost consciousness.

And she dreamed.

In her dream, she was eating ice cream at Thusnelda's Burger Shack in Gnarled Oaks. Mom and Dad and Ethan were there, and her friends from the town, and the power was back on, with lights and fries and blenders making shakes. Everything was okay.

And then Ethan turned to her and said, "You left me."

She woke with a start, her leg jerking out and cracking a cornstalk. It toppled and fell.

She was lying in three inches of congealing mud, and something with many, many legs was crawling up her arm. In horror, she shook it off. Spat. Tried to stand. Couldn't.

She couldn't stay here. They would find her.

Overhead clouds obscured the stars and moon—she didn't know which way to go. Her thirst almost closed her throat.

She tried to crawl, but the pain in her hands and her knees made any progress impossible. Sometime that night, it began to rain again, a thin, cold rain that soaked her again and made her shiver, huddled on the ground in the middle of a cornfield.

By morning, she was so stiff she couldn't move. Her lips cracked, but there was no water to relieve her thirst. All day the sun beat down on her, and all day she lay there under it, drifting in and out of consciousness. Her skin began to blister.

Just before she lost consciousness, she thought that it was a shame her brother had been right. Now she would never get to tell him.

Mom and Dad Tuttle got one more message out on the radio—they were stuck in a farmhouse, just inside the Wyoming/Nebraska border and couldn't get any farther. Bern heard it and ripped off the headset, sprinting out into the camp and yelling for Ethan.

He got there in time to talk to his parents. They were in good spirits. They were going to be fine. They just couldn't go any farther at the moment.

No, they hadn't seen Emily.

Afterward, when the power came back, and the MAG slowly disbanded, with its members going back to what was left of the world, Ethan got on one of the vehicle caravans making its way west. He made it to Nebraska and found the farmhouse where his parents had last been, but they weren't there anymore.

Tacked to the wall was a note: "Ethan and Emily," it read, "We love you. Remember, we'll see you again."

Ethan never went back to Spoonerville. Like so many others, he couldn't go back to the remains of a life that had been so sweet and now was so bitter. He found his way to Gnarled Oaks, though, where Grandma welcomed him and kept him fed until he recovered enough to try being human again.

There were a lot of people like that.

Years later, a package arrived at the Little Pink House, bulky and thick with no return address. In it were photographs taken from the walls and scrapbooks of the old house in Spoonerville, all that remained of their possessions and keepsakes there.

That was when Ethan was able to cry.

THE END

Fred said, "Ethan, sit down. Right here, next to your sister. I want to talk about this."

Ethan was reluctant, but this was Fred. Their teacher. The wisest man they knew. How many times had they sat on this couch and discussed things? Too many to count. He sat, but he kept a little distance from Emily.

"There are so many reasons to fight. So many. I don't need to list them. You both know that we could fight, and one of you wants to. Maybe that's the right thing to do—we're certainly justified. We might have to do it anyway, no matter what we decide. But I've been in battle. I know what it looks and feels like to kill, and what it does to a man. You're children. What it would do to you would be worse. Even if you were my squad mates in Vietnam, I would still say this same thing—if there's ever a chance to make peace, take it."

Ethan looked down at the floor for a minute. He waited for Emily to say something. But she didn't. The silence stretched.

It was *so* quiet. No cars. No humming of refrigerators. No chirps, no beeps, no pings. No airplanes cruising through the atmosphere. Ethan thought he could hear the buzzing of the bees as they went about their business.

Fred didn't say anything, either. He just waited patiently and let the silence do the work. Ethan didn't want to be the one to break it, but finally, he couldn't stand it anymore. "So how do we do this peace offering thing?"

Emily said, "I've been thinking about that. The trouble is minimizing the chance that they'll take it as a sign of weakness and come after the rest."

"But that's what it is—a sign of weakness," Ethan said. "That's why I don't think we should do it."

"Does it have to be, though?" Fred said. "We've decided that we're going to do it. So how do we do it that shows strength?"

"We booby-trap it with grenades." Ethan was joking, but not really.

It got a laugh from Emily, at least. "I did the food storage inventory. I must have missed those."

"I put them in with the pinto beans. You probably missed them."

Fred had a faraway look in his eyes. "You know, there might be something there."

"*You* have grenades in your food storage?"

"No, no," Fred said, laughing, "No grenades. But what if we did something surprising, something that would show... maybe not *strength*, exactly, but humanity. People don't kill other people. They kill animals. They kill *others*. That's why soldiers—and demagogues—have to demonize the enemy. They have to make the "other guys" not human. If they don't, then their soldiers won't be as ready to kill them."

"Right," Emily said, snapping her fingers. "In the movies, they make all the bad guys unreal. They wear masks or, you know, stormtrooper armor. Anything to keep the audience from seeing them as human beings."

"Aliens," Ethan said, picking up the thread. "I get it. And right now... we're not human?"

Fred shook his head. "We aren't. None of the people on this block are. So we need to do something to become human to these people. Something that will forge a connection."

"A humanity grenade," Ethan said, rolling his eyes, but he was smiling. "Now I really have heard everything."

Ethan lugged a bucket of sugar out the front door and down the steps. Sweat pooled on the end of his nose and stubbornly refused to drip. He couldn't wipe it. It just dangled there to annoy him. "Okay, you talked me into the olive branch. But did we have to give them the good stuff? We have dehydrated spinach, you know. I'm sure they'd be grateful for that."

"You mean you'd be grateful you don't have to eat it," Emily said. "It's okay. I promise to include our last barrel of freeze-dried beets in our offering."

"That will be satisfactory," Ethan said, setting the bucket into its place in the pile and finally getting to wipe the sweat from his nose. The sun beat on him like a hammer. He was sure he could smell the blacktop melting.

Fred came out of the house with a manila folder, the old kind that was tied with a clasp. He unstrung it and reached in, drawing out some photographs. He held them out to Ethan. "Look through these, will you? See if there are a couple that will do the job."

Emily jogged by, headed for the Tuttles' house. "I'll get some of ours. We'll see if we can't persuade these people that we're human enough to be treated decently."

Ethan thumbed through the sheaf Fred gave him. He stopped on the second photo, drew it out, and held it up. "Man, I remember this one. You, Fred?"

In the picture, two very young kids held oversized fishing rods, casting from a dock out into a pond. Behind them, pointing, was a younger Fred. Sunlight slanted from their backs, lengthening shadows across the water. On their right, a stringer of fish dangled in the water.

"How could I forget?" Fred said. "That was a very good day. There are a lot more of those."

A few minutes later, Ethan had a small pile of photographs, mostly from lessons they'd had, though a couple were from family picnics to which Fred had been invited. Ethan had picked the ones where the Tuttles' faces could most clearly be seen and where it was most obvious that they were having a great time.

Emily had two large photos from off the wall in the front room—one big family picture with Nana and Grandma Tuttle and aunts and uncles and another that showed just the two of them, arms around each other in the sunshine. Their heads were tilted back, and they were laughing up a storm.

"I remember this one," Ethan said, taking it gently from her. "We were supposed to be posing and you told the worst joke I ever heard."

"Yeah, well, I didn't think the photographer would take the picture right then."

"This is Mom's favorite picture of us. We can't put this out here. What if they do something to it?"

"I thought of that," Emily said. "I digitized all these last year, and we put the record on disk and stuck it in a safe deposit box. Plus, we sent copies to Grandma. We have backups. It's okay."

"Not that we can get to the backups," Ethan said, taking his baseball cap off and running his fingers through his sweat-damp hair. "But I guess if the power never comes back on, we'll have bigger problems than having sacrificed Mom's favorite picture." He set the photo on top of one of the buckets.

"I hope this works, Fred," Emily said. "It's risky."

"Not as risky as trying a shootout with an armed gang," Fred said. "Is this all the food we're sharing?"

"Not quite," Ethan said. "We have two large buckets of honey to add to the pile."

"Honey. Oh, man, that's going to be a winner," Fred said.

Ethan smiled. "That I don't mind giving away. We have minions making more even as we speak."

By evening they had the display arranged the way they thought would work best. On every bucket was a photo, sometimes with a note identifying the people in the pictures. There was no way for anyone to come and take the goods without seeing the pictures and reading the notes. They stood at the front window, looking out at the cache in the fading light.

"Great thing about notes," Fred said, "if you can read, you can't stop your brain from processing the words. They'll have read them before they realize that they don't want to know who these people are."

"But they *do* want to know who we are," Emily said, "that's just the point. They might think they don't. It's easier to harm people you don't know, just like you said. But I bet most of these guys aren't bad people. I bet they had jobs like regular folks, and now all they're trying to do is survive. We'll help them do that, but in return, they're going to learn a little about us. And they want to, even if they don't realize it."

"I never heard of fighting a war with kindness," Ethan said. "Seems almost unsportsmanlike."

"It is," Fred said, retreating to the kitchen. He came back with a bag of pretzels, ripped it open, and crunched down on one. "It's supposed to make this as unlike sports as we can get it."

He held out the bag to them. Ethan had never really been much for pretzels before, but now any snack food tasted like a bite of Heaven. "Well," he said, "I guess now we wait. Someone should be on watch. I'm going down to the radio for a bit—Fred, will you put some juice in the generator?"

Fred nodded, chewing. "Pretty soon, we'll have to cut back to just once a day. At this rate, we only have enough gas for another two weeks. I want to stretch it."

Emily took the first watch. And nothing happened.

In fact, nothing happened for three more days.

Rain threatened all day on day twenty-nine, and Emily almost went out and took down the pictures so they wouldn't get ruined. In the afternoon, there was thunder to the northwest, but the rain came down on Malantown and left Spoonerville alone, which wasn't necessarily a good thing. They had all been longing to wash their hair again without using any of their precious water supplies.

But the skies cleared in time for a spectacular sunset, worth watching even, Fred said, if you were in mortal danger.

"There's an old Japanese legend," he said, the three of them sitting on the roof gnawing on loose pieces of beef jerky, "that goes something like this. One day a

Samurai warrior was walking through the forest when he heard the sounds of an approaching bear. He held very still, hoping the bear wouldn't notice him, but it did and began to chase him. He ran with all his might but shortly came to a cliff. With the bear almost in claw range, he had no choice—he flung himself from the lip of the cliff and plummeted down. As luck would have it, from the side of the cliff, a root had grown thick and sturdy, and he grabbed it for dear life, dangling just out of the reach of the bear above."

He swallowed, grabbed a handful of peanuts, and continued. "The cliff turned out to be not very tall, and he found he was only fifteen feet or so from the bottom. Just as he was about to let go, though, a wolf came sniffing the ground below him. It saw him and called to its fellows, and soon there was a pack of wolves circling him, jumping and snapping at his dangling heels.

"So there he was, trapped on the cliffside—a bear above and wolves below. And then, all at once, the root began to crack, threatening to drop him into the slavering wolves. But then, just at the moment of greatest peril, he looked to the cliff face and spied a flower, a sunflower just turning its face to the sun. He gazed at it and thought it the most beautiful thing he had ever seen. A tear slipped down his face at the loveliness of it."

Fred reached over and took a sip from his cup, then put it back down. He leaned back and watched the dipping sun. He said nothing more.

"So… then what?" Ethan said. "The sunflower became a giant eagle and flew him to safety?"

"You've been reading too much of *The Hobbit*," Fred said. "No. Nothing happened. That's the end of the story."

"What?!" Emily said, jumping to her feet. "That's a terrible story! You can't end it like that!"

Fred put his hand to his chest in mock surprise. "Me? I didn't end anything. That's the story. But you shouldn't be so quick to dismiss it. There's a powerful lesson there. I only told it because this sunset is so beautiful."

"If only we didn't have wolves below us," Ethan said. "I'd appreciate it a lot more."

But Emily sucked in a breath, and her eyes got wide. "Wait… no. It's *because* we have wolves below us that we have to see this sunset as beautiful. *That's* what the story is trying to say. The beauty of the sunset is unaffected by the wolves or the bear or the power going out. Beauty is worth appreciating just for itself, no matter what the circumstances."

Fred was silent. Emily put a hand to her head, trying to process what she was thinking.

"It *is* beautiful," Ethan said softly. His face was red in the glow of the fading sun. He kept his eyes to the west for a long time.

At about midnight, the gang arrived.

Emily was on watch, and never had she been quite so vigilant, either. In the half-light of a waxing gibbous moon, she saw a shadow flit forward toward the cache of food. Behind the lacy curtains, she knew she could not be seen from the street. She turned and called out softly, "They're here."

Moments later, Ethan arrived, rubbing sleep from his eyes but already fully armed with the 12-gauge. Fred was right behind him, carrying a pistol and a shotgun of his own.

They didn't need to ask anything—they could see just fine what was happening.

The first man reached the food, crouching down to the west side of it. He didn't touch it. His head swiveled back and forth as if he was counting, then he turned and flashed a light back the way he had come. One pulse of light—a signal.

He turned back. He paused. He reached out toward the pile and very tentatively plucked a photo from the top of one of the bean barrels.

Click went the flashlight on. Pause. Clicked off again.

He kept the photo in his hand.

"That's the one with the three of us," Ethan whispered.

"He's still got it," Fred said.

One at a time, the whole group assembled. They seemed to feel exposed in the middle of the street and

congregated closer to the pile of food, using it as cover. Though the front door was cracked a bit, they couldn't hear any voices, though the group was clearly talking. Heads rose and fell. The picture was passed around. One of the men opened a barrel, looked in, and closed it.

Then they found the note.

Fred had written it, but it had been heavily influenced by the kids. It wasn't long, written in Fred's neat hand, less than a full page. It offered the men the food and said that they—the twins and Fred—would share all they could. It invited whoever found the note to share as well so that everyone could make it through the dark time.

It detailed the food in the pile. And it made sure to identify the people in the photographs.

The men passed the note from hand to hand, reading it with a red-colored flashlight. One or two cast glances at the house. The discussion was growing heated, judging by the waving and gesticulating from the knot of men.

Then one of them started toward the house.

He was carrying a gun, a pistol of some kind, but he didn't have it raised as if he were threatening anyone. It dangled at the end of his arm, and in the other hand, he held a picture.

Now they could hear. More than one of the men by the curb shouted, "Reggie! What the—"

But Ethan had no ears for that. His eyes were fixed on the man coming toward them and he wasn't listening to anything. "That's... that's Reggie Walters. He's my baseball coach."

"What?" Fred said.

Reggie took a few more steps toward the house, putting him just a few feet from the steps up to the front porch.

Men at the curb cocked their weapons.

Reggie looked up at the front window, eyes locked on as if he could see through the curtains to the people inside. "Ethan! Ethan Tuttle! Is this your house?" he shouted.

Fred put his hand on Ethan's arm. "Don't answer him," he said. "Remember, there are still ten more armed men out there."

But Ethan wasn't listening. "That's my coach," he said. "He's nice." He shook off Fred's hand and stepped to the front door.

"No!" Fred shouted, but it was too late. Ethan tugged, and the door came open.

From outside, he must still have been very deep in shadow, probably too deep for anyone to see him. Reggie's head came around toward him, but there was no recognition in his face.

The gang at the curb leveled their weapons at Ethan.

Ethan dropped flat like a marionette with its strings cut.

As he fell, he called out, "It's me, coach. I played third base for you except when you made me play right field. I hated it out there."

From the curb, a shot rang out. The rifle's report was thunderous in the silence of the street. Simultaneously, a crack sounded inside the house, and plaster rained down from a hole in the ceiling.

"No! Don't shoot!" Reggie cried and mounted the steps in one great leap to stand in the doorway, arms and legs spread, blocking it. He faced out, back toward the gang, so that Ethan's head was about a foot behind his back.

"Hi, Coach!" Ethan said brightly.

"They're going to kill you," Coach Reggie said. Then, to the men outside, he called out, "Don't shoot these people. We don't need to hurt them. They gave us food. They're friends of mine."

Fred was the only one who saw what happened next. A couple of the men put up their weapons, obviously not wanting to fire on Reggie. But more than one kept guns sighted, and one of them pulled the trigger just as another man bumped into him. The crack of the gun split the night.

Reggie screamed and dropped to the ground on top of Ethan.

Emily chambered a round and leveled the shotgun. But Fred put a hand out. "No," he said. "Wait. You'll be ineffective at this range anyway."

The Tuttle Twins and the Days of Darkness

Reggie wailed, thrashing on the ground, holding his arm. Ethan did his best to get up and get his arms around his coach. Two men from the gang started toward the house, shouting to the rest of the gang to give it up and go back to base. The other men shouted back at them, waving their arms, telling them to clear the field of fire. But they marched up to the porch and stood there, looking down at Reggie, obviously trying to make up their minds about what to do next.

It was Ethan who broke the stalemate. "He's hurt, guys. Help me get him to our medical supplies."

They didn't move. One of them, tall and thin like framing lumber, clenched and unclenched his hands uselessly. But Ethan had practiced this and knew what to do.

"You, tall guy, in jeans. What's your name?"

"Me? Uh, Lenny."

"Lenny, kneel down right here and grab his legs. You, in the flannel shirt. What's your name?"

"Marcus. My friends call me Mark," he said, adding to the unreality of the scene.

"Mark, then. Can you hold your hand right here?" Ethan nodded to Reggie's upper arm, which bled all over the floor.

Mark took up his position.

"Okay," Ethan said. "Stay right there until I get back with some bandages. Keep pressure on the wound, or he'll lose a lot of blood."

"You shot me!" screamed Reggie.

"Not me!" Lenny said, holding Reggie's twitching legs. "It was Austin that shot you."

"Austin! You sack of horse dung! You better run, or so help me—"

Mark clamped down harder, and Reggie screamed again.

Out at the curb, one of the men—Austin, almost certainly—broke and ran.

"We're going out there," Fred said to Emily. "Put down the gun. I'll take my pistol, but I think we're done with the shooting for tonight."

Emily was frozen for a second. But then Lenny said, "I think he's right. This didn't go down the way we thought it would."

"Not at all," Mark said, shaking his head. "No offense, Reg."

Fred took her hand. "Come on. It will be all right."

Ethan dashed back into the room with a box of gauze just as his sister and Fred went out the front door. He looked at Lenny, holding white-knuckled to Reggie's calves while they twitched spasmodically underneath him. "What are they doing?" Ethan said.

"Going out to talk," Lenny said. He shrugged. "It might work. Austin is the one that burns the houses, but I don't think he's up to doing that tonight."

Fred and Emily held hands as they went through the door. Fred had the idea that might be even less threatening. They stood on the porch for a moment, glad that there was enough moon to see something by.

The gang was still clustered around the food on the far side, crouched to keep themselves from being easy targets. Fred called out, "We're taking care of your friend here. He's a friend of ours, too, it turns out. This is Emily—" He gestured at her. "—and I'm Fred. This is my home. We're hoping to stay here, and if you let us, we'll share what we have with you."

They let that statement sit there for a minute before taking another step down toward the cache. Nothing happened, so they went down the stairs to the front walk, slowly and deliberately, not wanting anyone over there to get the willies and lose their discipline.

"That's far enough," a voice said.

Emily and Fred stopped walking.

"We just want to talk," Fred said. "There's been enough shooting tonight."

"And we haven't even done any of it," Emily muttered.

"I heard that," the voice said. "I'm sure you *could* do it if you wanted to."

Emily said, "That's just it. We *don't* want to. We offered our food and our names so you would know we don't have to fight one another."

"You don't know what it's like out there," the voice said, and Emily saw the top of a man's head poke above a barrel of wheat. He was balding, hair very thin on top. She thought it might have been red hair, but the light wasn't good enough to tell. She caught a whiff of gasoline from somewhere.

"No," Fred said, still slowly and carefully, "we don't. I'm not sure we want to. But we do want to keep living here, and we do want to keep living, period. Can we? Will you let us?"

The voice said nothing. Behind them, they heard Ethan's low voice reassuring Reggie and Reggie's strained answers. His arm must be very bad.

"What's your name?" Fred said, taking another step forward. "We already know Reggie and Lenny and Marcus."

"And Austin," Emily said. "Don't forget him."

"Right, Austin, too. Who are you?"

"Not important," the voice said. "I don't want to get to know you. You don't want to get to know me."

"The food is still yours," Emily said. "We left it for you. We don't have a lot more, but you are welcome to this much."

There was a long pause, and the voice said, "When you get hungry enough, you can do awful things."

Fred smiled that big, hearty, wonderful smile of his and said, "Then let's not get that hungry, okay?"

A few minutes later, a pickup truck rolled down the street, and five men—the part of the gang that was still outside—loaded the supplies into the back of it. Austin had not come back, that Emily had seen.

Ethan still knelt by Reggie's head as he lay on the floor. They had a pillow under his torso, and he looked more comfortable, though his arm was a mess. Lenny and Mark sat against the wall, their legs sticking out into the room, heads swiveling back and forth like they'd never seen the inside of a house before.

"I'm sorry," Reggie said between clenched teeth. "Carmen and the kids were visiting their Great Aunt Mabel when the power went out. I haven't heard from them. It's driving me crazy."

"*Drove* you crazy, I think you mean," Ethan said.

He considered that for a moment, then nodded. "Guess so. I mean, I didn't have any storage at all. Just what was in the fridge. That was gone in a couple days, and I got very hungry. I bumped into these guys at the

Stuff-Mart. One of them is a guy I worked with down at the warehouse on the water, you know, just one of the guys, and he said they had a group that went around looking for abandoned houses and scavenging food from it. They had a pile, and if I'd come and help, they'd share it with me. It sounded good. Then I found out some of the houses weren't empty after all. But... I was just so *hungry*, and I was all alone."

He stopped talking for a second and shifted his back a bit, hissing when he had to move his arm. "It's not really an excuse," he said and closed his eyes.

"No, but it is a reason," Ethan said. "Where is the Great Aunt your family went to visit?"

"Charlotte."

"North Carolina? We've been talking to some people there," Ethan said.

His eyes flew open. "What? How?" He tried to sit up, the pain in his arm forgotten.

"We have a radio."

"Shortwave?"

"Ham. Fred has a license."

"Can we try talking to them right now?" Reggie's voice was frantic.

"At 1 a.m.?" Ethan said. "Not likely. And anyway it's not like making a phone call. We never know who's on the other end."

"How do you have power for it?"

"Generator in the garage," Ethan said. "But we're getting really low on fuel."

Lenny interrupted, "We have fuel." It was in the same tone of voice someone uses to say, "Sun's coming up."

Ethan's heart skipped a beat. He didn't want to appear too eager. "Generators burn a lot."

Lenny barked a laugh. "Not this much, they don't. Anton out there, he's the foreman at the refinery. He can get all the fuel you could burn in a lifetime."

"He's stealing it?" Ethan said.

Lenny shrugged. "I don't know. There's nothing happening at the refinery anymore. The gas just sits there. They don't have the power to run the turbines, so they don't do any refining. Besides, no one is bringing in any crude, and they can't get trucks in to ship out what's already in the tanks. Hundreds of thousands of gallons of gasoline, just sitting there."

"Don't you have generators?"

"Of course we do, kid, what do you think, we're stupid or something—"

"Hey—" Reggie said, raising his head with a wince, "this is my star third baseman. Take it easy on him."

"Sorry, kid," Lenny said. "We got power. We got all the generators you could want. What we don't have is a radio. We tried to get one, but the fella that had it smashed it up before we could, uh, persuade him that he should let us take it."

Ethan nonchalantly laid his hand on the pistol in his waistband. "I might do the same under those circumstances."

"Relax, kid. Reggie says you're okay, you're okay. You got nothing to fear from us. Besides, we have all that food now. Unless you poisoned it." Lenny fixed Ethan with a baleful eye. "You didn't poison it, didya, kid?"

Ethan took Lenny and Reggie downstairs to the radio. Fred and Emily were out front with the rest of the gang, negotiating exchanges of goods and services. It turned out that once they knew the names of the people in the houses, the gang wasn't so bent on driving them out. Emily had taken that hint and gone down the street to the Cunninghams, bringing them back to the confab. She told them to bring some family photos. Hey, if it worked once, it could work again.

Also, the gang had brought gasoline with them, so the generator was full, and they'd gotten new reserves (in exchange for the food outside). Ethan suspected the gasoline had been for incendiary purposes, but he didn't ask, and no one volunteered anything except for Reggie, who said, "It's a lot more pleasant having this conversation than the other activities we had planned for tonight."

This early in the morning, the radio was able to connect with Europe, where the sun was already up. In Budapest, Imre (K36VGG) said they had no power issues at all. Their power was the same as normal. Jean-Claude in Lyon (YY4BNS) said the same thing. No power outages. But he had heard that the states were in complete chaos, and he thought that not having the Americans to trade with was going to cause serious problems in Europe before too long. "Get your American act together," Jean-Claude said. "We don't like you, but we need you, ok?"

Try as he might, Ethan couldn't raise anyone in North Carolina, let alone pin down Charlotte. "But I'm not that good at the radio. Now that we have power for the generator, we can try a lot more and see what we can find."

Before long, Reggie nearly fell off the stool from weakness. He'd lost a lot of blood, and Ethan said he should go to the hospital. "The bone might be broken. I can't tell."

"Not gonna be pitching batting practice for a while, am I?" Reggie said.

They carried him upstairs and laid him in the bed of the pickup. Fred had made a friend out of Anton, the leader of the group, and a tentative agreement had been struck—the gang would get access to the radio in exchange for gasoline to run the generator. They would take the cache of food but leave all the rest of the houses on the block alone, including the Cunninghams'. And when Reggie had recovered he, Lenny, and Anton were invited to dinner.

"Probably we'll feed you eggs," Fred said. "But they're healthy."

The gang also had news of Spoonerville and Malantown. "The center of Spoonerville looks like a max security prison now," Anton said. "It's an ugly place. But it's not as ugly as Malantown. There are fires there all the time, whole blocks burning. The refinery shut down and chained its doors shut, and the whole thing is patrolled by dogs now. Nobody in or out other than the plant managers. We don't know if we'll ever be able to restart things once the power comes back—if it does."

"But it has to come back," Ethan said. "I mean, eventually. Doesn't it?"

Anton raised an eyebrow. "Does it? Where is that written?"

"It seems a small thing to bring a mighty nation to its knees, yet here we are." Fred took a bite of one of their last apples. No more until the McMurtrys' apple tree bore fruit in the fall. Though that fruit would be wormy—they didn't have the right kind of spray to keep the moths from laying eggs on the apples.

"Bringing the power back right now would probably be fairly effective. We wouldn't have too much disruption. But in another month? There's equipment that needs maintaining, but we can't maintain it without power because electricity gives us the tools to maintain it, and also shows us when parts have to be replaced. We turn that power on in a year, and the whole system will blow again, like a breaker tripping because we haven't found the cause of the short. Not to mention that whatever caused this in the first place might happen again."

"Cyber attack," Emily said. "Or that's what we were told."

Anton looked off into the distance. "Maybe. If so, do you think we learned our lesson?"

With the new agreement with the gang, living by themselves at Fred's wasn't impossible anymore. The gang kept them supplied with fuel, and the chickens kept the protein coming. Once in a while, the gang came up with other things, too, like new books.

"I'd give them *all* our food if they'd keep those coming," Emily said.

One day they brought a case of mandarin oranges, which they traded for lessons on how to use the radio. Although it was illegal—to use the ham radio required passing the FCC test, but since the test was taken online, there wasn't any way to pass it anymore—Fred thought it would be okay for Lenny and Reggie to learn the basics. Soon they were consuming huge amounts of gasoline to run the radio, searching for Reggie's family.

And one day, the search paid off. An operator in North Carolina had coordinated a kind of clearinghouse for missing families in the state and had a list.

Lenny hit the transmit button and said, "We're looking for a woman named Carmen and three small children, six, four, and a toddler. They'd be in the Charlotte area."

The radio crackled, and QT9BBF replied, "I have them on my list. They're still in Charlotte. Sorry, I don't have anything more."

But Reggie didn't care. Tears streamed down his cheeks. "I'll go to them. I have to."

"You might not make it," Emily said.

"But I'm going to try. There's nothing for me anywhere without them."

So in the weirdest collaboration ever seen in Spoonerville—or pretty much anywhere else—the Tuttles and Fred and the gang from Malantown loaded up a lime-green pickup truck with gasoline and food until the springs sagged under the chassis. Reggie couldn't drive very well because of his arm, so two other men from the gang volunteered to go with him. Duncan and Reese played rock/paper/scissors for the right to ride in the cab while Reggie strapped himself into the passenger seat and tried not to be miserable with pain and worry.

"They'll be there," Emily said.

"We'll stay on the radio until we hear something about what happened to you," Ethan said.

And then they were gone.

After that, the twins didn't see much of the gang. It was a good collaboration until it wasn't, and by day ninety-three, they hardly saw each other anymore. That was until day 103 when QT9BBF reported that Carmen and her three children were not in Charlotte anymore.

"Where did they go?" Ethan said, alarmed. If they weren't still there, they could be anywhere, and how would Reggie find them?

"My info says three men in a pickup truck ran a blockade and took them from a government security camp. They disappeared south, toward Georgia. I have no more information."

Emily sighed. "I wish our parents would run a blockade and come home." But they didn't, and there was no more chatter on the radio about them.

On day 127, a brown pickup truck several years newer than the lime green one pulled up in front of Fred's house, and a very thin, haggard-looking man got out carrying the yellow flag that the Tuttles and the gang had decided was the signal not to shoot.

Emily was on watch and hurtled down the steps toward the street, yelling for Ethan and Fred to come as quickly as they could.

It was Reggie, all right, bearded and weather-beaten. He couldn't give a proper hug with his left arm, and his clothes were tattered and faded, but the truck was nice, and his eyes shone like lamps. "I found them," he said. "I had to break them out, but we made it."

"Duncan and Reese?"

He smiled. His teeth were very white against his tanned face. "Reese met a girl in Tennessee and decided to stay. But Duncan made it back."

"All's well that ends well, I guess," Ethan said.

"Well, I guess," Reggie said. "See, the thing is, the gang really isn't the environment for the kids. I was hoping… well, I was hoping… "

"You want to come up here and live," Ethan said.

Reggie didn't nod. He made some curious motions with his hands, tugged on his ear, and wiped his forearm across his brow.

"You want me to steal third?" Ethan said.

Reggie looked annoyed. "No, that was the sign for 'it's up to you.'"

"It was not. What happened to the clap before the ear tug?"

"*Anyway,*" Emily said, "we'd be thrilled to have you, if we had water."

Reggie's smile got bigger. "I know where there's all the water we need for a while."

"What?" Ethan said. "Where?"

"Three blocks over there's a house with a red picket fence. Ugly thing. Rotting, too, and the house is even worse. The thing should be bulldozed. But in the back there's a barn and in the barn is a pumphouse. The pump doesn't work, of course, but it's on a well. There's a hand crank and the sweetest water you ever tasted comes up."

The Tuttle Twins and the Days of Darkness

"A pint is a pound the world around," Emily said.

"What?" Reggie said.

Ethan rolled his eyes. "She means water is heavy."

Reggie patted his truck. His truck, Ethan guessed, had belonged to someone else fairly recently. "That's why I have Bertha here. She can fetch and carry most everything we need. I just need my family to have some company."

Ethan looked up and down the street. "There are a few places available, I think," he said. "Though people might want them back when the power comes back on."

"I'll take my chances," Reggie said.

Reggie and his family moved onto the Tuttles' street on day 130. They moved in across the street, two doors up from the Cunninghams.

So it was that six kids were out in the street playing stickball when Emily came pelting out of the house, screaming her lungs out. "Ethan! It's Mom and Dad! It's *Mom and Dad!*" She skidded to a stop on the front lawn, chest heaving, waving her arms.

Ethan was up next but tossed his stick in the gutter and charged back to Fred's house. "Where? Are they here?"

"No. On the radio."

They took the stairs down two at a time and heard Fred talking to someone on the set. "If you can make it to Malantown, we can get you the rest of the way. We have friends there."

Dad's voice was 5x9 (a strong signal) from the speaker. "We don't think we can get to Malantown tonight. But tomorrow, or the next day, probably. There's a chain of people ferrying passengers along the I-70 freeway, and we're working with them.

Ethan punched the button for the microphone the second there was the slightest pause. "Dad! Dad, it's Ethan! Where are you?"

Dad's laugh was music. "Kansas. We're just south of Lawrence. Coming to you."

"What took you so long? It's been weeks!"

"It's not easy finding a radio out here. We had to find rides, then work out payment… it wasn't easy. But we knew we had to do it. We couldn't leave you there by yourselves."

Ethan put his head down on the table, too overwhelmed to speak. Emily took over. "Can we come out to meet you? We have gas. We could come up the freeway toward you."

"No, stay there," Dad said. "Anything could happen once you get out on the road. We know. We've seen about everything there is."

"Tomorrow? Did I hear you right?"

"There's a small convoy leaving here this afternoon, and we're going with them as far as we can get. We'll stop short of Malantown tonight, I think, but in the morning we'll get to the Malantown exit."

They did. And the twins and Fred were there waiting for them.

Eventually, the Tuttles and Fred had a relatively peaceful year, staying on their street and keeping a low profile. Their bees made honey, and their chickens laid eggs, and their garden had its best year ever.

Oh, they were hungry. They were dirty and always got less than they wanted to eat. But they were together, and that was what was important.

And then, one day, the power came back on with a spark and a shudder.

The first thing Emily thought was that it was very loud.

THE END

The prospect was just too much. Ethan remembered later that it hadn't even been so much the gas—though that was super important—but he felt like he hadn't had a treat in so long that he started shaking at the thought of peach ice cream.

And then the sign, hand-painted, that read, *We have gas!* broke it for him. Before he knew what he was doing, he had clicked the turn signal and begun to turn into the gas station.

It almost looked like the power had never gone out here.

The pavement was clean. The grass at the border by the street was trimmed tight and uniform. The pumps themselves were practically gleaming. And there was a kid sitting on a low wooden bench in front of the gas station, eating an ice cream cone.

In days to come, Ethan and Emily both would look back on that scene and know they should have smelled the rottenness of it. But at the time, the whole scene did precisely what it was supposed to do—attract flies to the trap.

They drifted to a stop at one of the pumps, pulling up so that others could reach the pumps behind them. They weren't entirely careless. Emily had her hand down low where the rifle was, eyes up and watchful, but she saw nothing to be concerned about. Ethan took a moment to scan the front of the store. The windows were dark but wiped shiny, just like everything else. The front door's sign read *Open*—it was a wooden sign, not neon as it probably would have been before. But it invited just the same.

"It looks good," Ethan said. He checked the pump. It was a new-fangled digital job, and the numbers appeared to work. A paper sign covered the credit-card slot, and read *Please pay inside! Sorry!*

It was what he expected. Power to the pump or not, there wouldn't be any connecting with credit-card payment services.

Ethan leaned back in the window. "Give me fifty bucks," he said. Emily peeled a twenty and three tens off the roll under the seat and handed it over. She tucked the rest back in its place.

"Stay in the car," Ethan said. "I'll be right back."

He slid the money into the front pocket of his pants and kept his hand there as protection. His eyes never stopped moving. Light was pouring down warm from above. Birds flitted back and forth in the trees to either side of the gas station, singing to one another. Ethan could smell the gas, along with the scent of something cooking, probably from farther down the block. Houses lined the street on both sides, with big trees along the street edges so that their limbs made a kind of tunnel.

Here at the gas station, though, there was plenty of blue sky above. It was going to be a beautiful day—sunny and not a breath of wind.

The kid watched Ethan come across the oil-slick asphalt. The cone was turning his tongue pink. Strawberry. It looked good. Ethan thought the kid looked about ten, thin, with an unruly mop of brown hair over a freckled face, shirtless, overalls, and boots.

"Hi," the kid said.

"Hello," Ethan said. "How's the ice cream?"

"Cold. Good breakfast, Mom says. As long as it's strawberry."

"Is your mom here?" Ethan said, stopping a few feet away. He could practically taste the ice cream—cold, fruity, and creamy.

The kid tossed his head toward the windows behind him. "Inside. My folks run this place."

"You have power. I haven't seen any of that for a while."

The kid took another lick. "It's the solar. Dad had it put in last year. We got all the power we want. We can even run the freezer."

"So I see." Ethan took two more steps toward the tinted front door, reached out, and pulled the handle.

It wasn't well-lit inside, but there was enough light coming through the windows that Ethan could see the layout of the place. Snacks and drinks stood in racks to the right, with the counter to the left. No one was behind it. The lights were off. To the far right, the fridge doors all gaped open like mouths, but there were still drinks in the slotted racks. They might have had power for ice cream but not for the wall of refrigerators.

"Hello?" Ethan called. His voice echoed.

A door in the rear wall read *Employees Only*. Ethan crossed to the door and opened it.

It was dark inside. "Hello?" he said, sticking his head in.

There was a metallic click, and something cold and hard was pressed to the back of his neck.

"Easy now," a voice said. "No reason to get hurt over nothing."

Ethan stood very still. A pair of hands patted him down. "Hands out of pockets," the voice said. It was low, a man's, and not a young one. As soon as Ethan's hand left his pocket, the man fished out his $50. Ethan heard the crinkle of it as it disappeared.

"Don't hurt me," Ethan said. "We're just trying to get to my grandparents'."

"Well, that's not going to go well from this point," the man said. "At least it won't go how you expected. Turn around."

The pressure left Ethan's neck. He turned. Behind him stood a large, wide man with a month growth of beard. His face was tanned and lined, and his small dark eyes did not look friendly. He held a pistol in his hand, a Glock, probably, or some other 9mm. It pointed unwaveringly at Ethan's middle, a dark, malignant mouth.

"We'll just wait here a bit," the man said. He wasn't much taller than Ethan, only an inch or so. His sandy hair was unkempt, stringy, and greasy. One whiff told Ethan he hadn't been washing. Not that Ethan had.

Ethan quickly tossed a glance out of the window toward the truck. Maybe Emily had taken off. That would be good—saving herself.

But he instantly saw that she had not. The truck was there, all right, but it had four people around it, two men, a woman, and the kid, who stood with his belly button pressed to the front bumper.

"That's my sister," Ethan said. "Let her go."

"I don't think that's gonna happen."

"We don't have anything you want."

"What do you know about what we want?" The man scowled at him. "Everyone has something to give."

A minute later, the woman poked her head in the front door. "Mort," she said, "We need the kid. The girl's not playing ball."

He waved Ethan outside with the barrel of the gun. Ethan marched obediently into the rising sunshine. Mort stood to his right and pointed the gun at his head.

"Roll down the window!" one of the other men yelled.

Emily did. She'd slid over into the driver's seat.

"Now get out," the man said. He carried a shotgun, a massive thing, ugly and dangerous. Emily popped the locks on the truck and climbed out. The man herded her over to where Ethan was.

Then they ransacked the truck. Everything they found they tossed out onto the pavement, except for the twins' phones (which held their precious maps), the rifle, and the pistol, which they laid gently on the hood.

"Just let us go!" Emily said. "We're no threat to you."

"Of course you're not. But that ain't the point."

"What *is* the point?" Ethan said. A lead weight settled in his gut as they took the empty gasoline cans from the bed of the truck.

"The point is we want things, and you have those things, so we're going to take them."

"You steal from defenseless children?" Emily said.

"You had guns. You just weren't smart enough to use them."

"We don't use them on innocent people!" Emily said. The water—they were taking the water, too.

Mort laughed, a thin, reedy sound. "We ain't innocent, Missy. But no shame, you didn't know. Now you do, but it's too late, ain't it?"

The truck had been relieved of all its possessions. It stood forlorn and empty, doors open as if it, too, was being held at gunpoint.

"That's all of it," the woman said.

"Okay, you can go," Mort said.

The twins exchanged a glance for the first time with some hope in it. They started for the truck.

The other man moved in front of them, shotgun held akimbo across his body. "Nah, nah," he said, his voice raspy and hoarse.

"Not in the truck. That belongs to us now," Mort said.

Ethan turned back, mouth open. "But... we need it! How can we get to our grandma's without it?"

Mort took his fingers and made a walking motion.

"You can't be serious!" Emily said. "It's more than fifty miles!"

"You'll want to get started, then," Mort said. The rest of the gang—because that's what it was, a sophisticated gang that laid a trap the twins had walked right into—smiled at their misfortune.

"You can't do this!" Ethan said, his voice shrill.

"We *are* doing it. Are you dense?"

"At least... " Emily said, thinking fast, "At least give us our 72-hour kits. If we go walking now, it's three or four days at least. We'll starve or something worse. You have to give us a chance."

For the first time, Mort's face showed indecision.

"You have everything. You took our water, our food, you took our guns, our gasoline, you even took our money. You're taking our truck, too. A couple of backpacks won't make any difference to you, but they might mean we can survive."

Mort's gun dropped to his side, but he didn't say anything.

"Please," Emily said. "Think of what you're teaching your son."

Mort made a face. "Grandson," he said.

"Grandson, then. Simple mercy. Don't send us out into the wilderness with nothing."

For a while—it felt to Ethan like a month—nobody said anything, everyone standing still like a painting, not even breathing.

Then Mort said, "Any weapons in the packs?"

"No. Well, there's a pocketknife. It's about two inches long. I don't think it's anything you need to worry about. But it could keep us alive. We might be out there a long time."

Mort didn't seem convinced, but he finally nodded his head at the other man. He went over to the pile of goods, picked out the backpacks, and tossed them at the feet of the twins.

"One more thing—" Emily said.

"No." Mort chopped at the air with a hand.

"Our phones. We need our maps. We can't find where we're going without them."

"You have thirty seconds to get off my property," Mort said.

Ethan opened his mouth to say something, but Emily crouched, picked up the backpacks, and slammed one into his chest. "Come on. We have a long walk ahead of us."

They shouldered the packs and started toward the road. Ethan couldn't resist a parting shot. "Great role model, Mort. You send a couple of kids off into the wild without a map. You didn't even give us ice cream. Sleep with one eye open—you know what they say about karma."

"Keep trying, kid. I admire that. Oh, and by the way, I wouldn't walk much farther down the main road. There are people on the other end of town that like backpacks."

It was all Ethan could do to stop himself from picking up one of the rocks on the gas station verge and winging it through one of the gas station windows.

But he *did* stop himself, and that impulse control would come in handy many times in the next few days.

They crossed the street at the crosswalk where a single blinking light used to be. It was probably silly, but it felt like the right thing to do. Emily wanted to stop at the opposite side and talk through their options, but Ethan grabbed her arm and said, "Keep moving. We need to be out of sight of them as soon as possible. I don't want them to change their minds."

"Dad will be sad about his truck. Grandpa gave it to him."

The corner of Ethan's mouth turned up a half inch. "I'm going to love telling him this story. And coming back down here with him."

But all that was for another day.

As for this one, it was going to be hot. The town they were in—Accord Landing—was tree-lined and pretty, a thing they would have appreciated if they hadn't been so mad. Summer flowers were out, and the overhang of the trees created long stretches of shade. Rolling hills raised and lowered the road and kept them from seeing very far ahead, except on-top the next rise, where they could see that the sidewalk ended about a half mile farther on where the road narrowed back to a single-lane highway.

"That's probably where the people on the other side of town are waiting to get us," Emily said, still walking. The gas station behind them was hidden by the masses of foliage and a slight rise they'd just descended. She took off her backpack and rummaged for a second. Her hand came up holding a compass.

"Get yours out, too," she said and shuffled until the sun was directly at her back. Then she turned 90 degrees to the left, north, and set the direction of travel on her compass.

Ethan did the same.

They stood in the middle of a stretch of blacktop and tried to figure out how to make the next leg of the journey work.

"I remember a little of the map," Emily said. "This town is close to a river—it's called Accord Landing—and there's a crossroad ahead that goes out to the riverbank. We know our orienteering skills from summer camp. All the rivers and creeks run down into the Monongahela River, eventually."

"So we follow the river to the Little Pink House." Ethan sighed. "I just think it would have been a lot easier to do with a truck, that's all."

"Spilled milk. No use crying."

"Good thing we went through these 72-hour kits last month. We know the jerky is fresh, and the batteries are good."

"That's the spirit. Come on. Let's get to the road and see where it goes."

It went down a long, winding lane, growing progressively more weedy and gravel-strewn until it forked southeast and southwest. The right-hand fork descended into a shallow valley where horses galloped, and cattle grazed in the field, and a man in a cowboy hat kept watch. He was little more than a speck below them, but both twins felt as if he could see them clear as day. They kept to the far side of the road and tried to make as little noise as possible.

The left fork went up over the top of the hill. They climbed it just to see where it went and found that they could see quite a way. A mile or two distant, at the bottom of the hill's east side, their road struck another blacktopped road at a right angle. "The landing road," Emily said. "A lot farther away than I thought, but at least there it is."

Beyond the landing road, there was a belt of trees running mostly east and west—large, full-grown sycamores and oaks, thick and impenetrable, like Mirkwood.

"That's the river," Ethan said.

"How do you know?"

"Basic reading of the land. Dad taught me on one of our long hikes. Most of this is pastureland, and it's been cleared, so when you see a group of trees, especially if they're in a line, that usually means water. I'd bet that's the tributary river that will lead us to the big river by Grandma's house—the Monongahela."

It was encouraging to both of them to think that their walk had brought them to the place they sought most—or at least to something they could use to find that place.

They sat for a bit and had some beef jerky. Both of them were tired and thirsty, but there was no water, and their halozone tablets were no good without a water source. They had to make the river.

"Not too far," Ethan said. "We can be there in an hour and get a good drink. We can use the road, too. It will go faster that way."

But as they started down the hill, a glint of sunlight brought them up short. There were vehicles on that road. More than one, by the look of it. Now that they listened closely, they could hear the roar of engines—trucks. Big ones, by the sound of it.

Emily had a pair of low-power binoculars in her pack. She got them out and trained them on the road. "Two... no, three trucks, cruising back and forth. It's like they're waiting for something."

"Or someone," Ethan said, tapping Emily's shoulder for a turn.

Emily wiped her brow. She was parched but still sweating, which meant she probably wasn't to the level of heatstroke yet. "They can't be waiting for us. What would be the point?"

"What's the point of taking a rusting old truck from us? But Mort and his pals were just fine with that."

The hillside was deeply grassy as it sloped to the valley floor, but the trees had mostly been cut, and only a few larger bushes provided cover. Worse, the road they were on pointed ruler-straight at the landing road and offered no cover at all. If they went down it, they'd be seen.

But cutting across country wasn't much better. Ethan's shirt was a bright blue, and Emily's pink—both would show up like a blinking sign against the deep green of the pasture.

"I hate to say it—" Ethan began, lowering the binoculars.

"Then don't," Emily said. "I could use a nap anyway. Maybe they'll go away."

"Maybe... I don't know. We can maybe go another few hours before water is a serious problem. But if we don't go now and they're still there later, we'll be in more need and still be no closer to the river."

"If it is a river. We still don't know that for sure."

"Well, yeah."

"Or we could go now and get caught by whoever that is, stuffed in the back of a truck and sold to slavers."

Ethan wrinkled his face. "I don't think we're quite to that point yet in the decline of Appalachian civilization. The power only went out a few weeks ago. Give it at least through July"

Emily found she could laugh a little, which given their circumstances, was a surprise.

"Okay," she said, "so what do we do?"

If you think the twins should make a break for the river, go to page 244.

If you think the twins should hide and sleep a bit and try later, go to page 299.

If they left, Mom and Dad might not be able to find them. Perhaps not ever. If they went to Grandma's—assuming they made it—that would be good, but they'd have to leave Fred behind, and he was obviously so tired he was falling off his chair. He looked closer to eighty than sixty, and his face—Ethan tried not to think it—looked like something from the Michael Jackson *Thriller* video.

Ethan's heart gave a little jump at that. Fred had never been anything but generous, kind, and helpful to them. So the moment things got rough, they ran out on him? No. That wasn't happening.

But as much as Fred seemed to trust the people in this mutual assistance group, Ethan was wary. Amihan Legaspi might have been okay—he didn't have any reason to think she wasn't—but what was the guarantee about the others? Away from their base of resources, Ethan didn't give two figs for their chances of survival. What skills did they have? Pamphleteering? Marketing? Debate? Those weren't exactly survival skills, not in a desperate situation. They could shoot straight, that was true, and they had some weapons and food, but once those had been blended with the general resources of the group... what did they need the twins for, or Fred, for that matter? Although Ethan had a suspicion Fred was capable of a lot more than teaching history.

No, the smart thing would be to stick close to home, stay in Spoonerville, and give the government a chance to do one of the few things it was actually supposed to do—protect them. They had plenty of resources. If they were vigilant, they could stay there for several weeks.

Ethan opened his mouth to say this when the radio crackled again. This time there was a voice. It came in staticky but strengthened and resolved itself. "Break channel GP2IWQ, Golf Papa Two Iowa Walter Quebec, we're in Malantown, and we need assistance."

Emily's eyes grew wide. She looked at Fred. "What do I do?"

Fred said, "We listen. See who responds. Maybe we'll learn something."

The voice, a woman's, grew increasingly desperate over several minutes as she tried to raise someone with no success. Finally, Emily couldn't stand it any longer. She keyed the mic. "NX7JCS here, GP2IWQ Malantown. We read you five-by-nine. What's the trouble?"

"Oh, thank Heaven," the woman said. "I didn't know... where are you, NX7JCS?"

Fred intercepted Emily's hand as she reached for the mic key. "We don't know these people," he said.

"But they're in trouble!"

"Are they? That's what they say."

"But we saw a big column of smoke in Malantown. There's a fire there. The police radio said there was a fire at the refinery on the waterfront." At least, that was what Emily thought the radio had said.

"And maybe there is, and maybe these people are really in trouble. But how can knowing where *we* are do them any good?" Fred said, arching his one non-swollen eyebrow.

Emily hadn't thought of that. "Malantown, we're in touch with emergency personnel. Give us your location, and we can get assistance to you." It wasn't precisely a lie—they *had* recently been in touch with emergency personnel, and she was pretty sure they could use the radio to alert them—the CB in Fred's truck.

A few moments went by, and another voice cut in. "AH1TTL Malantown breaking channel, we have a massive fire on the waterfront and no emergency vehicles to fight it. Requesting assistance, repeat, requesting assistance."

Emily looked back to tell Ethan to get on the CB and radio the police, but he was already on it.

"Break 9, break 9, I have an emergency at the Malantown waterfront. Calling any Malantown or Spoonerville officer or any state trooper. Repeat, emergency at Malantown waterfront, fire and injuries."

The response was immediate. "Whoever you are, this is a restricted channel. Get off and stay off."

"I'm calling in an emergency because there is no 911 anymore."

"We're aware of the emergencies. Thank you for your concern. We will respond as appropriate. Please vacate the channel so that authorized personnel may use it."

Ethan clicked off. "Well, that was rude."

Fred shook his head. "Wish I were surprised."

The chatter on the ham radio, however, hadn't abated at all. There were so many people trying to talk that the channel was effectively blocked. Even if Emily had wanted to comment, she couldn't have.

So instead, she switched to another band. Another voice was calling for help, this one identifying itself as Peachtree, just outside Atlanta. What could Emily do about that? They listened for a while and then went to another.

It was a long evening, and it didn't get any prettier. When Emily did find someone who wanted to talk—someone who was not currently in a life-threatening emergency—the news they had was universally bad. Large cities, stranded without water, had caught fire in some places. Where that hadn't happened, refugee waves had poured out of them into the suburbs, seeking food and water, and protection from gangs and other criminals who were preying on the weak.

Almost no one had any food storage, not even a couple of weeks' worth. Medicines were in short supply. Emergency personnel had, in many places, stopped responding altogether.

"It's like nobody was ready for trouble, even though we knew—everybody knew—that it was coming one day," Emily said. She had finally given up and moved to the sofa to sit and have some chocolate.

"Humans are very odd, historically," Fred said. "If you ask a hundred of us, 'Do you think things will go on perfectly for the rest of your life?' absolutely no one will say yes. But if you ask us, 'How much preparation have you done against the day things go to pieces?' almost all of us will say, 'Not very much.' It seems impossible, but it's true."

Ethan chewed a candy bar slowly. There were only a few of them left, and he wanted it to last a while. Who knew if there would be any more? "Even our family. We were a lot more prepared than most, but we didn't see this coming. We're okay for now… but not for long." He looked hard at Fred and Emily. "Not for long. We all know it."

Fred cleared his throat a little. "I, uh, haven't wanted to mention it, but I've been thinking a lot about exactly that. I'm feeling… weak. No, no, don't get all fidgety. I'll be alright, and I'm getting better. But it would only take one slip, one fall, one cut… just one thing, and I'd be down. I don't think I can stay here."

Emily hung her head but then sucked in a big breath and smiled. "Well, that'll make three of us, then. This last session on the CB radio really has me spooked. The police can't help us as long as we're here. And as Fred says, there's not much between us and the end, like, the *real* end. I think we should go into town. To the camp. For Fred's sake. And for ours."

They kicked the idea around a little more, but in the end, they all felt there was only one thing to do.

The next morning they went down to the center of town. It had been radically transformed. Where once there had been open parkland with trees and grass, ringed by the biggest buildings in town, now the high school, City Hall, the library, and the police station were surrounded by what must have been miles of chain-link fence, broken only by a gate at what had been the road that split the park and Spoonerville High.

Every dirt or grass surface inside the fence had a tent on it. They were arranged in neat rows that stretched hundreds of yards, and hundreds—maybe thousands—of people milled about between them.

"I gotta admit, it doesn't look very inviting," Emily said.

"We're not here to get inside yet," Fred said. "All we're trying to do is find out what we can bring and what would await us."

Apparently, they were not the only ones who had those questions because before they even got to the gate, a young red-haired man drove up to them on a golf cart, holding a sheaf of papers. "Are you from Spoonerville?"

"Yeah," Ethan said. "We're just, um, browsing."

The redhead broke into a big smile. "You're gonna want to come here. I have some information if you're interested." He held out a paper.

Emily took it. "Thanks."

"My pleasure," the man said and drove on.

The paper wasn't an advertisement by any stretch, but it was a fairly cheerful paragraph about safety and security—and food—with a short list of who was eligible to "camp" in the Compound and what those eligible were allowed to bring.

"Sleeping bags," Emily read. "Pillows—one each; one week's worth of clothing; reading material—to be held in the library. All campers are required to give access to their properties and surrender any supplies therein to police and other government officials for the duration of the camp."

"Sounds lovely," Ethan said in a voice that meant the opposite.

"Sounds typical," Fred said. "Anything else on there?"

"No. That's all. But then, that's about all anyone *could* bring."

Fred turned left and headed back up the hill to their subdivision. "Anything about radios?"

She flipped the page. "Oh, yeah. Here it is. 'No radios or other communication devices allowed, as they interfere with official channels.' I'll bet they do."

"Why would they ban radios?" Ethan said. "I would think they'd want all the comms they could get."

"They do. But only if they control them. Uncontrolled communication means uncontrolled people. That's why it's the first amendment in the Bill of Rights. Make no mistake, in the Compound we won't be in control."

"Control?" Ethan said, mock horror in his voice. "At such a nice resort camp? Who would need such a thing?"

Despite the rather dismal aspect of the Compound, none of them seriously suggested they wouldn't go back. Fred pulled into the driveway and shut off the truck. He rested his head on the steering wheel for a moment, then said, "Okay. Nine a.m. tomorrow morning, we go down there and check in. Enjoy yourselves tonight."

'Enjoying themselves' consisted of eating the rest of the candy bars and deciding what to bury in the backyard where, presumably, the police wouldn't find and take it. Fred locked his radio into his gun safe along with the rest of his weaponry. Emily told the bees they were on their own—*they understand a lot more than we think*—and let their scavenged chickens out to fend for themselves.

"They'll last a week," she said.

"They'll last an afternoon," Ethan said. "If they're lucky."

They made sure to pack their best books into boxes to donate to the compound library—ones that Americans before failed to read, and learn from—Bastiat's *The Law*, Adam Smith's *Theory of Moral*

Sentiments, Read's *I, Pencil*, and Hayek's *The Road to Serfdom*. Maybe without the distractions of electrical entertainment, more people would read them and be ready to rebuild a better world after the lights came back on.

Finally, they walked slowly through the house, touching all the things they might never see again. Never had they more powerfully missed their parents, whose smiling faces stared out at them from every picture frame.

"I'll miss being able to do what I want," Emily said. "Liberty. Freedom. You know we're going to have a lot less of that starting tomorrow."

"And we're trading Fred's life, potentially. Maybe our own."

Emily picked up a recent family photo and brushed a thin layer of dust off the top. "Is it worth it?" she asked nobody in particular.

Ethan was asking the same question and had the same lack of answers.

"I guess it is," Emily finally said, "or we wouldn't be doing it. And if you're dead, your liberty is pretty thin, too, so there's a strong incentive to protect your life if you can."

The intake officer at the Compound was not as cheerful as the redhead recruiter had been. His table sat just inside the gates, and he sat just behind it, sweating profusely in the sunshine.

The Tuttle Twins and the Days of Darkness

"Name?" he said, apparently bored out of his mind.

They gave their names, addresses, phone numbers—not without a giggle—and next of kin. Medical condition. Allergies, both food and chemical. The heavyset man reached over to a stack of papers and wrote on three of them, then stamped them with a complicated red seal.

"These are your papers. Keep them on you at all times. If you lose them, another set will not be provided and may result in your expulsion from the camp. Do you understand?"

They said they did.

"No violence in the camp, either physical or verbal. Any breaking of these or any of the other posted rules in the camp may result in your expulsion. Do you understand?"

They said they did.

"Have a nice stay." He turned to a uniformed woman behind him and said, "27 R and S".

And they were inside. Carts were provided for them to wheel their belongings to their tent site, which was fairly easily identified as Row 27, Sites R and S, on a grid marked out on the wide lawn of the park. Each site was a 15' square lined up with 26 other rows and letters of the alphabet. It was enough room to pitch their tents and have a small amount of space left over. Most people pitched their tents in the middle of their slots. The Tuttles and Fred pitched theirs on the extreme edges so that there was about 10' of clear space in between, a kind of patio to which both tents faced.

They moved in their sleeping bags and their pillows and blankets. Ethan insisted that a number of books were smuggled in as well and kept in their bags. "I don't want to have to go to the library for my own books," he said.

And that was that. They were in.

At first, there was a lot to occupy their attention. About ten minutes after they got situated, a family of three came to occupy Site T. They introduced themselves and had smuggled in chocolate bars. They were excited about the Tuttles' books. They seemed nice.

The other neighbors kept mostly to themselves, which made getting to know them difficult, but eventually, they established a cordial relationship.

The camp smelled like a lot of unwashed people had been crammed into an area too small for them, because it was. It was hot and getting hotter. Every two hours, a cart would come by and provide water. "You should always get some," Fred said. "Even if you're not thirsty."

The only shade was on the edges, by Row 1 and the A sites. Those were a long way away. A lot of people stood around there, chatting or just sitting on the grass under the giant willow trees. So Emily and Ethan sat on the grass by their tent.

And that was that.

Absolutely nothing happened. For hours. For days.

The Tuttle Twins and the Days of Darkness

Oh, certainly, some people would come in—nobody left, that was one of the rules—a steady trickle of new people every few hours or so during daylight. Meal carts came down the rows, distributing MREs to the camp at 8 a.m., 1 p.m., and 6 p.m. One day it rained. That was interesting. A lot of the tents were not terribly waterproof, to put it lightly. Some people opted to simply stand in the rain.

Other than that, nothing. Fred tried to go to the communication center of the compound for news, but he was met with "Everything is under control, sir. Go back to your tent."

They caught up on sleep. They went to the library and were informed that there was a two-book-per-person rule in effect.

The librarian, whose name was, improbably, Marion, was very nice, if terribly overworked. She remembered the boxes of books the twins had brought in and said they could volunteer, restocking shelves for a few hours a day. The library was a mess, with books everywhere. Hundreds of new books had come in, and there was nowhere to put them but on the floor and in tall stacks. Not as many people came to borrow them as the twins would have expected. They didn't really know the Dewey Decimal system, but almost all the new books were fiction anyway, so those were easy—alphabetical by author. With a long day of work, the compound library was in perfect order.

After that, the twins noticed several kids and a few adults came in, not just once a day, but twice or three times—they were apparently burning through books at a pretty high rate—the kind of rate the twins read at.

Thus it was that two weeks after they arrived at the Compound, Fred started a school.

He started with the kids who read like demons. They were, as he suspected, bored out of their skulls. History class might not be the most exciting thing to do in the summer, but it beat doing nothing at all, which was the other option.

On the first day, nine kids showed up.

By the fourth day, there were twenty. And that got some people's attention.

A uniformed policeman rode up on a motorbike as Fred was teaching about how the American colonists rebelled against the Stamp Act. He watched for a minute, then told the kids to go to their homes.

One of them had a smart mouth. "I'd love to. You won't let me."

"Watch it, kid, or the food truck will skip your row. You," he said, pointing at Fred. "What do you think you're doing?"

Fred put a bookmark carefully in his copy of *Conceived in Liberty*. "I'm teaching, Officer... Tandy."

"You can't do that."

"The rules don't forbid it. I checked."

"Well, you can't do it, anyway. The rules say you have to comply with uniformed officers in this camp."

"The rules actually don't say anything about uniforms, but I understand where you're taking this. May I ask why you're making this decision?"

Tandy tried to come up with a reason. He wasn't successful. It basically boiled down to "I don't like it."

"But they do," Fred said, indicating the children, who were watching the exchange with great interest.

"What are we hurting, Officer?" the smart-mouth kid said. His name was Justice. Fred liked that.

"Nothing… it's just not… what is he teaching you, anyway?"

"Right now, he's teaching us about how we got the Bill of Rights and the Constitution."

Tandy spat, just missing one of the tents in Row 28. "That's a dumb thing to learn about. Look around you. The power's gone. Your rights aren't going to bring it back."

Fred smiled, and if Tandy had been a policeman long enough, he would have understood right away that this was precisely what Fred wanted. But he'd only been on the force for two months, and his most important job up to that point had been to stamp forms.

"The Bill of Rights was written when there wasn't any power—any electricity, anyway. And the Constitution is not about how to build things or fix things. It's a set of rules for keeping people free so that they can build and fix things on their own."

"How is that working out?" Tandy said, "Look at the mess we're in."

"We're in this mess because the wisdom of the patriot generation was rejected. A centralized electrical grid, funded and managed by bloated bureaucracies, and a clownishly out-of-control national government… But we'll get out of it by using things we *can* control—our minds, our will, and those constitutionally protected rights that you swore to protect. So, we *will* continue here, Officer Tandy. Have a nice day."

Tandy had had enough. "Okay, smart guy. You'll find out how this really works—not the book theory, but how it works on the ground, right here in this mess that *we're* trying to keep you alive in." He jumped on the motorbike, kicked it to life, and rode off.

When the noise faded, Fred made sure the kids understood what they had seen. "Why didn't Officer Tandy arrest me? He clearly didn't like what we were doing."

"He couldn't," one kid said. "You didn't do anything wrong."

"The second part of what you said was true. But the first part wasn't. He *could* arrest me. He still can. I don't think he will, but he might. Even though I didn't do anything wrong. So why didn't he?"

"He looked afraid?" another kid tried.

"Of me? What for?"

"Of all of us. We're pretty scary!" The kids laughed. They were pumped up, filled with adrenaline.

"You certainly are," Fred said. "But I don't think that's exactly it. See, true authority isn't something you can take. It has to be given to you. A leader can

lead only when others choose to follow. *Consent of the governed* is what Thomas Jefferson called it.

"We held our ground and didn't comply with his unreasonable mandates. In order to enforce his will, he would have had to escalate to full-on violence. If I stood alone he may have made an example of me, but with all of you here, standing with me, he wasn't willing to continue with his aggression."

He stood up and threaded his way through the mass of kids, looking down at them. "I think his bosses will probably want to have a chat with me. But the truth is that those documents are still powerful, not because they can't be broken—they can, and they are—but because they're *right*, and what is right is powerful. All of us in this country—and all of us in the world—know something that we didn't before the Declaration. That we have rights. Everyone has them. Not just kings and queens and government officials, but all of us. Humans are meant to have life, liberty, and the pursuit of happiness. Even where we don't have these things—" Here he spun and held his arms out wide. "—we know we *should* have them."

"And that's the greatest power of all."

Emily woke in the dark of morning to the sound of buzzing—not the buzz of a bug, though. It had been so long since she had heard anything like it. The sound of electricity. Her phone. A text? Was it over? Was the power back on? Then she felt something soft against her fingers. The softest cotton sheets, not her sticky, stinky sleeping bag. She was in a bed. Her *old* bed in her *old* house.

Disoriented, she sat up and looked around the quiet room. How did she get there? Where was Ethan… Fred? "Text!" she said in a groggy whisper.

She picked up her phone to look, but was blinded by its bright blue light in her still dilated pupils. Through her squinted, sleepy eyes she read the contact: Mom.

"Ethan! Ethan!" she yelled out. She ran to her brother's room, hoping he'd been transported back to the house too. He was there—and startled from dead asleep.

"Wha…what happened?" he said, wiping sleep drool from his lips. "What's wrong, Em?"

"A text. From Mom and Dad. They're alive!" Her eyes had finally adjusted so she could read. "*On the plane. Landing in an hour. See you guys soon!*"

"That's what you woke me up for?" Ethan said, flopping back down on his pillow. "Oh, man. I was in the middle of an awful nightmare. So many hornets."

It was then that she realized what really had happened.

THE END

All the options involving leaving made some kind of sense. Grandma would be the ultimate safety blanket. She had food storage and livestock to feed a small planet, all the water you could want, and surely the aunts, uncles, and cousins would go there. Mom and Dad, too, if they got to Spoonerville and no one was there, they'd know right away to go to the Little Pink House. They could even leave a note for them.

The other options were good, too. Staying with Fred felt right. He had always protected and encouraged them; how could they leave him just when he was in need of protection and encouragement?

But.

They'd have to leave *home*.

No matter how attractive any of the other options were, home was still home. Everything they knew was here, everything they'd stockpiled and prepared. Their generator, all their food storage, water, medical supplies—everything. Fred's radio setup, too, which wasn't portable in any meaningful way. There was just no way they could leave all that.

The government would surely come around looking for them and demand that they come to a shelter, but they knew the law. They didn't have to go. The government couldn't make them. The worst they could do was threaten to leave them without protection. Well, the twins knew what to do. They had guns and ammunition. A lot of people would be leaving their houses empty, and those would be much softer targets. After all, they didn't have to make their houses secure. They only had to make them more secure than the houses down the block.

"I want to stay," Emily said. "I'm grateful we have the other options, but Fred's in no condition to go hiking into the woods, and we can't leave him. I'm for staying right here."

"Me, too," Ethan said, coming over to stand behind Emily. "This is where we planned to ride out any emergency. Our supplies aren't portable, anyway. We've got gas and water and everything right here. It's our best option."

Fred sighed heavily, and his shoulders sank. "I can't argue with you about any of that. I can't argue at all tonight. Too tired."

"You should go to bed, Fred," Emily said, taking one of his hands. "Let's go. I'll walk you up. Then Ethan and I will stand watch tonight so you don't have to worry."

"As long as you get sleep, too," Fred said.

"We will." Emily snapped the switch and turned off the radio. "There will be a lot more time for listening in tomorrow. For now, we should all go to bed."

Fred needed no more coaxing. He went straight into his room, pulled down the covers, and got into bed. Emily made a mental note that she'd need to wash sheets eventually and wondered if they had a washtub large enough to do the job.

When she got back to the front room, Ethan was arranging pillows on the big, soft couch that faced the wide front window. "You sleeping first, or am I?"

"You do it," Emily said, running a hand through her hair. "I'm too keyed up. Also, I'm going over to the house to get a few things."

"Bring back the shotgun," Ethan said. "And a box of shells."

The night was quiet, but the smell of smoke was more intense, and there was an unnatural glow over the northern sky in the direction of Malantown. Emily shuddered and picked up the pace toward the Tuttles' house.

They'd left the door unlocked, but as far as she could tell, the house was undisturbed. She got a couple of pillows, a blanket, her Enfield .303 rifle, and Ethan's 12-gauge shotgun, both with a box of ammo. It seemed a bit silly. There wasn't really any danger. Not tonight. Was there?

When she left this time, she locked the door, forgetting that the power was out and reaching for the light switch to turn on the porch bulb. The switch did nothing, of course, and the porch stayed dark, just like every other house on the block.

No more cars on the road, either. People were conserving gas as much as possible.

Ethan had already laid down when she got back. She carefully locked and deadbolted the door and drew back the heavy curtains, leaving a wispy patterned interior curtain in place.

"Anyone passing won't be able to see in, but we'll be able to see them," she said in response to Ethan's quizzical look.

"I'm not used to the streetlamp being off. It's so dark," he said. But he was asleep in minutes.

Emily sat near the front window and tried not to doze off. She had a very good look at the night sky as she sat there, and it was filled with more stars than she could believe. They had been there all the time, and it had taken a catastrophe to show them to her.

Sometime in the quiet and the dark, Emily's focus wandered, then drooped, then drifted, and before she knew what was happening, lights flashed outside on the street and woke her. How long she'd been sleeping, she did not know without going into the library and looking at the grandfather clock. But there was no thought of that, not with red and blue lights bursting through the curtains.

Two police cars stood nose-to-nose in the middle of the street. Their doors were open like the wings of some clipped bird. A pair of policemen crouched in the shadow of the open doors, guns drawn, occasionally peering over the metal to see through the windows.

Their attention was focused on the house across the street and down one to the east.

"Ethan!" Emily called. "Wake up!"

Behind her, Ethan stirred, rolled over, and went back to sleep.

"Ethan!" she called again, and this time she was rewarded with a "Huh? Wazzat?" and a thump as his feet hit the floor. He staggered over to stand by her. "What's going on?" he said.

Emily pulled him down to kneel on the floor. "Get down. The cops are after someone across the street, at the Brogans' house."

They didn't seem to be very aggressively pursuing whoever it was, but a minute or so later, two of the officers broke the cover of the car and shuffle-ran, crouched all the way, to the shelter of the bushes that lined the front walk of their neighbors' house.

"What did the Brogans ever do to them?" Ethan said, coming fully awake.

"I don't think it's the Brogans. Remember they weren't at the party a couple days ago. I think they're out of town, and the police are after whoever is in the house now."

"Who *is* in the house now?"

"How should I know? Just watch."

But the action had fizzled. The officers scuttled up the walk to the front door, called out something the twins couldn't hear, and kicked the door in. Then the remaining two officers charged the house, weapons at the ready. The twins waited for gunfire, but nothing happened, and after a few moments the police came back out. One of them stood on the front stoop and scratched his head.

"Guess they didn't find what they were looking for," Emily said.

But they weren't finished looking. The police had a chat in the middle of the street, their faces purple and black in the rotating lights. Then they turned their attention in another direction.

Toward the Tuttles' house.

At first, it was just glances, looking over their shoulders at their house next door to Fred's, where Emily and Ethan kept watch. But then one of the officers turned and tilted his head as if he had seen something. He bobbed his neck, speaking into the microphone strapped to his upper chest. He listened. Emily could imagine what they were saying: *Check it out.*

The officer nodded in response and said something back.

"What's the deal with our house?" Ethan said. "Why are they looking over there?"

Taking tentative steps, the officer moved toward the Tuttles' house, gun drawn and face tight. The other policemen turned from their confab and formed up behind him.

"We have to go out there," Emily said. "That's our house they're going to."

"If we go out there, we're going to get shot," Ethan said. "We stay here."

"There's a window in the garage. We can watch from there."

They pelted through the house and out the door to the garage. The window was on the far side of the truck. It hadn't been cleaned in some time, and cobwebs laced the glass. Emily caught a whiff of night air where the pane was improperly sealed. Despite the grime, they could see the police moving slowly, cautiously, step by step up the front walk and onto the stoop.

They vanished, one by one, into the house.

"They're inside," Ethan breathed.

"What could they be after?" Emily said.

"Must have seen something."

"What could they have seen? Our house is dark. We're over *here*."

Someone—or some*thing*—was in their house— along with four armed policemen.

"We have to go," Emily said, wild to know what was going on, to… *defend* their house or something. They couldn't just stand there and do nothing. *Those people were in their house.*

"Get Fred," Ethan said. "He'll know what to do."

"You get him. I'm going over there."

Ethan grabbed her arm above the elbow. "You are *not*. There's nothing you can do over there except get hurt."

She turned to him, eyes wild, but then she nodded. As if a string was cut, Ethan whirled, ran around the truck, and disappeared. Emily spun back to the window. Every so often, a beam of light lanced out the windows of their house and grazed the front lawn. Flashlights, sweeping inside. She held her breath, listening, hoping to hear… something. And hoping not to. Her heart pounded blood into her ears like a hammer drives a nail.

"Emily." Fred's voice floated out from behind her. "Come away from the window."

She didn't move.

"Come on, Em," Ethan said. "You can't do anything."

As if she were tearing off a layer of skin, Emily finally turned her body and began to walk, but her eyes remained riveted on the side of their house until she rounded the truck, and its metal sides blocked her view.

They sat in the library. Fred looked as if he'd been dug up from the grave. His hollow cheeks and bruising made him look like a playdough model of himself, but his voice was steady.

"We don't know what they saw in your house or what they're doing in there now. Ordinarily, you have every right to go over there and ask questions, and get them to leave, if you want them to. But this isn't the ordinary. Things aren't the way they were. What you have a right to doesn't matter when the power goes out."

"It still matters," Emily said. "It has to matter."

"To us, yes. To many others, probably. But to everyone? Can we count on that? Suppose one of the policemen mistakes you—or any of us—for a scavenger. For a gang. He shoots. Down you go. What then? Do you think we're going to sue? Where will the justice come from? There aren't functioning courts. No one will blame a policeman for doing what he thinks he has to do to protect the town."

"But... *we're* the town," Ethan said.

"Not anymore. The town is the central gathering place. The people the police have collected. They're the town. We're not part of that, so we are outside, and anyone that is outside is a threat."

"We aren't a threat. We just want to be left alone!"

Fred sighed and put his face in his hands. "I know that. You know that. But they don't know that, and there might not be any way to get them to. Not in the dark, in a dangerous situation, when they're already on edge."

Ethan got up and went to the library window, the one that faced out onto the front lawn. The police cars still sat in the street, gull-wings open, lights flashing. None of the officers had returned.

They waited another ten minutes by the grandfather clock. By then, surely the police would have found whatever they were going to find or given up the search.

What if they caught someone? What if they *didn't*? They had to have seen something, or else why would they have gone into the Tuttles' house? Was someone in there?

Fred went into the kitchen and came back with a bag of pretzels and some potato chips.

"Might as well eat them," he said. "I don't think there will be very many more for a while."

The salt and carbs did make them feel better, but nothing could extinguish the burning in their gut when they thought of what might be happening in their house. Would they find the place trashed? What if the police decided the house had been abandoned?

Seventeen minutes. One of the policemen came out the front door and back to his car and radioed in. He shook his head a lot, which Emily took as a good sign. One by one, the rest of the officers returned as well. They didn't carry anything. Their weapons were holstered. The twins had heard no gunshots.

The cars drove away in opposite directions.

Nothing happened. No one rushed across the street through the void left by the retreating police. No shouting. Nothing caught fire or exploded. It was as if the police had never been there.

"Now I really *am* going over there," Emily said, "and I think you two should come with me."

They needed no encouragement. Fred seemed to drag himself along by sheer force of will, but once he got a jacket and a rifle, he was moving better. Ethan carried the 12-gauge, six shells loaded in the barrel magazine. Emily had her rifle. They all knew how to use them. They all prayed they wouldn't have to—except Ethan had to admit there was a part of him, a new dark part he hadn't known was there, that itched to have something to *do*, even if it was to shoot someone.

His breath came short, and he had to force himself to calm down. It was one thing to talk about going back over to what should be an empty house and another thing entirely to go in the pitch black to see if it really was.

But he went. Behind him, close enough that he could feel her body heat, came Emily. Fred brought up the rear, falling into a kind of stance the twins hadn't seen him use before. Ethan remembered Fred had served in the military and wondered if the training ever truly left.

Their front door was open.

Ethan couldn't decide if that was good or bad.

"Careful," Fred whispered unnecessarily. Ethan had never had such an urge to be careful in his life.

He brought the shotgun up across his chest, in a resting position. There was nothing to shoot, and he didn't want to lead with the barrel.

They crept up the front steps, ears pricked. They heard nothing. Ethan had never been so tired of silence.

Perhaps they should announce themselves? Give whoever might be in there a chance to leave before they came upon him?

No. Stupid. The cops had just been there. If anyone *had* been there, they'd be hiding, thinking about perhaps coming out. The last thing they wanted to do was alert an intruder to hide again.

The open front door was a black mouth, swallowing even the small light of the stars. A breeze stirred the bushes and brought the smell of burning oil. Ethan's mouth was so dry. When had he last had a drink?

He stepped through the door.

The living room was just as it had been, undisturbed right down to the pillows on the couch. He half expected to see muddy footprints on the carpet, but that was silly; it wasn't muddy out, and this wasn't the movies.

He heard a slight shuffling behind him and guessed it was Emily coming through the door. He risked a glance backward. Fred had taken up a position just inside the door, looking out. His rifle was raised but not sighted.

Ethan took a few more steps, quietly, willing the rug to sponge up the sound of his footfalls.

Through the passageway into the kitchen. Pitch, stygian dark. He could hardly see anything. If it weren't for the wan starlight leaking through the big bay window, he wouldn't have been able to see a thing.

Emily's breath was in his ear. "Thome thingth have been moved." She turned the "s" sounds into "th" to keep its sound from traveling. And by the weak light, he could see she was right. Some of the containers. The bag of popcorn leaked onto the table.

But the house was quiet, and Ethan began to grow bolder.

Room by room, he and Emily searched. Their bedrooms had been searched—their bedcovers pulled back and the blankets strewn on the floor—and everywhere there were signs of intruders, but whether those were the police or the people the police had searched for, they couldn't tell.

"Here," Fred said from the master bedroom. "This is what they were looking for."

Blood spattered the floor. A crimson handprint, minus two fingers, showed on the shower tile. Much of the roll of toilet paper and all the towels were heaped up in the bathtub, streaked with black. Ethan turned on the flashlight on his phone. Not black. Red.

The bathtub had been drained, too, and the sink and the toilet water had been slopped all over the floor.

"Someone was here, all right," Fred said. "But he wouldn't be here now. If he'd left enough of a trail, the police would have found him, but they didn't, and now he's gone."

"How do we know that?" Emily said, voice high and strained. "He could still be here."

The Tuttle Twins and the Days of Darkness

"Or she," Ethan said, shotgun at three-quarters, pointed back toward their parents' bedroom door.

But they searched—and the twins knew all the hiding places in the house, places that no one who didn't live there could have found—and whoever had been there, bleeding pretty badly, was gone now.

They assembled in the front room. The door still stood open.

"No one stays here tonight," Fred said. He was hoarse as if he'd been yelling. "Back to my place. Bring some of the loose food, maybe some of your bedding."

"Toothbrush," Ethan said.

"Deodorant," Emily said. "For all the good it will do."

Fred looked forlornly around the house. "Lock everything up tight. Tomorrow we'll put another couple of locks on your food storage, what all we can't move over to my place. It's too dangerous to split up anymore."

They carted over their goods. Ethan got the wheelbarrow out of the back and used it to wheel over some of the water storage that they couldn't put in the basement. It filled up a lot of the empty space in Fred's garage. When they locked the front and back doors of their house, it felt final, as if they were leaving forever.

"We're just next door," Emily said.

"It's a lot farther than I thought," Ethan said, staring at the door with bloodshot eyes.

Emily thought she would never be able to sleep, but fatigue dragged her down almost the moment she hit the pillow. Ethan said he'd stand watch—Fred certainly wasn't going to be able to.

It wasn't a good night's sleep, but it was mostly restful, and no one bothered them.

Over the next few days, it became clear that the neighborhood was emptying. Tuesday—day five, numbering everything from the time the power went out—there were kids out playing in the newly-emptied streets. Generators buzzed away. Parents sat on front porches and rocked and munched on dwindling snacks.

By day seven, most of the children were gone. The ones that were left had dirty faces and unwashed hands—they did not seem to mind this very much—and their games were quieter. They scattered when the twins came down the block.

On day eight, Ethan was awakened by the clucking of chickens. Looking out the front window, he saw three of them grubbing for worms and other bugs, raking the front garden. He went out onto the porch to watch them. They didn't seem to notice that he was there.

Emily came out a few minutes later. "You found some friends, I see."

"They followed me home. Can we keep them?"

Emily squinted up into the sun. There was a haze to it today that felt like rain later. "We probably *should* keep them. Where did they come from?"

"Robinsons had chickens."

The Robinsons, like most of that end of the block, were not there anymore. Their dark house sat lonely in a growing patch of unmown grass.

"That's a couple hundred yards away. Why would the chickens come down this far?" Ethan said.

Emily shrugged. "Who can say with chickens. All I know is, they lay eggs."

"Eggs. If only they laid bacon, too."

"They lay drumsticks if you slaughter them."

"But then no eggs," Ethan tsked. "Don't you know your golden goose?"

"Always more eggs as long as you have a rooster. We should go see what the deal is at the Robinsons."

The deal was that they were gone, and their coop stood open. The twins decided that the chickens probably hadn't learned how to unlatch it by themselves, so the Robinsons must have left it open so the chickens wouldn't starve. There had been more than three of them, judging by the pile of eggs in the henhouse. Where the others were, they couldn't say.

"What's the opposite of an apex predator?" Emily said.

"A sandwich," Ethan said. He scratched at his waistband. He itched everywhere. "Let's take the eggs back and talk to Fred about what to do with the chickens."

The three that had come to visit on day eight had decided to stay since Fred had cracked some wheat and scattered it in a bread-crumb trail into his backyard. He had instantly agreed that keeping all the chickens they could was a great idea. The Robinsons had left most of their feed behind, and they had quite a bit, enough for several weeks.

Two dozen eggs made a welcome sight on Fred's counter. The twins went right back out to comb the neighborhood for any of the rest of the flock they could find. By afternoon they had found four more and caught three of them. It took a good deal of work, but they broke down the Robinsons' coop and ferried it a bit at a time to their own house, where they deposited all six chickens they'd found.

The rest had disappeared, probably down the throats of one of the dogs that now began to trot through, right down the empty street, noses down and ears flat. Most of them had collars. They still looked cared-for and groomed.

That would not last long.

Fred shot the first dog on the night of day twelve. His health had recovered somewhat, though Emily privately thought he still wasn't his old self. He had insisted on standing watch after day eight, and the twins had to admit he had skills they did not. At about 2 a.m. on day twelve, they were awakened by the flat *crack* of a rifle. They bolted from their beds and skidded into the dining room, where they found Fred crouched in the back doorway, rifle leveled, shoulders tense.

"Fred! What—"

"Shhh," Fred said without turning around. He might have been made of wax for all the movement he made.

After a few heartbeats, he finally let the rifle go slack and breathed out long and sadly. "I think I got it," he said.

"What? What did you shoot?" Emily said, dearly hoping it was a *what* and not a *who*.

"Dog. I think. It's plenty dark back there, but I'm pretty sure it's canine, and wolves aren't really part of the wildlife scene around here. Not yet, anyway."

"Couldn't you just have, I don't know, shooed it away?" Ethan said, a bit sick to his stomach at the thought of their having shot someone's pet.

Fred turned his head, then went back to staring into the dark of the backyard. "Not without risking being bitten. You happen to have a store of rabies medication in your old house?"

"No."

Fred rolled his shoulders. "I couldn't risk it. Anyway, there's nothing moving back there now."

It was morning before he would let anyone go out to look. When they did, sure enough, it was a dog, a labrador mixed with some other breed. It had a collar that read *Sandy* and gave an address.

"I guess we should try to bring the body back to its home," Emily said, but Fred was adamant they bury it in place.

"Take a look." He prodded it with his toe. Ribs showed through the hide, and the coat was spattered with mud. Around the muzzle, a thin layer of dried blood crusted. "No one lets their family starve like this. They left the poor thing when they abandoned their house."

"It was just trying to get a meal," Ethan said, kneeling. He wanted to reach out and stroke the animal, but it would certainly have fleas, and they'd love a chance to get onto him.

"Sadly, there will be more of this," Fred said. "Remember, it's not just trying to get a meal, but everything we have here is *your* meal. It didn't get in."

Near the dog's front paws was a shallow depression by the fence where it had begun to dig. Fred shook his head. "Better fill that back in. A dog this size would have a time digging deep enough to get under the fence, but a weasel or a ferret could almost squeeze through it now. We're going to have to step up our defense."

By day fourteen, packs of hungry dogs could be seen roaming the streets—mangy, underfed, and feral. They'd seen cats skulking around the coop as well—it was almost as if their coop was a magnet for predators. Fred said he thought that would continue for another couple of months until most of those predators were dead. "The local wildlife scene can't support that many dogs or cats. Right now we're likely in the middle of a population crash. They'll get rarer."

The Tuttle Twins and the Days of Darkness

They did. But other predators began to crop up in greater numbers, and they were far, far more dangerous than the dogs.

By day seventeen, the neighborhood had settled into the pattern it would keep for a while. On the Tuttles' street, there were twenty-eight houses, fourteen on each side from east to west. Three houses still had occupants if you didn't count the Tuttle house itself. Up on the eastern end, two in from the corner, the Van Gaals had also refused to go to the central refugee camp.

"We spent all our life earning the money for this house. We're not leaving it," said Mrs. Van Gaal in her thick Dutch accent. They had four children, but they lived in other states, and they didn't think any of their children would try to come for them. They had good water but not very much food, and Fred offered to share with them when they ran out. Mr. Van Gaal nodded at that but said he thought they could manage.

Across the street and four doors down to the west was the Chamberlain house, and they had also decided to stay. Mrs. Chamberlain had died a few years back of a nasty cancer, and Mr. Chamberlain wouldn't leave the only house they'd ever lived in together. They had three children, a 12-year-old boy and two girls, nine and seven. As luck would have it, Mr. Chamberlain's brother Ike had been in town when the power went out. They had a generator, too—a big one that could power the whole house—and a 50-gallon drum of gasoline.

Sometimes the twins could see light from their house at night, and not flashlights, either.

The rest of the block was dark, the people gone, the yards getting overgrown.

But some of them had planted gardens, too, and those had continued to grow, though they were getting a little weedy. The twins tended the peppers and tomatoes up and down the block as if they owned the whole thing. "Why not?" Emily said. "We're the only ones around to eat it."

The three families that remained set up a kind of territorial system. The Chamberlains had everything west of the Tuttles on their side of the street. The Van Gaals had the east side from the Tuttles to the corner, plus the house on the north side that faced east. The Tuttles and Fred had everything on the north side of the street, and it was plenty to keep them busy.

Every night, and for a couple hours during the day, the twins and Fred would take turns monitoring the radio. They hadn't heard from Mom and Dad since that one day, but there was plenty of noise from the local bands. Fred had found the net the Mutual Assistance Group used, the one Miss Legaspi wanted them to join. They were quite active, and from their chatter, the twins learned some interesting things about how the town was doing. Not as much as they would have liked—the group spoke in a kind of code that the twins didn't understand—but some. Malantown had melted down, and it was not a place anyone wanted to go. The police were holding a six-block area around the central downtown, but the rest of the city wasn't doing well at all. Water had failed, and it wasn't long before violence erupted around the waterfront. The twins could hear gunshots all day and night from there.

"As long as they're out there doing well, we have someplace to go if we need to," Fred said.

But that turned out not to be true. Or perhaps it was, but they never had a chance to test it.

On day twenty-two, the Van Gaal's house caught fire and burned to the ground. Emily smelled the smoke and went out to see what was happening. A group of men stood in a bunch on the sidewalk, not doing anything about it—though what could they do, anyway?

The Van Gaals were not home, as it happened. Ethan noticed that their car was not in the garage. But they never came back, either, and the twins never saw them again.

On day twenty-four, Emily went out scouting and came back with news.

"They're working their way down the block," she said, tossing her backpack on the floor and slumping into one of the library chairs.

Ethan put his book down. "Who are, and which block?"

"This block, and... well, I'm not entirely sure. But I think it's some gang or something. Remember the men standing in the street watching the Van Gaals' house burn? Those guys."

"That wasn't a gang, it was just a... group of... bystanders." Ethan could hear in his own voice how naive that sounded.

Emily grunted. "They did stand by, yes, but I think they also were the ones that burned the house. Now they're going from house to house down the street and stripping it of everything they can use."

Fred came in and sat on the loveseat so that the three of them made a triangle. "What makes you say that?"

"I went up the street to tend Garden One," she said, using the terminology they'd developed for keeping track of the plots where things were growing. "When I got there, I noticed footprints in the dirt that hadn't been there the day before. Big ones. Boots. I looked around a bit but didn't see anyone. Then I saw that the house across the street didn't have a front door anymore."

"What happened to it?" Ethan said.

Emily shrugged. "It just isn't there. The front of the house gapes like a mouth."

"Maybe it's just open."

"Maybe," Emily said, walking over to the end table by the bookshelf and pulling one of the wet wipes from the pack. She bathed her face with it, saw the grime on the wipe, and grimaced. "But I don't think so. Because the top five houses on the street—including the Van Gaals'—also have no front door. And if you look inside, you can tell the place has been ransacked. There's trash on the floor and broken bits of furniture."

Fred and Ethan exchanged a look. "Okay," Fred said, "but when would this ransacking be taking place? We keep watch. We would have seen something."

"That's what's bugging me," she said, throwing the wipe into the wastebasket. "I can't figure it out. If it's really a gang of marauders, why not just go up and down the block and take what you want? And if it's not, then who is it and what are they doing?"

On day twenty-five, they found out.

Mid-morning, a knock sounded on the door. This was unusual enough that Ethan had to think a second before he registered what that meant.

"Should I answer the door?" he yelled.

"Bad guys don't knock," Fred said from the kitchen. All the same, Ethan heard Fred rack a round into the shotgun.

Standing on the doorstep were two uniformed policemen. "Good morning," one of them said. His badge read *Officer Cappeletti*. "May I inquire who lives in this house?"

"You may inquire, but I don't think I'm required to answer you," Ethan said. He took half a step backward and kept his hands in plain sight. Fred came into the room behind him. Ethan didn't take his eyes off the policemen, so he didn't know that Fred didn't have his shotgun until Fred stepped around him to take over.

"What seems to be the trouble, officers?" Fred said. As always, when dealing with the police, Fred was cheerful and even friendly.

"We're requiring all citizens in the area to come to the central community zone," Officer Cappeletti said. "Will you and your children comply?"

Ethan thought Fred would correct him, but he didn't. "We will not. Thank you very much for your concern."

The officers frowned but didn't go back down the steps. They did, however, turn and hold out their arms toward the Van Gaals' house—or the blackened ruin where the house used to be.

"See that?" Cappeletti said. "I'm sure you know what that is, a man of your experience."

"It's a burned house. The fire department never responded."

"Nor will they, not outside the central community zone," Cappeletti said. "They tried to help people like you once too often and lost a whole fire station of men in one night."

"Not people like me," Fred said. "Nothing like me."

"What happened?" Ethan said. He thought Fred wouldn't like it, but these men would know things, and Ethan wanted to know them, too.

Cappeletti's face showed some sort of internal conflict. Apparently, the good guys won, because he said, "A gang from Malantown set a fire and waited for the fire brigade to show up. Then they gunned them down. Plus two policemen. That's their M.O.—they go to a house, if it's empty they take what's there, and if it's not, they set fire to it."

Ethan swallowed. But the Van Gaals had not been home. He was sure of it.

Or was he? Had he seen them go?

"It sounds to me like you have your hands full dealing with this gang," Fred said. "I would hate to take you away from that important work just to chat with us."

"You need to come down to the town center," Cappeletti said, setting his face hard. "I won't ask again. We're not going to come protect you when you need it."

"Understood. Thank you for your concern," Fred said.

The police and Fred stared at each other for a long moment, then the officers turned to go. But Cappeletti turned back at the bottom of the stairs, "Sir, please. You've got kids. This gang won't care about that. I hear chickens in the back. That will draw them for certain. Maybe not today or even tomorrow, but it won't be long before they get to you. You can't hold them off. *They will kill you.* They won't even hesitate."

Ethan could hear the concern and sincerity in the man's voice. But he also knew this man wouldn't be in charge of the camp down in town. And the people that were in charge of such things might not be better than a gang.

Behind them, Emily stole quietly into the room. She'd been listening, Ethan was sure.

"Thank you, officer. We'll take your words to heart. Good day." And Fred shut the door.

Then he leaned forward on it, his arm crooked to make a pad for his head. His eyes were closed, and his breathing shallow, quick.

"You heard, Em?" he said.

"I heard."

"I think he's right about this gang. I think they'll be vicious and ruthless. And we're not exactly equipped for a firefight."

"Or to fight a fire," Ethan said because he couldn't help himself.

Emily sat down on the couch. "We have one more chance to choose," she said. "Stay and probably fight for our lives, or go downtown and lose control of them."

"Some choice." Ethan sat down beside her.

Fred shoved himself back upright and squared his shoulders. "Okay," he said, "three people, one vote each. What's it going to be?"

If you think the group should head for the Central Community Zone, go to page 136.

If you think the group should stick it out, go to page 295.

The whole idea was completely insane. They had a good thing here in the MAG. People liked them. They had food, safety, and as much comfort as a sleeping bag on the ground could give. Even the weather had cooperated, with a few showers that didn't penetrate the tent and some good breezes to keep the heat down.

To leave... on foot. Ethan couldn't believe he was even entertaining the idea. But Emily had shown him the work she'd done, the preparation. It was extensive. She'd been thinking about it for a long time, obsessively, and Ethan knew how obsessive she could be. She was also meticulous, thorough, and driven—when she wanted to do something, even something incredibly difficult, she did it.

And Ethan realized he was going to help her.

But he wasn't going to do it without telling Fred.

He'd been their friend so long he was like a part of the family. The twins couldn't leave without telling him, especially because if they disappeared, he would possibly decide he had to come find them.

"Okay, Em. If you think we can pull this off, I'd have to lock you up to get you to stop. I can't let you do it alone, so I guess I have to come with you. I only have one condition."

She had stopped breathing, it sounded like, during Ethan's declaration. But now her voice was apprehensive. "What condition?"

"We tell Fred."

"No! He'll make us stay. He'll tell on us!"

"Fred? Are you serious? Come on, Em—you know him almost as well as you know me. He wouldn't do that to us."

Emily scrambled back to her side of the tent and curled up in a ball.

"You're acting irrationally. We have to tell him. He brought us here, and when we go, the fallout lands on him. We can't do that to him without warning."

Emily uncurled a bit. "That's probably true. I don't want to get him in trouble." She sat back up. "Okay. We can tell him."

Sometime later that night, Ethan realized how glad he was to be doing something, even if it was something insane, to bring his family back together.

It made it a lot easier to get to sleep.

"I know," Fred said.

"You... we... wait, *what!?!*" Emily spluttered.

They stood in the woods fifty yards or so down the hill from their pair of tents, speaking as low as possible to keep from being overheard. Still, Emily was sure her surprised squeak would carry to the moon and back.

Fred shrugged. "I know. I knew two weeks ago. I think the two of you have been very patient."

"When were you going to tell us?"

The Tuttle Twins and the Days of Darkness

"When was I going to tell *you*? You're the ones with the secret. Can I help it if I know you very well by now?"

Emily's mouth flapped open and closed like a landed fish. She couldn't think of what to say. She had all her arguments lined up like toy soldiers, ready to march, and now she didn't need any of them. Or maybe she still did. He said he knew, not that he would let them go.

It was dark, but not as dark as it would be an hour from now. The western sky still showed a band of orange where the sun had gone. They had a minute.

"We're going tonight," Emily said. Ethan stood off to the side, arms folded. He didn't say anything, but he also didn't argue, and Emily had thought he might, for all that he'd gone along with hoarding food and working out a route for them to take.

Fred spread his hands. "I suppose you expect me to argue that you shouldn't go."

"Well—"

"Are there any arguments about that you haven't heard? You know it's a bad idea. You know the chances of success are small, especially without a vehicle. But you decided that you didn't want to live a life without your parents. A wise man once told me that if I couldn't afford to lose, I couldn't afford to bet. But what he didn't tell me was that there were going to be times when I couldn't afford *not* to bet because not to bet meant losing anyway. This is one of those times for you."

And there it was. He understood. Emily threw her arms around him and sobbed into his shoulder. He just held her while Ethan kept a vague watch on the camp in case anyone was curious. No one was.

Eventually, Emily said, voice muffled by Fred's shirt, "I should have known you'd understand."

"I'm glad you told me, finally."

Emily sniffled through a laugh. "Ethan made me."

Then they all laughed, low, privately, but the way friends do when they're saying goodbye.

"What can I do to help?" Fred said.

"Lookout duty while we steal the tent," Ethan said. "It's way too far to try to make it without a shelter. We consider it a fair trade for the truck and supplies our family has donated here."

The three of them made their way through the bracken to the camp, where most of the people in the main square were roasting s'mores over a good-sized fire. *That will make them night blind*, Emily thought. *That's good. No one will see us.*

The tent stakes came out without too much difficulty, and the tent collapsed, folding down with a wheeze to where they could stuff it in one of the packs. The packs were heavy—a lot heavier than Emily had wanted them to be, but they couldn't spare any of the things inside. They hung everything they could on their belts, including two precious handheld BaoFeng radios Ethan had smuggled out earlier that night. If they hoarded the batteries, they might make it three or even four stops on the Rescue Railroad, as they called it.

They had to go. Right now, before the radios were missed, before the fire died down, before the rational, sane parts of themselves reasserted their claim and made them quit being so stupid.

They hugged Fred again, shouldered their packs, and started down the hill on foot.

When they were out of sight of the camp, they bent back toward the lower parking lot, where they had arrived weeks earlier. The brush dragged at them, and Emily couldn't imagine trying to slog through it for two miles, let alone two hundred.

The moon's gleam off the windshield of their old truck showed them where the parking lot was. Taking it would have made their mission possible, even simple, but the keys were no longer in their possession, and they wouldn't have enough fuel to make it far down the road anyway. They stepped out of the woods and crouched between two cars, listening. They heard nothing. There was usually a sentry there, guarding the drive that led back to the main road, but they couldn't see one. Maybe he didn't come on duty until later.

"Come on," Emily said, leading out.

The moment they stepped into the open, they were pinned by two high-beam headlights.

"Don't bother running," a voice said. Emily recognized it. Amihan.

"You couldn't outrun us with packs on, anyway," said another voice, and that one froze Emily's blood.

"Fred," Ethan whispered. "He ratted us out, just like you said."

"If you're wondering whether I ratted you out," Fred said, stepping into the high beam and blocking some of it, "I didn't, and I never would."

"I knew something was up with you two," Amihan said. She also stepped into the light and spread her hands. "Too many whispers. Too much secrecy. Too much false camaraderie. Forgive me—I was in intelligence in the Army. You two weren't obvious, but it wasn't hard to figure out that you were up to something, and even easier to figure out what that was."

Emily just sat right down where she was. She was determined never to move again.

"Oh, come on, kids. Cheer up. First off, I'm not arresting you. Second, I congratulate you on your planning and your determination. That's rare in anybody but especially rare in teenagers."

"Told you they were exceptional," Fred said.

"Yes, you did. And you were right. In fact, I don't feel much like turning them in at all. I believe that initiative should be rewarded, not punished."

Emily raised her eyebrows. This wasn't going the way she thought it would.

Amihan strolled across the parking lot toward them, prowling like a jungle cat. "Fred told me you had a conversation about disciplined initiative."

Emily could only nod. Ethan seemed to be carved from wax for all the movements he made.

"I had a commander named Parker Winters, and he was big on that, too. It's a good principle. You're showing that kind of initiative with this hopeless stunt of yours."

"It's not hopeless."

"It is indeed," Amihan said, still in that conversational tone, "but it's also very disciplined. I like that."

"But initiative has to be in support of the objective," Ethan finally said. "And this is, um, outside that somewhat."

"Ah," Amihan said, "that's where you're wrong. Oh, the objective of the camp isn't supported by you guys stealing a bunch of stuff and vanishing; I admit that. We're going to have a chat about that presently. But the rest? The camp isn't the objective. Preservation of life, family, and goodness is the real objective. Your mission does support that. I believe it does so without too large a cost to the preservation of the MAG."

"You... you're letting us go?" Emily said, incredulous.

Amihan crouched down to look her in the eye. She frowned, a thoroughly creepy look when backlit by the headlights. "No. I'm not letting you go."

Ethan slumped against the car and slid to his knees.

"I'm helping you go."

He shot back up again. "You're *helping* us?"

"I told you. I think disciplined initiative should be rewarded. You're taking one heck of a risk, but you're doing it in support of a cause I believe in, and you're doing it... mostly... the right way. As you are my personal responsibility in this camp, it is my decision whether to let you proceed. I have decided to do more than permit it. I'm going to enable it. I'm going to *augment* it." She stood up and extended a hand to Emily to help her to her feet.

"But I think there's a chance others might not agree with my decision, and I don't have the patience to explain it to them this evening. So if we could continue this conversation in this lovely four-door extended cab truck," she said, motioning like an MC introducing a performer, "that would be preferable to standing in the open like this."

Once they were rumbling down the road, Amihan said, "I did tell Cap I might be on the move tonight and that I couldn't explain at the moment. That should keep the motorbike patrol off our tail."

"He let you go?" Emily said, surprise evident in her voice.

"He's a good commander, one of the best I've ever served with. I wasn't surprised. He trusts me."

"Will he still trust you after this?" Fred said.

"Absolutely. I'm doing the right thing." She sounded very sure of herself.

The Tuttle Twins and the Days of Darkness

After a couple more minutes, Ethan said, "Um, I don't want to spoil the mood or anything, but what exactly *are* you doing besides helping us down the mountain?"

"I'm giving you transportation, equipment, and guidance."

That was stunning enough that Ethan couldn't even ask what all that entailed.

Fortunately, Amihan was only too happy to elaborate. Emily thought she seemed positively cheerful about it.

"First, wheels. You can walk, but it's slow, and with those packs, it will take you about an hour before you're blistering and hoping you die. So the logical thing to do is to provide you with a vehicle."

"This *truck*?" Ethan said, far too excited and hopeful.

"Oh heavens no," Amihan said, laughing. "This thing is way too valuable to the MAG. It's a dual-fuel, so we can run it on almost anything, and we have huge reserves of natural gas that don't require electric pumping. No. Not this truck. But I do know where there are a lot of other vehicles, most of them with only a little fuel in them, but it all adds up. I'm taking you there right now."

"The second thing?" Emily said.

"Equipment. I'm afraid I can't let you take those radios." She waved at their belts. "Those belong to the MAG, and we may need them. But they're the wrong thing for you anyway—you don't need comms. You need positioning. And that I can help you with. The glove box, Fred, if you please."

Fred opened it, and two small units fell into his hand, about the size of a pager, with LED screens—dark, of course. "Are these—" he said.

"Handheld GPS units. Yes. They don't need cell reception, and they run off batteries. There's nothing wrong with the satellites, so they should work perfectly." She swiveled her head to look at Emily. "You have maps? Of the places you're going?"

"Yeah."

"Were you smart enough to get GPS coordinates for those places?"

"Uh, no. But Ethan was. I thought it was overkill because we'd have the BaoFengs."

"Great!" Amihan said. "Use the GPS units to find the bases. That will be a lot more helpful, and a lot less potentially dangerous, than talking in the open about where people are and how to get to them."

"Thank you, Amihan," Ethan said. "I'm... this is so much more than I thought possible."

They rumbled out of the forest and into town—not Spoonerville, but a different one. The sign read *Micawber*.

"I know a guy here," Amihan said. "He'll help us."

"How do you know he'll be here still?"

She laughed again. "He'll never leave his lot. It will take more than the apocalypse to pry him off his place."

His place turned out to be a large car dealership, with cars spread out for an acre or more, a bit dusty, but still there, locked behind huge gates. Amihan rolled up in front of one of them and honked a complex series of beeps.

After a couple minutes, a round mound of a man rolled down the concrete toward them. He peered through the gate, and Amihan stuck her head out the window.

"Legaspi!" the man shouted in surprise. "Never thought I'd see you again."

"Need your help, Micawber."

He opened his arms wide. "You name it, sweetheart, and it's yours."

They rolled through the opening gate, and it closed silently behind them.

"What you need, honey?" Micawber said, leaning on the open driver's windowsill.

"I need a truck."

His laugh rolled out like an avalanche. "Even for you, my darling girl, I don't give away my children."

"Not asking you to give me one. Or even loan me one. I want to buy it."

The laugh was even bigger this time. "Oh, honey, you're making an old man half drop his britches. You know none of the bank machines are working. I can't take your money."

"But you know I'm good for it. You *know* I'll pay."

His face got thoughtful. "I do, yeah. After what we've been through, I'd take your word that the sun went out."

She nodded. "Here's what we need, then." And she laid out some serious requirements—extra fuel tank, offroad capability, spare tires, fuel economy.

He beamed at her as if she was his own child, which she simply could not have been. "Darlin'," he said, "I know just the thing."

The truck was midnight black, long, bulging a bit where the extra tank went, and gleaming like a new-hatched snake. It was perfect.

Amihan haggled with him a little over the price, but in the end, she shook on what Emily thought was an unholy sum, and he handed her the keys.

"And a full tank of gas," she said.

"You're gonna think the world spun backward, but it's full. I filled up everything the moment the power went out and flagged down Pete to get his tanker in here to top off our reservoir. I'm solid on fuel. I should add another grand to the price, but I'm just that nice of a fella."

When they rolled the beast out through the gate, Emily hopped out and wrapped her arms around Micawber, as far as she could, at least.

"Oh, now, no call for that. Y'all come back when this is over and tell me what you did with Bessie here. That'll be payment enough."

"They can't pay you back for this," Fred said. The twins nodded.

"We'll see. Survive. Bring Bessie back. Then we'll talk."

Ethan scuffed his shoe on the concrete. "You said there were three things. This is like ten things all by itself, but… "

"Guidance," she said. "The last thing. But honestly, my guidance wouldn't be worth very much. I don't know what you'll face. I don't know what you'll need in order to survive and find your folks. So I'm sending a guide with you."

She handed Fred the keys. "Him," she said with a wink.

Fred reared back. "What? I can't—"

"You can and you will," Amihan said. "To make it official, I won't be taking you back to the MAG. Therefore you must go on with these kids. I know you've been giving them advice and guidance for a long time. This is just one more opportunity."

"We don't have enough food for three," Emily said.

"You do now. On foot it was going to take you, what, a month to get out to Cheyenne, if you were lucky? Now it won't. If you're very lucky, it won't take more than a couple of days. You have enough food for all three of you, plus your parents when you find them."

She grabbed each of the twins firmly by the collars of their shirts and yanked them in close and spoke sternly. "Listen to me. You're walking into the worst nightmare you can imagine. You've been on the radios. You know what's out there. Fred here has every skill you might possibly need. Not to take him with you is even stupider than going in the first place. Okay? You get me?"

They nodded as if their heads would fall off.

Then there wasn't anything more to do but get on the road. Amihan pulled her truck around and met them window-to-window. "Oh!" she said, "I almost forgot." She handed over a box carefully, with both hands. Fred took it. It was heavy and clanked.

He unwrapped it. "Guns," he said. "You really do think of everything."

"I'd have been happy to give back your rifles and shotguns, too, but then I really would have had to explain myself. So the handguns will have to do. I pray you never need them."

The extended tank got them all the way to the Nebraska border before it ran low. The first three farmers they tried ran them off with dogs, but the fourth one was willing to trade a full tank for one of the handguns.

The Tuttle Twins and the Days of Darkness

The GPS functioned flawlessly, and it was in a little town called Tarry Park that they got their first big break. They found the home belonging to MF4GKY, and in their well-stocked root cellar, they got some good sleep. At 9:30 p.m. on the dot, the radio they were monitoring squawked, and there was Mom's voice.

They were in the middle of nowhere, Nebraska. And they were stuck. Their vehicle had broken down. They had crawled, essentially, to a farmhouse that happened to have a radio. But they couldn't go any farther. They were at least 40 miles from anywhere, they had no food, nor could the farmer spare any to take with them.

The twins used their radio to call ahead on the route and explain their predicament. They used code phrases, circuitous language, anything to keep prying ears away from where they'd be going.

Everywhere the news was the same. The interstate highway had been unsafe to travel due to ambushing gangs, but the secondary, smaller roads would work. They arranged fuel as they could, and word spread in the remaining ham community. People banded together to help them.

When the twins finally found their parents they almost didn't recognize them they were so thin—near starvation. They had made it just in time.

At the last radio stop, before they made the Monongahela crossing to Gnarled Oaks and the Little Pink House, a familiar voice came on the radio.

"Ho, Starbuck and Apollo. This is Caprica."

The twins' faces lit up. "Bern," they said.

Bern went on. "I have a very interested party here. We've been following you all the way. You're both crazy, and the whole camp agrees." Then she broke, and a new voice came on. It was Amihan.

"Hope you're taking care of my truck."

Mom took the microphone. "You're a saint. If we were having any more children, we'd name one after you."

"Ma'am, it's an honor to make some good in the world. Y'all take care, and come see us when it's all over."

And when it was, they did.

THE END

The three of them were silent for a long time. Outside, a bird began to sing, loud and long and beautifully, as if all were right with the world. Three weeks before, Ethan would have stopped whatever he was doing to listen. Now he shut it out. It had nothing to do with the world as it was.

Fred sat with his eyes closed, breathing deeply as if meditating. Ethan wanted to shake him to hurry him up.

Finally, he opened his eyes. They were bright but moist. "I think Ethan is right that these people won't stop. They're not likely to be influenced by any olive branch from our side. And there is the bare chance that they don't know we *have* any food. They might leave us alone anyway. If they don't, better that we be ready to discourage them from coming down this street. We should do it with the minimum loss of life, whatever that is."

Ethan pumped his fist. "Yeah! I knew Fred was on my side."

Ethan might not have seen it, but Emily did. If he *was* on Ethan's side, he wasn't happy about it.

Fred turned to her. "You okay with that? Because this will never work if we aren't all on the same page."

"I'm not happy about it, and I think we're making a mistake. But I won't sit idle and watch you two try to defend us by yourselves. I'll do my part."

The corner of Fred's mouth turned up. "You always did like John Dickinson."

Emily didn't bother to hide her smile. "Yeah, I did. If he can speak against the Declaration of Independence, then politely bow out to let it pass and follow that by enlisting in a patriot militia, then I can pick up a rifle and defend my home. Or, you know, your home."

"*Mi casa es tu casa*," Fred said. "As you know."

"Then *mi arma es tu arma*. Let's get ready to use them."

It was the rooster that finally did it.

Sometime in the early hours of Day 22, a cock crowed and woke the house. When Emily looked out the window, she saw it silhouetted against the rising sun, singing its heart out. Her first reaction was that she wanted to shoot the thing for waking her up. Her second was just as practical, if less violent—the rooster could fertilize the eggs, and they could raise more chickens, meaning meat as well as eggs.

The rooster was a vicious, nasty thing that flew at them and clawed at their faces whenever they went into the backyard. Red-streaked feathers, like a murderous comet, streaked toward them whenever they showed their faces. Emily took to carrying the lid of a trash can as a shield to fend him off. They named him Lucifer. Emily thought that name was perhaps a bit short of the evil the bird contained.

The Tuttle Twins and the Days of Darkness

But he patrolled the backyard and twice had set up a ruckus when a feral dog arrived on the scene, saving a good number of the flock by summoning assistance. He had taken command of the flock and herded the chickens toward the coop in the evening, which had saved Ethan and Emily a good amount of work. They obviously hadn't seen any eggs hatch yet, but there didn't seem to be any reason why that wouldn't happen at some point.

Day twenty-eight dawned overcast, with dark thunderheads on the western horizon. Fred went out early to make sure the rain barrels were positioned correctly under the downspouts of as many houses as they had barrels for. Collecting rainwater was a major priority, even with the recently-discovered bounty of the kidney-shaped swimming pool in the back of the house at the end of the block. Emily hated that it was so far—water, as she had said, was heavy, and carrying it in buckets lashed to poles was her least favorite chore of all.

Ethan cracked eggs into a pan for breakfast—they had modified the stove to run on propane now, which Fred had a good supply of—while Emily ground up some wheat with the hand-cranked stone grinder. Her stomach growled. The smell of the eggs always did that to her. She didn't think she was eating that much less than she had before, but she always seemed to be hungry these days.

Fred came back a little later and reported that no more houses had been ransacked that he could see. The gang's progress had halted two doors up the street from the Cunninghams', and it had been quiet for three days now.

"Maybe they found easier pickings," Emily said over her shoulder.

Fred dropped into a kitchen chair. "Easier than this street? How is that possible?"

But calm was welcome, and for a moment that morning, all three of them started to wonder if things were going to be okay. As long as it rained. And the generator held out. And they kept finding gas cans filled with fuel.

Problems for the future.

At two that afternoon, the skies let go, and a regular gullywasher tore through Spoonerville, dumping sheets of rain down as if the heavens were trying to cleanse the earth.

It didn't matter to Emily whether the earth got cleansed, but she knew that rain like this would do a great job on *her*. "I'm going out back to take God's shower. Nobody come back there for, oh, as long as it keeps raining."

"What if it goes on for days?" Fred said.

Emily sighed so loudly and happily that Fred couldn't help busting up with laughter. But then he got Ethan outside as well, and they stripped down to bathing shorts and took their own shower, soap, shampoo, and all, right there on the driveway. The rain was so heavy they could hardly see to the end of the street. No one was going to come out on a day like this.

The relief of it, the chance to let down their guard, almost got them killed right away. But the rooster was vigilant.

The rain slacked off and stopped around four, and despite her threat before, Emily found she was as clean as she wished to be after forty-five minutes. But she was gloriously, deliciously clean. She'd done wash outside as well, hanging up the clothes on the line and soaping them down, scrunching them, with the rinse water provided by the Almighty in a soaking deluge. Sun finally cut through the clouds at five. Ethan had gone for a nap, and Fred, for the first time in a couple of weeks, sat in the library, calmly reading a book. Emily hummed to herself as she kneaded bread in the kitchen, a tune she once would have queued up on her iPod.

And then, at dusk, the rooster shrieked.

This was not the call of the Lord of the Flock, summoning his chickens back to the coop. Neither was it a cry of superiority to let the world know who was the top chick. This was alarm. Outrage. Challenge.

Something was in the yard.

They all heard it, and at once weapons were in hand. Ethan stepped toward the back sliding door, prepared to take aim, as they usually did when a dog or another sort of varmint came roaming, but this time the flat crack of an unknown pistol rang out.

The color drained from Emily's face. "It's them."

Fred boosted himself up on the counter and looked out the sink window. "The intruder is against the house. I can't see him." But they could all see the rooster, still in the fight, flapping and screaming and crying out like the devil he was. Feathers flew. The pistol cracked again. But the rooster did not fall, did not quit.

"We have to help Lucifer!" Emily said and reached for the door handle.

"You can't! You'll be shot!" Ethan grabbed her and held her back.

"It will be a lot easier for him to do that once he's shot Lucifer! Let me GO!"

"He'll know we know he's here," Fred said. "But we can still get him, I think. Ethan, hand me the shotgun and get ready to open the slider door. Emily, go to the front window—no, you mind me now, we talked about this—and get low and angry with the rifle. Use the scope. They're all out there right now. You have to get them before they come running and put the fear of God into them. Go now."

Emily gave Fred a quick hug and jogged out of the kitchen. Ethan stood by the slider door, hand on the handle. They looked hard at each other. There wasn't any going back from this point. Fred wouldn't fire warning shots. He wasn't shooting to scare the intruder off. He'd be trying to kill him.

"I'm sorry you have to do this," Ethan said.

"I'll be a lot sorrier if I don't."

Ethan nodded solemnly and jerked the back door open.

Fred was already in a crouch. In one smooth motion, he stepped sideways out to the little porch, and the moment his muzzle cleared the doorframe, he pulled the trigger.

The shotgun boomed like a cannon. The recoil knocked Fred sideways and off the porch stairs onto the patio. The rooster stopped cackling.

Fred didn't fire again, but he didn't lower his gun, either. Then he got up at a run and headed for the scene under the kitchen window. Ethan risked a look.

What was left of a man was there, slumped against the siding of the house, covered in scratches and feathers, and a dead rooster. He had a hole about the size of Ethan's fist in his chest.

Fred swore, which Ethan had never heard him do before. "I didn't want to get the rooster," Fred said.

Two cans of gas lay at the dead man's feet. The smell of gunpowder mixed with the definite smell of gasoline. "He was lighting us up," Ethan said.

"Now we have more gas," Fred said, checking the man's pulse. "He's very dead."

"Ethan! Fred!" screamed Emily from the front window. They heard her rifle and the sound of splintering glass. Then the world seemed to come apart.

Emily would never be able to recall exactly what happened that day. When she tried to explain what she witnessed, the description was like a kaleidoscope spinning, with colorful images breaking apart and recombining, but never creating a coherent story.

She remembered Ethan's shadow on the fence by the garage—she couldn't see him properly—as he raised his shotgun and pulled the trigger. Dark-clad shapes swarmed up the driveway, up the walk, and the front steps. One went down, then another, under the *chunk-chunk* of the 12-gauge. Three of them peeled off toward Ethan, leaving five or six to assault the front door.

They had prepared a surprise for the gang there, a heavy washtub filled to overflowing with their daily waste, and they walked right into the trap, tripping the wire and bringing a hundred pounds of latrine pouring down on their heads. They shrieked and beat on the door, but it was steel and repelled them while all the time Emily's gun went *bang, bang, bang*, and at this range, she couldn't miss. Emily noticed one of them was wearing a t-shirt with their summer camp's name on it "Camp Hope." They fell off the stoop like leaves falling from a tree. She'd have seen more, but her eyes were blurred by the tears pooling in them.

The Tuttle Twins and the Days of Darkness

She remembered Fred, who planned to defend from the roof though she couldn't see him. Or hear him—her ears were thunderstruck from the blasts of her rifle. But lightning flashed from above, and her vengeful guardian angel struck down the gang's reinforcements as they came boiling out of the cars along the street.

There were too many of them, in the end. Which one got Ethan, Emily never knew, but she heard Fred's scream, and then another muzzle flash from up the street, and a body fell from the roof, a body she knew. They had so many men. Where did they all come from?

Most of them were down, still, unmoving. Emily was good. Fred was good. Ethan's shotgun left many on his side moaning and writhing on the ground. But there were more, still more. Not so many, now. Three. Four maybe.

She heard stomping at the back door. Retreating from the window, she dropped behind the overturned couch and abandoned her rifle for a sawed-off shotgun. The daylight was nearly gone, and she couldn't see, so she fired early. The blast of her new weapon knocked her back against the wall. Her shoulder erupted in fire. She was sure she'd broken her collarbone. But she succeeded. The enemy invaders were down, writhing and screaming though she couldn't hear their voices through her burst ear drums.

Except she wasn't finished, after all. One more dark mass dashed into the room. She had one more shell, and she fired it.

But he had slipped on the bloody floor and fallen, and the shot went high—her last shot unless she could get the pistol out of her waistband.

There wasn't time. She saw the round hole of his own pistol swing toward her and knew it was the last thing she would ever see. A bright light shone far ahead of Emily. She heard of this—she was dead. But at least she'd soon be at rest with Fred and her twin, Ethan.

Then someone shook her—quite gently, really—and asked her if she was okay. She realized she could hear them. There was a flashlight shining in her eye.

She didn't answer. What if it was one of the bad people?

The flashlight shined upward to the face of the one holding it. A woman with curly brown hair and green eyes. Emily knew that face. It was someone she knew. Who was it? Names didn't come to her.

There were other people there. A man. Two men. A boy actually. Twelve? She didn't know. But then she remembered his name—Richie. It was Richie Cunningham from down the street.

"She's okay, I think," the woman said. "Not physically hurt, that I can see."

One larger man—that must have been Mr. Cunningham—said, "I didn't know she was there or I would never have... did she see? They'd have died anyway without medical care. What other choice did I have? She must have hit them with a shotgun… sawed off?"

Mrs. Cunningham—it had to be her—held up her weapon, sawed with Fred's hacksaw so close to the chamber that you could almost see the shell down the barrel.

The boy whistled. "That's a wicked piece. Effective, though."

"They took out half the gang over here," Mrs. Cunningham said, her tone like fizzing acid. "Enough for us to stand a chance at our end of the street.

Emily sat slumped against the living room wall. She heard them, but none of it processed. She didn't ask where her brother was because she didn't want the answer to that. She knew where Fred was, and he was probably just as happy lying there among his flowers he loved so much.

The Cunninghams did what they did, going back and forth through the house, in and out, and Emily finally got tired of sitting against the wall and lay down instead.

The Malantown gang, now destroyed, wasn't the only one active in the area, but the word got out how the neighborhood had been blooded, and none of the others dared come. That left the whole street's resources for the Cunninghams, and they made good use of them.

Emily did what she could to help.

The Tuttle Twins and the Days of Darkness

First, she moved in with the Cunninghams, and they used the Tuttles' house for storage. When they carried Emily out the front door of Fred's house, that was the last time she was ever there. She had no desire to go back. It was Richie that went and got her things and brought them down the street.

The one thing Emily did want from Fred's house was the radio. Piece by piece, Alex Cunningham brought it down and set it up in a back room. Emily didn't say much anymore, but she did help with installing and calibrating the system, and once it was operational, she spent most of her time there, calling around the country, looking for news, and hoping—the one hope she still had—that she'd hear her parents' voices again.

On day twenty-nine, the day after the attack, they held a funeral for Fred and Ethan. The other twelve bodies—*twelve*—were dumped a couple of streets over in a shallow pit that it took a whole day to dig. Fred was buried in his garden in the back, about where Emily figured he would have wanted to end up.

With Ethan, the task was harder. The Cunninghams asked Emily over and over where she thought he should be laid to rest, and all she would do was shrug her shoulders. Eventually, they chose a spot in the back of the Tuttles' yard by the beehives. It rained that day. Emily stood in it, trying not to remember the previous afternoon when she'd enjoyed the rain so much. This time she hoped she would get pneumonia and die.

But she didn't, and gradually the stupidity of it got through to her. It was as if she could hear Ethan saying, "Geez, Em, get a grip. You think I want my noble sacrifice to be for nothing?"

The situation around the country was dire. Most of the west coast ham operators had gone off-comm, along with most of those in the East, but not before describing fairly awful scenes in the big cities. Lack of water was the biggest killer, and people had gotten desperate very fast.

The Tuttle Twins and the Days of Darkness

From Oregon, Emily did hear some more positive news. The Richardsons—the family the Tuttles had stayed with—remained on the channel a couple of times a week, just for a few minutes. Their generator fuel was running out. But Medford seemed fairly quiet, with the Rogue River running through it. The people were sharing food, and there was plenty of water.

But the Tuttles had gone. To the East, Mandy Richardson said. She hadn't heard from them since.

Neither did Emily. Her generator fuel was running out as well. That prompted foraging trips to try to find gasoline. All the stations were picked clean, of course. But here and there, a house would have a gas can in the garage. They found twenty more gallons one day in a pool house next to a scummy, algae-overgrown pool half a mile from home. It kept the radio on for another month.

And that kept Emily alive.

Until day sixty-eight, when a crackle and a CQ brought a familiar voice on band.

"Emily... Emily, are you listening?"

The static was terrible, but it was Dad. She slammed down the transmit key, forgetting all the protocol, forgetting everything but that she needed to talk to him, to have him talk to her.

"Dad! Dad, I'm here. Dad—" She tried to say more, but what could she say. Tears blotted out her vision and cut her voice off.

"Emily. Oh, thank God. We're alive. Both of us, your mother is right here."

"Hey, Em. Where's Ethan? How is Fred?"

What could she tell them? How could she tell them? "They're... outside. Where are you? We have almost no fuel left for the generator. I don't know how long I can stay on."

"We're in Nebraska. We're coming to get you. Where are you?"

"Home. I'm still home. We're waiting for you."

"Can you get to—" was all there was time for. The generator shuddered to a stop, and the radio went dead.

That was the last time Emily ever heard their voices.

The day did come when the power came back on. But by then, there weren't very many people left to care. Broadcast messages from the federal government said that all critical functions of civil order were being restored and that the government had continued to function throughout the crisis.

Shortwave and ham radio told a different story.

THE END

"Mort and his gang deserve to get pounded into the ground. But I don't believe premeditated killing is the solution." Ethan sounded disgusted with himself but resolute.

"I don't like it any better than you do. People are going to die from this."

He nodded. "And I want to be in Gnarled Oaks before it happens."

Telling Faraday was simpler than they thought it would be. When they were ushered into her office in the terminal, Faraday barely glanced up from her maps. "So you're out, then," she said.

Now that it came to it, the twins stood sheepishly, toeing the floor and thinking that this wasn't a great way to repay someone who'd shown them so much kindness.

Emily felt she had to explain. "It's not that we don't think your cause is just. We do. You've been really nice to us and probably saved our lives."

Faraday straightened up and fixed her signature glare on them. "But."

Emily tried not to flinch. "But we don't believe this kind of violence solves the real issue."

"Even when that violence is perpetrated on you by someone bent on your destruction?"

"With all due respect, he hasn't perpetrated any violence on you…yet."

Faraday snorted. "He has on you."

"But we're choosing to walk away from the situation, because revenge isn't the same as justice."

Faraday didn't rock back on her heels. It wasn't that dramatic. But Emily could tell, absolutely, that this point hadn't occurred to her. There was a tightening of the eyes and a half-audible intake of breath before she spoke again.

"I admire your convictions. But I have people to protect. I'm going to do that protecting the best way I know how. It will probably be messy. But there's no way I can think of to keep my people safe that doesn't involve some kind of mess."

Emily could only nod. There wasn't time for a long discussion of non-aggression, and she was pretty sure Faraday wouldn't be in the mood anyhow.

"At least you came to me and told me directly. I can respect that." Now she blew that breath out like a balloon deflating. She leaned back down to her map and dismissed them with a wave. "See Alton. He'll fix you up with some supplies. If you want, there's a map here you can copy if you can find some loose paper. That's the best I can do for you."

"And it's more than you have to do," Ethan said. "Thank you, and best of luck."

They found Alton on the way out of the hangar. He looked at their faces, looked away, then back very quickly. "What?" he said, worry on his face.

"We're leaving," Emily said simply.

He goggled at them. "Before the battle?"

"Well, before, if we can. We want to be out of here before we're either in the way or a blow to morale. If we're moping about, we'll be noticed. If we're just, you know, *gone*, nobody will miss us."

"We're not really a part of this place yet," Ethan said. "And we won't be part of the attack on Accord. It won't end well for anyone."

Alton took all this in with his characteristic calm, then shrugged his shoulders. "Captain Faraday gave you permission?" It wasn't really a question. They couldn't leave without her say-so, and they all knew it.

"Told us you'd help us with some supplies," Emily said.

"I'll go copy that map," Ethan said, heading back in. "Won't take long."

"None of it will," Emily said as Alton turned on his heel and began walking to one of the storage sheds. He didn't look back to see if she was following him.

The sun was getting toward its noon-day zenith before they got out of the front gate. Alton drew it aside just wide enough for them to get out, then stood back, watching them with that same mildly curious expression he let them in with.

"Don't run into that bear again," he said.

"No promises." Emily stopped just outside the gate and turned back. Alton cocked his head a bit, waiting.

"It's not… I would have liked to stay," she said. "I don't even think what you're doing is wrong. I just don't think it will work, and I think there are better ways."

"You could stay and make those points," Alton said. He seemed to genuinely wish she would.

But she shook her head. "I couldn't. Not now. Cap is doing what she believes is right, and she's got a lot more experience than we do. All we would do is sow dissension, and that's not… I don't want that." She stopped and looked about wistfully. "I'm really grateful to you. You didn't have to let us in."

He nodded, acknowledging that. "And you don't have to go. But here we are. Godspeed."

He rolled the gate shut and padlocked it, turned, and without pausing or looking back, headed for the terminal.

"Well. That went great," Ethan said.

The road from the Field back to the river was quiet, baking gently in the summer sun, and they were eager to get off of it, and head into the trees again. This time, though, the map showed that there was a dirt road that paralleled the river for quite a ways. They found it without trouble and headed east, heads down, putting as many miles as they could between themselves and Faraday's Field. They didn't talk at all the rest of the morning.

Every now and then, Ethan took some of his frustrations out on an unsuspecting loose stone in the road, sending it spinning into the underbrush with a kick.

No bear molested them. They saw squirrels and birds and even a fox slinking through the underbrush, but nothing larger. And especially no humans, which was a relief. The entire day passed without them saying more than a couple of words to one another.

Compared to before Faraday's Field, they made good time. There were some landmarks on the map that made it fairly easy to know how far they'd come. At first, that was encouraging—for once, they knew where they were and how far they had to go. But as the day wore on and they made little progress, it weighed on them the distances they were attempting to cover.

Over dinner—some tinned stew, eaten cold—Ethan made some calculations for how long it would take them to reach Gnarled Oaks. "Two more days, give or take," he said.

Emily grunted as if that were about what she'd expected. Ethan couldn't decide if that was a good or bad thing.

Late that night, camped in a thicket of young maple trees, they heard what might have been gunshots echoing off the nearby hills. They rolled over and tried to go back to sleep.

Their food ran out on day four. They must have misread the map, somehow—or maybe were completely lost. They had fancy filtering cups that let them drink much more than the tablets would have and without the terrible taste. That let them keep going, but they needed food and could not find any.

The river widened until it became difficult to figure out how they could cross, but they knew they'd eventually have to. The time came later on that day. The river met another, a huge river, what was surely the Monongahela.

"Now we're on the wrong side of this river, *and* the Monongahela," Emily sighed.

The silt from their tributary river had piled up as it met the resistance of the stronger moving Monongahela. This effect created a delta. They spent the next hour swimming from sand bar to sand bar, until they reached the other shore of the smaller island. After a short break, they continued their journey north.

"Great. Now we'll get to Grandma's and be able to wave from across the river." Ethan chucked a rock into the swirling water.

"If it comes to that, we'll swim, and you know it. The trick is to get there in the first place."

The woods had thickened with brambles and downed, rotting trees, making their progress slow. There were mushrooms, but neither of them thought much of their woodcraft in that department, and hungry as they were, they still didn't think it would be fun to die from fungal poisoning.

Their packs had been liberally stocked with foodstuffs when they set out, but there was only so much food they could carry, and it was gone. The Faradays had not seen fit to provide them with firearms—though they did get a pocketknife, and that gave Ethan an idea.

"Remember that hike with Dad and Fred where we built a lean-to to sleep in?" Ethan said as they sat on a log sipping filtered water. He slapped at a bug and smashed it against his shoulder. It stank. He sighed. Just one more lovely smell to add to his growing stench.

"We've built a few since then on this journey," Emily said. She picked at the bark and peeled strips off when it came loose.

"Yeah, but after we built them, Dad showed me how to build a snare for rabbits or squirrels. I think I remember how to do it."

Emily contemplated the lengthening shadows of the forest and thought about the empty state of her stomach. "If you think it will work, yeah. We're not going to have much energy if all we're eating is bark."

"It would have been better if Faraday had given us fishing line and some hooks, but she didn't. This is the only thing I think will work."

Emily reached into her pocket and pulled out the knife. "Okay, well, what do we need to do?"

It was an old-fashioned whip snare, with shoelaces for the catch and a flexible tree branch for the whip, baited with the last of the peanuts from their packs. It wasn't much. It looked, in fact, like a waste of time, until the third hour of their rest, when a cottontail rabbit hopped into view, nosed about for a moment, and stepped in the wrong spot. The branch whipped up, the snare tightened, and the rabbit dangled from the nearby tree, neat as you like.

The twins stood in open-mouthed shock, staring at the struggling animal.

"I don't believe that worked," Ethan said.

"Yeah. It's been so long since something worked out well for us I was beginning to think it would never happen again."

They had even less experience rendering the coney, gutting, and skinning it, which turned out to be a thoroughly foul process neither of them was keen on repeating. But hunger drove them on until they had, at last, a half-rabbit each on sticks over a small, but hot fire.

The Tuttle Twins and the Days of Darkness

At the riverside, the thick woods loosened, and tall reeds grew instead. They could look over them across the water to a similar vista on the other side. Up the river, north, there was hardly a break in the forest as far as they could see. The spot where they stood was dry and cool under the spreading branches of elms and chestnut trees, with a blanket of leaves that made even the ground soft and inviting.

"We could stay here a day or so. Rest up," Emily said, turning her rabbit.

Ethan's stomach growled. He resisted the urge—growing powerful now—to rip the coney off the stick and devour it half raw. "We can't. We have to move on. There's no rest for us until we get to Gnarled Oaks."

Emily sighed, knowing he was right. She was just so *tired*. Just a hundred years or so ago, people had lived like this all the time, trapping, hiking, and building shelters. How had they done it? She was wearier than she had ever been, and they'd only been on the trail for a week.

"We thought we were clever," she said, voice despondent. "We did those weekends in the woods and hikes and things. Playing at wilderness survival. Remember how proud we were of those lean-tos we made? They wouldn't have held out the water from a bare sprinkle for ten minutes, but you'd have thought we had built the Taj Mahal."

Ethan ran a grubby hand through his matted hair. "And how tired and hungry we thought we were after a few hours hiking. That was nothing compared to this. At least Dad taught us how to build a fire, or we'd be... well, we'd be dead. That's all there is to it."

"So many skills we could have learned. We thought we were prepared."

Ethan gave a low chuckle. "Remember that guy with the long hair and buckskin at the last 4th of July festival in Gnarled Oaks? The one preaching about survival and mountain man skills? We marched right on by with our fat hot dogs dripping with relish. Thought we had no need for that stuff. He'd come in handy right about now, don'tcha think?"

Emily inspected her rabbit, found it cooking a little too much on one side, and moved her stick to a different part of the fire. "All it took was the power going out. No pandemic. No zombie apocalypse. Just... no power. And everything fell apart like tissue paper."

Later, tearing all-too-thin strips of greasy meat off slender bones, Ethan asked, "What happens when the power comes back *on*?"

"Don't think I haven't thought about that every two minutes for the last month!"

"Well, then? What happens?"

Emily licked her fingers and looked quizzically at him. "What do you mean, 'what happens?' We turn on our computers. We go for a drive. We... I dunno, take hot showers until the water runs cold."

"I've been thinking about that," Ethan said, cracking a bone and licking at the marrow inside. "I don't think it will work that way."

He chucked a bone into the river and picked up another one. "Think about it. The whole system is down right from the source. After this long, a bunch of equipment is going to need repair. To repair it, trucks and supplies are going to have to roll out. But they can't roll out because there's no fuel. It's all been used up at the business end of things.

"And there's more. The computers will need to reboot. They'll be looking for other machines that have information, but the networks are down. They won't come back all at once. A lot of them won't work. If the power comes back in surges, a little at a time, systems will overload and crash."

He shifted uncomfortably and licked his fingers. Even the last dregs of the grease were like manna from Heaven. "In other words, the whole system was built around the idea that the power would stay on, or that at least some of it would. I don't think it's like switching on a light. I think you can't restart the system without power, and you can't have power unless you restart the system."

Emily looked stricken. "I wasn't thinking about that at all. I was wondering what's to stop this from happening again?"

Ethan sat up a little taller. He wanted nothing more right now than six more rabbits lined up to roast, but at least he wasn't starving. "What do you mean?"

"Something took down the grid. We don't know what it was, but it probably wasn't a massively unlikely event like a solar flare. So probably, it was human-caused. Maybe someone attacked us. Once we get our machines back online, what's to stop whoever did this from doing it again?"

"I didn't… that hadn't occurred to me."

"I wouldn't have thought of it either, except for that cybersecurity career day at the college. Thing is, an open hole in your security has to be closed, or it remains vulnerable. You have to have the machines on to find that hole. While the machines are on, they're vulnerable. You can take them offline, find a patch, and plug the leak, but you have to have the machines on to be able to do that. And who knows what damage was done to the systems before they went down. It's not a simple problem—and just like you were saying, the whole network depends on there being parts of the network that are unaffected. This? Nobody prepared for this."

They sat in silence after that, ignoring the birds, the quiet gurgle of the passing river, and the rustling of leaves. Would they ever go back to the way things were? No. They never would. They couldn't. And neither would anyone else.

Emily finally spoke, her voice like a whisper, barely audible over the forest noises. "Remember how Grandma always talks about how her mother never got over the Depression? How she was still hoarding rubber bands, socks, and bits of string right up until she died?"

Ethan nodded. He'd been thinking about that, too.

Emily wiped her hands on her pants. "This will do that to us. To everyone that lives through this. We're never going to be the same."

"I was worrying about whether I could beat a level in my video game, *Force Majeure*," he said. "That's what I thought was important a month ago."

"And I was frustrated that the latest vlog from Fashion Monger was taking too long to load." She laughed out loud, a little hysterically. "What an idiot I was."

"We're still idiots," Ethan said, standing and holding out a hand to help Emily up. "Only now we know it!"

She took his hand. "May we survive to use the knowledge."

They kicked dirt on the fire and poured water on it from their cups. It seemed almost silly. But good forest manners were hard to break, and besides, they'd look very stupid indeed if they ended up burned in a fire they had started.

The twins finally stumbled out of the woods to a shingle beach across from Gnarled Oaks three days later. They had been lost, far from where they thought they were on the map, but eventually the Monongahela led them there. They were thin, eyes staring out of shrunken hollows, lips cracked, skin coated in dirt and sores. Across the river was the place they knew so well, less than two football fields away. And they couldn't get to it. They couldn't call out—their voices rasped and refused to work. There was no way they could make themselves heard over the din of the rushing river.

On the point of exhaustion and starvation, Ethan finally got a fire to light and used it to set a sapling pine tree aflame like a torch. That *did* attract attention, and bodies came out of the Little Pink House and pointed across at the spectacle. It felt like hours before someone shouted that there were people on the other beach and longer before someone organized a rowboat to go get them. It landed a quarter of a mile or more downstream and had to be towed back, but finally, after ages and ages, Uncle Brock crashed out of the woods and practically fell over on them, lying on the stones, feet half in the water.

"Ethan?! *Emily*!?!? How did you get here? What happened to you?"

They were too drained to respond.

Mom and Dad had made it to Gnarled Oaks a week before and began hiking through the woods, hoping to find some trace of their children, though they knew

the chances were next to zero. They hadn't, however, imagined they would come from so far south.

Emily developed a cough while recuperating that never quite went away. Eventually, many years later, her children would call it her "Power Cough," and they thought it was silly that no one could cure it.

Ethan rallied quickly and began taking long hikes through the woods, living off the land, exploring, and learning to handle the outdoors, until, when the power came back, he found he couldn't remember why he'd missed it. For the rest of his life, he went from town to town, teaching basic survival skills to anyone that was interested.

There were many, many more attendees that came to listen and learn than there would have been before the Event.

And yes, the power came back on about a year after it had gone away. But it was never like before. People didn't rely on it the way they once had. They opted for smaller, more local systems over the giant grid that had once dominated modern life.

Nobody ever spoke of either *Force Majeure* or *Fashion Monger* again.

THE END

So. That was it.

Ethan knew Emily had been hiding something, something pretty big, for a few days now. He could read his twin like yesterday's newspaper. But he hadn't known it was *this* big.

She couldn't do this. It was stupid. Pointless. She would throw her life away, or possibly several lives, for no purpose at all.

And Ethan should tell her that.

But he had rarely been able to persuade Emily to do something once she set her mind against it. So it would have to be someone else to convince her.

Fred was the logical choice. His tent was right next door. They saw him every day. Ethan could find a moment and tell him what Emily was planning, then together, they could figure out what to do to keep her from being suicidally stupid.

All this passed through Ethan's mind in less than a pair of heartbeats. And all he said was, "Em, we need to think hard about this."

"I have. I'm done thinking. I'll have all the supplies I can carry before the end of the week, and I'm going."

"To walk a thousand miles on foot? By yourself?"

"Well," she paused, and he heard her blow out a breath. "No, I mean, that wouldn't be ideal. Obviously, I want you to come with me."

"But I haven't been preparing. It will take me some time to get gear together."

"I'll help you. We need to be gone in the next few days."

Why the next few days? What difference did a couple of days make? But Ethan didn't say that. "Okay. I'll see what I can do."

She squeezed his hand. "I'm so glad. I was worried you'd try to talk me out of it."

"When has that ever worked?"

She giggled a little and sighed. "Freeze-dried stuff is best. Some jerky. I have tons of tablets, so we can purify water. I stash the stuff under my sleeping bag. It's going to be great, Ethan. Imagine! A few weeks, and we'll be back together with our parents again!"

She slid over to her side of the tent, and he heard the zip of her sleeping bag.

Ethan didn't go to sleep for a long time after that.

The next day, Emily was assigned to the farm for the morning while Ethan had been assigned wood foraging duty. He watched as his sister went off with her group to the terraces, and as soon as she was out of sight, Ethan made a beeline for Fred.

"I have to talk to you," he said.

Fred tugged off his baseball cap and wiped his sweaty brow. "Okay, talk."

They stood about a hundred yards from the longhouse, down the hill toward the car park. Fred had been stationed there on guard duty.

"Emily's leaving."

Fred's eyes got wide, but otherwise, he didn't seem terribly surprised. "So that's it. I knew there was something going on."

"It's insane. I tried to talk her out of it, but when Emily gets an idea—"

"She doesn't let go of it, yeah, I know. I'm glad you told me."

Fred pursed his lips and thought a moment. Finally, he said, "If we try to stop her, she could just run for it, and we'd have the devil's time catching her. We can't be watching her all the time. And if she goes, I'm sorry, but she's going to get herself killed. So we need help, and I can't think of anyone better to help than Amihan."

Ethan recoiled. "I thought we could just keep this to ourselves. You know, deal with it as a family."

Fred gave a little smile. "That would be ideal, Ethan, but we can't. She's too smart and too determined. And if she won't listen to you, there isn't a lot of chance she'll listen to me. We need help. We have to face that."

Reluctantly, Ethan nodded. "Okay. I guess you're right."

Amihan was just down the hill, and she turned out to be a very good listener.

Cap rose from his meal, wiped his mouth with a paper towel, and held up a hand to the crowded longhouse. "Friends!" he said. "I have something important to talk with you about."

His voice commanded respect, and within a few moments, most people had quieted down. Nearly the whole camp was here for the evening meal and nightly meeting. Fred, Ethan, and Emily occupied their usual place at the end of the third table from the front, and they turned their faces to Cap for his announcement.

Most nights, Cap's lieutenants gave the briefings and made the announcements, so this must have been something special. Ethan thought he might know what it was and flicked a glance at Fred. Fred didn't look over; he just kept his eyes on the camp leader.

But Cap was having trouble beginning. Usually so sure of himself, his open, friendly face remained clouded by something, and his eyes swept over the congregation as if he was looking for help. He took a deep breath, held it, and let it out slowly. Then he rubbed a hand over his face.

"I... want to tell you what's going on out there. I'm sorry, my friends, I'm having some trouble with this." His eyes glistened, and he swallowed very hard. Now all conversation had ceased, and the Longhouse was as silent as if everyone there had turned to stone.

"You should know—I think you probably do—that most of the major cities are essentially gone. Even when the power comes back, it will be years—decades, probably—before New York and Los Angeles and Atlanta and Chicago are places people want to live again." There were nods around the Longhouse. Most people knew that.

"You should know—I think you probably do—that most of the middle-sized cities are also in chaos, though some of those have fared better than others. Maxwells, I know you're from Idaho—Boise hasn't done well, but Twin Falls seems to be okay. That's just one example." The Maxwell family sat toward the back and had four little kids. Emily played with them sometimes. They reached hands across the table, and all held each other.

"But even those towns that are handling things are going to be changed forever. There isn't any going back to what we had before. When this is over, America is not going to be at the top of the heap anymore, not for a long time. We'll get through it. We always do. But your children and grandchildren will listen with wonder when you tell them about five bars of Wi-Fi and things like Spotify and YouTube. We'll have a lot of rebuilding to do. It's going to be very, very hard. I want to make that clear—none of us, no matter where we're from, is going to have things easy."

His face had hardened as he delivered this news. It wasn't really *news*, in the sense that people had no idea about it. It was simply that no one stated it so baldly, and the blunt statement of the facts hit them like a hammer. Heads bowed. A couple of people were crying.

But Cap wasn't finished. "As much as I dislike talking about it, I want you to know the facts. Hiding from bad news only makes it stronger. We don't do that here. So we need to keep our shoulders square and our eyes on the prize—get through this with as much grit as we can, then get back to building this great country."

There were some "Amens" to this, like a revival meeting. A few people pumped fists. This was more like what they were used to from Cap.

"Tonight, though, I want to do something unusual with our meeting. All evening activities are canceled. We'll meet at the bonfire in thirty minutes, and tonight we'll have only a skeleton crew on guard so that everyone can be together. Usually, our evening meetings deal with who is here, what we're doing, and what comes next. Tonight, we're going to talk about who's *missing*. And I'm going to talk about my son."

Ethan glanced over at Emily. "He has a son?" he said.

Emily shrugged. Apparently, they didn't know Cap all that well. But it was obvious from the reaction at the head table, among the lieutenants, that this was something monumental.

"I'm hoping," Cap said, his voice raspy, "that you'll be willing to talk about who is missing in your life. To tell me about the holes in your hearts. You don't have to. It's not an order. But I'm asking you as a friend to let me share your pain. I'm tired of keeping mine to myself, I can tell you." His gaze swept the room again, and there was a lump in more than one throat.

"Okay. Chores. See you in half an hour."

Emily and Ethan buried the kitchen scraps in the latrine area. The whole camp was eerily quiet, with the only conversation being held in low tones as if everyone were in church.

Ethan's mind worked on the chain of events. He was pretty sure that his talk with Fred and then Amihan had something to do with this extraordinary meeting tonight, but he couldn't figure out how. Or what good would come of it.

"Are you going to say anything tonight?" Emily said as they walked back up the hill.

"I... don't think so. Are you?"

"No way. We're going to be with Mom and Dad soon. I don't have anything to say, and I don't want to draw any attention."

The bonfire blazed in the center of the common area in the middle of camp. This fire wasn't a particularly large one—they kept it low enough that everyone could see everyone else, circled around the flames three rows deep. Some people had camp chairs, and others had logs that they'd dragged out of the woods. Most people just sat on the ground.

As soon as everyone was there, Cap rose and began to speak.

"I started working on this Mutual Assistance Group more than two years ago. I learned all I could about survival skills, construction, food storage, man, you name it. I was obsessed with it. You know I was pretty involved in building a tech company—guess that's all gone now—but every free minute I was up here, working on this place. I had partners in crime, of course, Jackson here, and Amihan and Colleen, all of them were up here a lot, too. But mostly, it was me."

He shuffled his feet and continued. "My wife didn't like that. She thought I should be spending more time at home with my family, especially with my son, Todd. He was a young teenager and needed his dad to be, well, a *dad*. I didn't see it. I thought that what I was doing here was for our family, and he'd understand that. Eventually, Marie had to move away to get my attention. The kids went with her. But Todd, he didn't want to be with his mom. He wanted to be with me. So a month before the lights went out, he came to stay with me for the summer."

A breeze rippled through the woods and made the fire dance. No one spoke. Even the crickets had decided to listen, it seemed. "And then the power went out."

Around the circle, people dropped their heads. "I should have been at work. I should have been at home. But I wasn't. When the power went out, I was here. Now, my son was at work—he had a job at the Hard Leather store in Polk—and it wasn't a big trick for him to get home. But when he got there, I wasn't there. I was still up here—heck, I didn't even know that the power had gone out until I was halfway down the mountain trying to get reception on my cell phone. I didn't get any. But that was okay, I thought, because I have the CB. I'll call the house. So I did. No answer. But of course, there wasn't—the CB base station at the house is wired, and the power was out. Todd knew about the generator, but he also knew that we only used that in emergencies. He didn't think this was one, I guess, because he never turned it on."

Ethan could see that he wasn't the only one caught up in the story. It was all too familiar to nearly everyone. When the power went out, it cut people off from each other.

And those people were still cut off.

Now Ethan saw it, how his story had brought this story out into the open. Cap was trying to reach Emily— and maybe, probably, not just Emily. *I'll bet there are dozens of people in this camp that are thinking about heading out to find their lost ones.*

Cap brushed his hand through his short brown hair and tried to continue. But for a moment, he couldn't.

When he got possession of himself, his voice was quieter, harsher, and ragged. "I did hear... I, uh, did get through to him, just for a minute. He was in the other truck, driving. I told him I was coming down the mountain, and he said he was coming up to meet me, that something really weird was going on. I told him... oh, saints... I told him... " Tears began to flow down his face. "Not to come. That it was dangerous to be out. To go back home. Maybe he did. I don't know." He took a deep breath, swallowed, and went on.

"What I do know is that he never came home, and he never got here. He signed off on the radio, and sometime shortly after that, he was hit by a semi-trailer that didn't stop at a traffic light on the off-ramp to Polk. There weren't any emergency vehicles to come and get him. The truck was crushed, and the police told me he died instantly. He was probably one of the first... one of the first..." Cap put his hands over his face.

Amihan rose from her seat and wrapped her arms around him. Then Jackson did the same, and the three of them stood there while Cap's shoulders shook with grief.

And then, in the silence, one of the women stood up. Ethan knew her; it was Mrs. Perez, who was here with her teenage son, Rogelio. Her accented voice carried clearly in the heavy silence of the camp.

"My husband, Tomas, was driving a load from Malantown to Pittsburgh when the lights went out. He never came home. I don't know what happened to him. Maybe he's going to make it home to us, and maybe not. I left him a note on the table, one on the bed, one in the bathroom, and one everywhere he might look. He knows where the camp is, and every day I listen for a car to come up the road and bring my husband to me."

Rogelio's face was a mask of grief, but he stood up and put his arms around his mother. She did not cry; she was rigid as stone, but everyone could read the pain in her face.

And then, the floodgates broke.

"My mother and father were on a trip to New York..."

"My two sons run a business in Philadelphia..."

"My mother was in the hospital and couldn't get her medicines… "

The camp was an inferno of grief, as every single family poured the oil of their loss on the fire. But something marvelous happened. Where there had been dozens, scores, of individuals feeling the brutal pain of losing people they cared about more than their own lives, now the flame of that agony began to weld them together. The Perez family knelt and embraced the little Maxwell kids, who were sobbing their little hearts out. Mont Williams—a mountain of a man who had carried more wood and boxes than any three other men in the camp, had lost his wife who was battling a fatal lung disease in Las Vegas. He had flown to the area for just a day to meet with an expert about her condition, and now he couldn't get home. Without power for her medical equipment, she must have certainly died. Alone. His story moved two other men who had left their families for business… not to return.

And then Ethan heard a voice saying, "I know my parents are alive."

Emily stood up. Every face turned toward her. She wasn't very tall, so she had to move out into the center. "I heard their voices on the radio. I know they're alive. I know they need help, and I know they're trying to get to us."

Quiet sobs still rent the night air. Emily's bright hair seemed to glow from the reflected flames. Her face was hard. "I believe that they need me, and I think I can help them if I go."

At this, a few people shook their heads. Emily saw it and bowed her head a little. "I was… I was planning…"

The dam inside her broke. She lifted her head to the sky and cried out.

And the camp surged forward like a living thing and wrapped her from head to toe in love.

Ethan thought it was probably okay that it took him almost five minutes to make his way through the throng to his sister, but when he did, he threw his arms around her like iron bands and just whispered in her ear, "We're going to make it. We're all going to make it."

They both slept in the middle of the tent that night, with their arms still around each other.

The camp was never the same after that.

Tearing open the half-healed wounds of grief had been painful in ways few of them were prepared for, but the stitching together that happened after that made the pain worth it. It had been a happy place before but a polite, separate, distant one. That night made them a family.

Within days, plans were being laid to bring in more survivors, even if that meant taxing the resources of the camp. Chainsaws took out more land for camping and farming. One family went out and brought back six lost children—and four horses that needed a home as well.

Emily, for her part, returned the gear she had borrowed, and no one said a single word to her about it. She went to work with new energy and spent long hours on the radio trying to connect people to each other. In a way, the MAG became a clearinghouse for information about people who were missing and where they might go for help.

Ethan finally told her, a week or so later, what he had done. He thought Emily might punch him in the face, but instead, she just smiled and said, "My tattletale brother."

They did hear from their parents one more time. They'd gotten to Nebraska, where they were stuck, bogged down, and not able to travel any farther, at least for a while. By now, Emily, Bern, and Squawk knew everyone in the whole state with a radio, and they put out a message to the network asking for help.

An agonizing week went by when they heard nothing, but then a new contact a hundred miles south of Mr. and Mrs. Tuttle's location relayed a message—help had come through. They were on the move again.

And then, two months later, the radio shack nearly burst apart when WZ9YYN Gnarled Oaks reported that a skeletal Mr. Tuttle and a Mrs. Tuttle with a broken arm and two broken ribs had staggered into town.

The festival that night was the biggest the MAG had seen yet.

Most people never got their loved ones back. Most of them never even heard what happened to them—the people they loved were simply gone.

But from the camp came new families. Mont Williams and Amihan were married before the power came back on. Mrs. Perez adopted four of the orphan children, and she and the Maxwells built a cabin just outside the MAG that was big enough for both families. Everyone rallied to everyone else's aid.

The power did come back a year after it had gone, and everything Cap had said about it was true. The big cities were dead, well and truly. Malantown itself was a ghost town. Most of Spoonerville had survived, but the town did not recover for a long time, and the center of town, where the camps were, bore the scars of barbed wire and flame-scorching for years.

As soon as it was fairly safe to travel, the twins headed for the Little Pink House. They'd have extended an invitation to Fred to come with them, but after all they had been through there wasn't a need for one. Fred would be with the Tuttles for the rest of his days.

The roads were terrible, and the damage from the Dark Year was evident in every town they passed, but the small band did reach Gnarled Oaks at last. It had been good to chat with their parents on the radio, but nothing came close to the hour-long hugs they got when they finally arrived.

Safe at last.

THE END

"I could use a nap, too, but the more important thing is to get to water. We'll have both cover and water if we can make that tree line," Ethan said. "And besides, we don't know that they're watching for us, necessarily. What if they're just joyriding?'

Emily stared at him. "During the Apocalypse?"

"It's not apocalyptic. Not really."

Her stare didn't waver. "Okay," he said, "It is, but not for everyone. Mort seems to be doing all right."

She snorted. "Give me back the binoculars. I want to watch what they're doing for a minute. Maybe there's some kind of pattern we can use."

Ethan found a patch of shade and sat down on the tall, stringy grass underneath a spreading maple. He couldn't see the road from there, but he could hear the occasional whine of an engine. Not for the last time, he wished he had a vehicle of his own, that he had not stopped at the gas station, that he had ignored the ice cream sign and just kept going. He tried to make himself feel better by recalling that they had needed gas at some point anyway, but it didn't work. He put his head in his hands.

The next thing he knew, he was being shaken awake. "I got it," Emily said. "There is a pattern. If they're smart, and if they're looking, they'll probably still see us. But I think I can give us a fighting chance."

She led him back to the crest of the hill and had him lie down so he wouldn't present a profile against the sky. Then she listened and looked through the binocs and started counting. At seventy, she said, "This is when we'd run. There are three cars, and all of them are out of sight behind the curvature of this hill for forty seconds, like they are right now. Then they're back for seventy, then gone again. They're just driving up and down the road."

"Forty seconds isn't a lot. We won't get very far before we have to hide again."

"Even less actually… the further we go down the hill the more of the road is in view, and, the time the cars are out of sight gets shorter. After a while, we might have to just make a break for it. But I can't see anything to stop us between here and the tree belt. No fences. No barbed wire. Just open grassland, and we're going downhill."

They rummaged in their packs for something to camouflage themselves better, but there was nothing. In the end, they decided to chance it.

Emily counted, and when she cried, "Go!" they pelted down the hill. Not on the road, but straight across the field toward the tree line. At forty seconds, Emily called out, "Down!" and they dropped flat on the ground.

It was soft—or at any rate softer than the road would have been—but there were thistles and briars amongst the grass, and the seed heads broke off into their shirts and shorts. They were instantly miserable. But Emily reported that the truck noises had not changed on the road, and that meant they probably hadn't been seen.

After a count of seventy they went again, though Emily figured they would be visible for only part of the forty seconds. They reached the bottom of the hill and found that there was water after all, in the form of a bog that sucked at their shoes and legs and allowed them to make only the slowest, most agonizing of progress.

"Down!" Emily called, quieter this time.

Ethan fell headlong into the mud, and when he propped himself up on his arms, Emily took a hard look at him before she started rolling around. Clouds of biting insects rose up around them, but when Emily emerged finished, she was browner than a chocolate cake. Ethan was, too.

"Best disguise we could have," she said.

"That's good because we are never going to get there at this rate."

But the ground leveled out and was dry again, and they made better time after that, not bothering anymore to drop for the window of time since they could see the entire road now. But if the cars on the road were waiting for the Tuttles, they were either terribly unobservant, or the mud did a better job of camouflage than they had expected.

With one thing and another, they made the tree line and found that, yes, indeed, the trees were lined up on the banks of a shallow river about thirty feet wide. They wasted no time in jumping in, cleaning the worst of the mud off their faces and hands, and clothing, and letting the cool of the water wash their sweat and fatigue downstream.

A few minutes later, Ethan drew a packet of Halozone tablets from his satchel and dropped them into a collapsible cup. He dipped river water and set the cup on the bank. "Takes a few minutes to purify," he said.

By this point, the thirst was driving him mad. He wanted to duck his head under and swallow the whole river. But he knew that if he did that, the bacteria and microorganisms in the river water would make him sick. The Halozone, on the other hand, would taste gross, but it would purify the water so he could drink it.

Waiting was agony, but he managed it and took a long gulp. The chemicals made the water taste like rotten eggs. But it was wet, and it was cool, and it was the best thing he'd ever tasted. One glass wasn't nearly enough, so he got a second tablet out and filled his cup again when he heard engines getting closer.

"They're coming!" Emily said, dashing back toward the river, backpack flapping on her back. She plunged into the river and began wading across. "Quick, before they get here," she said, "We have to hide on the other side."

"They can just cross the river after us," Ethan said. The far side was much like the near—tall, stately trees with few low branches, no good at all for climbing. There was considerable brush, though, at the base of the trees, deep and thick enough that if they lay down, it would be hard to see them.

Ethan dumped the Halozone tablet into his cup and snapped on the lid, following Emily across to the other side. A few yards downstream, one of the large trees had slumped away from the river, exposing some roots and pulling up the bank to a dark cave at the base.

"Right here," Ethan said, pointing.

The engines abruptly cut off. The searchers were here.

Emily climbed the bank and dropped on her face. She vanished as if she hadn't been there.

Ethan snugged himself into the shadowed space at the base of the tree. His lower half remained in the river, which was only about two feet deep at that point, while his upper body, from the chest to the crown of his head, stayed dry. He instantly regretted the hole he chose to hide in. Spiderwebs clung to his hair and face, and he didn't dare brush them away lest the movement give his position to his chasers. The water had been refreshing when he first got into it, but now it was chilly and rapidly sucking the warmth from his body. The overhanging roots of the tree dripped moss and smelled of rot. And everything that remained in his backpack was now waterlogged and ruined.

Worst of all, he couldn't even take a drink from his cup. It was bright yellow and would be instantly visible to anyone on the opposite bank.

The only good news was that he had a perfect view of the other side, up and down the river, while he himself was as good as invisible.

A pair of watchers came through the trees, questing, heads on a swivel, looking for something—or someone. Ethan didn't know them—brown-haired men in overalls with farmer's tans wearing baseball caps turned backward.

"They went in here. I know they did," one of them said.

"They're close. We have to find them," said another voice, crashing through the brush a bit farther upstream. This one Ethan *did* know. It was the other thug from Verl's gas station, the burly one, that did Mort's dirty work.

All three men shuffled down to the river and tested its depth with sticks. One of them concluded, "They're not hiding in there. Like, you know, with straws for breathing and stuff. It's not deep enough."

"You sure you saw them come in here?" Gas Station Thug said.

The other two men exchanged a glance. "Uh," one of them said, "Yeah. Pretty sure. Running for their lives, they were."

"Probably kept going to the other side," the other added.

"Why we looking for them anyway? They're important somehow?"

Gas Station Thug said, "Mort says they are. I don't argue."

One of the overalls took his stick and whacked through some brush, more for something to do than any kind of search. "Mort's got a sweet deal going, that's for sure."

"Keep your mouth shut," Overalls Two said. "Mort's in charge now."

"I'm just saying—"

"Don't say it, then," Thug said. "He's paying for your gas, right? Your kids going hungry?"

"No."

"Then shut it. You got it better than you had it before."

Thug stopped and peered over at the far side. Ethan saw that he was wearing a new-ish pair of boots, leather, shiny. *I'll bet he doesn't want to get those wet.* The other two had good footwear, too. He began to hope.

"Is that a backpack?" Thug asked.

"Where?"

Thug pointed to roughly the spot where Emily had hidden. Ethan held his breath.

"I don't—"

"Get a rock," Thug said. Both other men scanned the bank but came up empty.

"No rocks here."

"Then go over there and look," Thug said, punctuating it by snapping his stick in half.

"Aw, Dan—"

"Don't give me any 'Aw, Dan.' You jump when I say, get it?"

Now it was down to the two other men. *Why don't they just toss Dan, the Thug, in the river? Together I bet they're stronger than he is. He's in charge because Mort is, but Mort isn't here.* They stared at one another, some sort of silent communication passing between them. Then one of them made a fist. Ethan thought they were going to fight one another.

Then he hammered his fist into his other palm once, twice, three times.

The other man did the same. On three, he made his palm flat. Paper.

But the first man had changed to scissors. "Ha!" he said. "I win. You go."

Paper looked down at his boots and hesitated. He bent and picked something up. A small rock, not much bigger than a marble. He threw it over, where it disappeared into the underbrush without a sound.

The Tuttle Twins and the Days of Darkness

If they actually went over there, they'd see Emily for sure. Her cover was maybe already blown, but as soon as they set foot on the opposite bank, they'd see her. Could Ethan make a run for it? Distract them?

Something crawled down his neck, hesitated by the collar of his shirt, and kept going inside. His shoulders jerked, spasming, as his mind conjured up all sorts of images about what it could be. Maybe he could drown it. Ethan sank deeper into the water, slowly, trying not to make ripples that would be visible from the other side.

Paper found a bigger rock and hurled it. This one crashed through the underbrush, but there was no cry, no yelp of pain. He must have missed.

The crawling between his shoulder blades stopped, but Ethan didn't know what that meant. He had stopped sinking with his chin touching the water. It smelled of mold, or maybe that was the little grotto he was hidden in. It was very cold and getting colder.

Dan pointed, eyes hard, arm straight. "Over. There. Go."

Paper pulled out a pistol and fired it.

Ethan held back a scream, fearing for his sister.

"It's not a backpack, look. It's a grocery sack," Scissors said.

Ethan's heat reserves vanished, and shivers began in his feet and legs. He had to get out.

He couldn't get out. Not with those three there. They had shot at his sister. He tried to clench his hands, find a rock himself, hurl it, and knock Paper out, but his hands didn't work.

Dan spat into the water. "Darn it!"

A car horn sounded. Once, twice quickly, and once more. The three men turned without a word and jogged back the way they came.

Ethan slid upward a little so that his chest was out of the water again. He waited. There was no sound, no crashing of boots through the foliage, no gunshots. Nothing.

He boosted himself ever so gently from the water, using his arm muscles because they were the only ones that worked, and a head appeared upside down above him, peering into his grotto.

"You alive?" Emily said.

"Are you? I thought they were going to shoot you."

Her head disappeared and reappeared a moment later. "They're really gone. I wonder what that horn was all about. They were never even close to hitting me. I put my backpack ten yards away, but I thought I had hidden it pretty well. Apparently not. But I am glad they didn't shoot it in the end."

Ethan's teeth chattered so hard that Emily heard it above the rush of the river. Her brow creased. "We have to get you out of there."

Ethan agreed, but it was now getting a bit hard to talk. He reached out a hand, and Emily took it. "Gack! You're like ice!" She hauled on him, and with him pushing and her pulling, they got him out of the water and up on the bank, where he lay down in a patch of sunshine.

Emily kept watch. "You have a mass of spiderwebs on your back," she said. Ethan groaned. He didn't want to think about that spider going down his back.

While Ethan recovered, Emily said. "They really don't see what they're doing, do they? I mean, we had good neighbors, and we all took care of each other. That's a successful long-term strategy. If you think you're going to be able to just take things from people and make a life out of it, you're going to run out of people and things real fast. Then you turn on each other. Looks to me like Paper and Scissors are starting to figure that out. There's nothing to stop Mort from siccing Dan on them."

"No honor... among thieves," Ethan said, voice coming back a little at a time.

Emily did think the trio would come back and look again, but after ten minutes or so, it was clear they wouldn't. She hadn't heard their truck go away, but by now, it surely had.

They stayed low, resting, waiting, watching. Above them, the sun moved lower, and a breeze started up out of the west, bringing the smell of woodsmoke mixed with something unnatural. It left a bitter tang in the back of their throats. Ethan felt his strength returning and munched on some beef jerky to help it continue.

He was dismayed by how much he'd already eaten of the stash in the pack.

The men did not come back.

As the sun touched the western horizon, Ethan said, "How far are we from Grandma's?"

"About 50 miles is my best guess. I don't know exactly."

"Wish we had the maps."

"Wish we had a truck. But instead, we have shoe leather jerky and a river that probably leads to another river that is possibly the one that leads to the Little Pink House." Emily stood up and shouldered her pack. "You need me to carry yours?"

In response, Ethan got to his knees and, testing his strength, stood up. He was wobbly for a second but not in danger of falling over. "No, I can get it," he said.

Now they were faced with a serious dilemma. They couldn't actually use the river as a walkway. It was shallow enough here, but it would get deeper and more treacherous quickly as it approached the Monongahela. And Ethan had already proved that it was cold, dangerously cold, after several minutes.

But the woods weren't passable, either. There were no trails leading east, no convenient paved or even packed-earth passages through the bracken and bush. The woods on this side of the river were thicker and denser and did not give way to fields as the ones on the other side had. Getting through the trackless woods would require a lot of time and effort, and the going would be slow, far slower than they had planned. Judging from the dwindling food supplies in their packs, they would run out of food sometime early on the third day since they'd lost the truck.

Ethan thought of all that food they'd packed in the truck and sighed.

But there wasn't anything they could do other than try. Squaring their shoulders, they set out together, the river on their left, heading for Grandma's.

They made very little progress before night which made it essentially impossible to continue. Some of the bush was thorny—blackberries or something else that hated them—and their legs were quickly scratched and raw. Emily was sure they'd wandered through patches of poison ivy, too, so tomorrow would be fun without calamine lotion or any way to make it stop itching. As they walked along, she could imagine the rash beginning on her lower calves, working its way up to her knees. She began to itch, though it was far too soon for the ivy oil to have its allergic effect.

The woods hadn't changed character at all in the few hours they'd been walking. If anything, it had gotten a bit more difficult, presenting an endless procession of moss-covered bark, scratching low bushes, and gnats. It was hard to know how far they'd come, but it wasn't very far. A few miles at the most, and probably less.

Ethan found a dead tree that had fallen over and began to mat down the local flora to make a kind of bed. Emily cut branches to use as camouflage, using the pocketknife in her pack. The night was dark and still, and Emily tried to remember what these kinds of nights had been like when she'd gone camping with the family. Was it always this dark?

Probably it had been, right? Only Dad's lantern would shine out from the central table so that wherever they were, they could see their way home.

A tear slid down Emily's cheek before she could stop it. Dad. Mom. They might never see them again. Her stomach rumbled. They might not see *anyone* again.

But she had Ethan, and he had her. They lay down together and were asleep before they could worry any more.

Morning came early, and stiff and cold as they were, it found them already awake.

"The only thing better about camping like this is that we don't have to take down a tent," Ethan said.

"We better pull the brush back out. We don't want this place to feel like home—or worse, to offer the bad guys a chance to track us."

They had more beef jerky for breakfast and chemical-tasting water. They were stiff and sore from the day before, and the prospect of another full day of walking was almost more than they could stand. But there was nothing to do but go on.

The sun had crested the hills in front of them when they heard something rustling in the brush. At first, they thought it might be their pursuers again, but there was no regularity to the sound, as there would have been with people walking.

But whatever it was, it was big.

"Bear," Emily whispered, freezing in place.

"Don't be silly," Ethan said. "There haven't been bears in these woods for a hundred years."

Still, he edged around to put a maple tree between himself and the source of the noise. It had progressed from rustling to crashing as if something very large were coming toward them through the bracken.

Above them, the branches were thick and sturdy, but reaching them would be a problem. Ethan stretched up, but his fingers were two feet short of the lowest branch.

Emily peered around the tree, and the color drained from her face. "Bear," she whispered again.

This time Ethan believed her. He jumped for the branch, and his fingers brushed it, but he couldn't grab on. The bear paused in the clearing thirty yards away and stood up on its hind legs. A black bear, fully-grown, scenting in the wind. Which was behind the Tuttles, though it was not blowing hard. Hard enough, because the bear quested nosily in their direction, then let out a bellow.

"Use your pack!" Emily said, bursting into motion. She dropped her backpack on the ground, stood on it, and leaped as high as she could. Her hand caught the branch. She slid her feet up the trunk of the tree and walked upward, grasping the branch with two hands and hauling. The bark bit into her palm and sap clung to her fingers, but her feet found purchase, and she was up. The next branch was much closer and easier, and then she was ten feet off the ground and a much less simple meal for a bear.

Ethan matched her feet, occupying a branch on the other side of the tree.

"But our packs… " he said.

The bear snuffled as it approached the base of the tree and their backpacks lying on the ground. It gave a low growl as if something about the packs bothered it.

The twins, who had a moment before felt like they were very high above the ground, now found themselves holding their breath as a huge bear—seemingly right under their dangling feet—considered their 72-hour kits.

They didn't have long to wait. With a moan that sounded remarkably like a laugh, the bear picked up one pack in its jaws and bit down. Something crunched inside the pack. Ethan winced. The binoculars, he thought.

But the bear wasn't having any trouble with whatever it was. It held the pack in its teeth and swatted at it with a massive paw. Once, twice, and the pack ripped open like a canvas pinata, and gear went flying—along with beef jerky, which the bear's sensitive nose detected immediately. In seconds, a week's worth of emergency food vanished down the bear's gullet, and it turned to the other pack.

"That's the last of our food!" Emily whispered, hoping the bear wouldn't hear.

Ethan just shook his head, not trusting himself to speak.

The bear wasted no time with the second pack, catching the straps in its three-inch-long claws and ripping it apart. The second bag of jerky suffered the same fate as the first.

After that, the bear took its time. It ran a nose over nearly everything it had scattered, slobbering on Halozone tablets and pawing at silver heat blankets. Nothing grabbed its interest. Having nothing more to do, then, it looked up.

And saw the twins dangling above it, close enough to touch.

It stood up. Now the twins screamed and looked for higher branches. None were within reach. The bear reached up and bellowed mightily, sounding for all the world as if it was yelling at them.

Once it was standing, though, Emily realized that it wasn't as tall as she had thought. In fact, unless it somehow learned to jump off its hind legs, she didn't think it could reach her branch. If she kept her legs tucked up, there was a decent chance she could ride it out.

Ethan saw the same thing and stopped trying to hug his way up the trunk of the tree.

"Well, we don't have to be quiet anymore. What do you want to talk about?" he said.

It was just such a stupid thing to say under the circumstances that Emily burst out laughing. "How about… the principles of non-aggression as they pertain to wildlife."

"Interesting," Ethan said, raising his voice over the bellowing of the bear. "So you think we shouldn't shoot this bear."

"I didn't say that." The bear roared up at them and sniffed the air, using the tree to help balance on its hind legs. Emily found she'd almost lost her fear of the thing. She was so tired and so hungry and so beyond any experience she'd ever had in her life that she almost couldn't believe it was real. "Of course, we don't have that option because we don't have weapons."

It took forever for the bear to decide to leave. Even after they could no longer see or hear it, Ethan and Emily stayed in the tree, wondering if it would be back, or worse, if it was waiting for them to get down. The entire prospect of ever getting down and walking

40 miles to Grandma's seemed less likely than being rescued by a flock of giant eagles.

The sun had set before they dared to try climbing down.

"You realize," Emily said, "that once we get down from here there isn't any getting back up. The packs are gone. If we couldn't jump up and grab a limb before, we certainly can't do it now that we're stiff and sore from sitting in this tree for three hours. So if we get down, and the bear comes back, at least one of us is going to die."

"On the other hand," Ethan said, assessing the jump to the ground, "if we *don't* get down, we're *both* going to die sometime in the night from falling out of the tree. So I'm willing to risk it."

And a moment later, he did.

He caught Emily as she jumped down herself. The packs were a total loss; not enough of them left to hold anything. Their pants had serious pockets, which they filled with everything from the packs that would fit. Tired and hungry, they made their way to the river and had a chemically sanitized drink.

Neither of them was ready to sleep, being too keyed up listening for any sound of the returning bear, so they decided to keep walking as long as they could.

That turned out to be quite a ways. It was a beautiful night, warm but with a cool breeze, and the river was lovely in the brighter-than-usual moonlight. If they had been on a night hike with their parents, they'd have thought it one of the best nights of their lives.

But now things were very different. They had not eaten since midday when all they had was a granola bar and a couple of mouthfuls of beef jerky. Those—wrappers and all—were gone down the gullet of the bear. There was no more. It was too early in the season for blackberries to be ripe, and even if they could have stumbled across a patch of wild strawberries, it would hardly have amounted to more than a mouthful for each of them.

They had no tools—not even a pocketknife, which had been lost in the brush. No weapons. Nothing but the clothes on their backs, plus a couple of spare jackets scavenged from the wreckage of the packs, a collapsible cup, and some chemical tablets that the bear had not been interested in.

They were hungry. They were, for all intents and purposes, lost. And they were a long, long way from anywhere that would shelter them.

All this went through their heads as they trudged, step after weary step, through the increasingly impassable woods next to what they dearly hoped was—or would at some point become—the Monongahela River.

They saw no sign of human habitation. Around them, the woods were alive with night sounds—small ones, fortunately, though half an ear was always kept for sounds of the bear—but none of the sounds they most wanted and needed to hear. Motors. Engines. The machinery that kept humans on top of the food chain and in the place where they could safely enjoy it.

And then they came to a road.

This one was bigger by far than the landing road. They approached it up a short, steep rise and were met at the top by crenelated metal guardrails, a gravel shoulder, and a wide, flat expanse with two lanes going each direction, with a central median dug into a kind of gully.

For a moment, they stood there, contemplating this intriguing artifact of human civilization.

"It's a road," Emily said.

"I see that." Ethan climbed over the guardrail. To the left, the road continued flat across a bridge that spanned the river, about thirty or forty yards wide.

"A road like this, there'd be cars along pretty regularly, I bet," Emily said. She could not keep the wistful note from her voice.

"Before," Ethan said, in just the same tone. "But it's still a road. A pretty big one. It must go somewhere."

They both were thinking about where the road might go and trying to decide whether they wanted to go there before they said anything.

The heat of the road, still radiating from baking in the sun all day, was welcome. Emily wanted to lie down on it. But the habits of civilization die hard, and she was not going to be comfortable on that road no matter how rare traffic would be.

Ethan said, "I wish I could remember the map better."

"I remember some of it, or I would if I could even think straight. There's bound to be a town in one direction or another."

"Yeah," Ethan said, bending over the bridge to watch the water glide slickly by in the moonlight, "There was a town before when we had a truck. That didn't go quite the way I had hoped."

"Not all towns are like that," Emily said.

"Really? Which ones aren't?"

"Gnarled Oaks." She was as definite as if she had it from the mouth of Moses.

Ethan shook his head sadly. "We don't even know that. We might be chasing shadows."

"It has to be," Emily said, her voice going ragged. "It *has* to. If not… " She didn't want to say it, but the prospect was there. There wasn't a safety net for them, not here, not now. There was the real prospect that they could die in these woods, even without a bear.

"All the choices I've made today have sucked," Ethan said, straightening. He plucked a chunk of gravel from the shoulder and slung it into the water. "So you make the call. Are we taking the road or keeping straight on through the woods?"

If you think the twins should take the road, go to page 386.

If you think the twins should stick to the woods, go to page 380.

Emily sighed. "I hate running away. I'm tired of it."

"Is that a good reason to go out and kill people?" Ethan said.

"No." Emily shook her head and batted at a cornstalk in frustration. "But it's going to happen, and we can't stop it, so maybe we can have some kind of mitigating impact. Keep things from getting out of hand. Offer some of our military advice."

Ethan broke into laughter. "Yes. Our military expertise. With our vast experience."

"Okay, okay, but we do know some things about history. And before you say 'Ethan Allen and Canada,' I already thought of that," Emily said.

"I wasn't going to. I was going to say 'Austria-Hungary and Serbia.' But it's the same thing. Defenders have big advantages, and attackers struggle to hold gains. In the end, she'll probably win, though. She's very good. A lot better than Mort will be, I think."

"And Mort's territory is much more diffuse. What's he going to do, defend the whole town?"

Ethan thought for a second. "No. He'll defend the gas station. He doesn't care about anything but himself." Then he thought a little more. "But... that also means that he won't waste any manpower until the central conflict. Faraday can take the whole town, but how can she hold it? She'll be extended. He could even... " His eyes got wild.

"What?" Emily said.

"I know what he's going to do." He was breathing hard.

"You do not. How could you? We met the man for five minutes."

"I don't know how I know. I just do."

Ethan broke into a run back toward the airfield terminal. He found Alton in line for chow.

"Where's the Captain? Where's your mother?"

Alton cocked his head to the side. "What's up?"

"I have something I have to tell her about Mort and the battle coming up."

Alton didn't look like there was much hurry about it, but he pointed toward the big entry doors. "She's in there, probably in her office, but—"

Ethan didn't hear any more. He didn't really understand why it was so important for this information to get to Faraday as soon as possible, but it was, and he knew it. He also didn't dwell on the complete lack of reasons for believing that he knew what Mort was up to, but he was absolutely certain he did.

Faraday was deep in conference with her senior leaders, huddled around a map when Ethan hustled in.

"Tuttle?" she said, looking up. "You're supposed to be eating. Or bugging out. Not bothering me here when I'm in the middle—"

"Mort isn't going to try to stop you. He's going to wait for you to leave, then take over this place. He's planning a swap."

"A what?" Faraday said, eyes narrowing. "You're not making sense."

Ethan forced himself to slow down, breathe normally, and speak calmly. "Your plan is going to be full frontal assault, dark of night, hit hard, and be done with it. Right?"

Even Faraday couldn't help glancing down at the map. "There were a number of plans on the table," she said, "but that was one of them."

"It makes sense. It seems like the best thing to do. Mort could probably even give us a pretty good fight of it if he weren't a coward and a trickster. He could just ambush people that come into the town. But he doesn't. Instead, he lures them in and takes them at their most vulnerable. That's his fighting style. And that's what he's going to do to you."

Faraday's eyes flashed. "He won't find it easy."

"He doesn't have to. He's not building for the long term. He's not thinking ahead. He's not trying to last indefinitely. All he's doing is hanging on until the power comes back. If he loses people, he won't care. If he destroys the airfield, he won't care. Even if he loses his gas station, as long as there's a trade-up, he won't care. But you care. You care about your people, and you care about this field, and you *are* trying to build something sustainable. You have far more to lose. He'll count on that."

Faraday turned to her brain trust. "Anyone here have experience with Mort?"

Most of them shook their heads. One man said, "I've known Mort for years. Mostly, he was good to do business with. But yeah, he always seemed to have an angle, and I didn't trust him to fight fair, if it came to it."

The map on the table had three markers on it. Now Faraday moved two of them back toward the airfield. "I don't think we can mount an offense if we're protecting too hard back here against a secondary strike." She looked up. "Thank you, Ethan, for your perspective. We'll take that into consideration."

She paused for a moment and straightened up. "Does this mean you're committing to the Field? You and your sister are staying?"

Ethan slid a toe of his shoe along the floor. "Yeah. I mean, yes, I suppose it does."

"Good," Faraday said, nodding. "We'll have the formal ceremony when this is over. For now, you know how to find something useful to do."

The next day was spent going over the battle plan, as well as guarding the perimeter of the field and doing all the other stuff that still had to get done. Plants that weren't watered were the same as dead. For the most part, the day was normal, except all eyes were on on the sky, the clock, and the tower. There was something big about to happen.

At dinner, Faraday had them all quiet down and spoke briefly, outlining their plans.

"We believe Mort will hit us sometime in the next few days. Our overflights tell us that he's running out of people to rob, so we're the next logical place. But," she said, with a flicker of a glance toward Ethan, "we believe he will try to get us to come out to him, then circle around and take the field while we're trying to find him. We're going to invite him to do that."

A murmur ran through the crowd. Ethan and Emily looked at each other out of the corners of their eyes.

"We're going to split our forces in two," she went on. "A small, mobile force will head out directly for the gas station in Accord. Their mission will be to destroy that place so that Mort can't use it as a base anymore—or at the very least, he'll have trouble using it as bait for unsuspecting travelers."

Ethan screwed up his mouth at that. He hated being reminded of it.

"The other group will stay right here, hidden in the hangars, until Mort's men show up. We can't know what direction he's going to come from, so we let him come because we *do* know where he'll end up—he'll end up right here between the control tower and the terminal. This is where the good stuff is kept. This is the place that's most defensible. So this is where we'll lure him, and we'll surround him and finish him off."

A hand went up near the front of the crowd. "When do we go?"

"Tomorrow night. I want everyone in bed early tonight, then we'll have a light day tomorrow and get some rest in the afternoon. I'm not going to sugarcoat this. There's real danger, and I'd be surprised if everyone survived the operation. But I'll be there with you every step. I won't ask you to do something I'm not willing to do myself."

She had a little more about how those with military or police training would go on the Gas Station raid, and everyone else would stay here, how they'd use the generators at maximum for one hour to make sure they had a lot of light to illuminate the bad guys. She explained their positions, fields of fire, and the desire to keep casualties—on both sides—to a minimum. The rest of the details would be given by the site commanders tomorrow so they could specifically address what everyone was to do.

"We're all going to participate, except the smallest of the kids, and you guys will be in the safest place we can put you." Faraday looked over her group. "I know you'll do the best you can. We all wish it hadn't come to this. Heck, we all wish we were at home binging movies or playing video games right now. But we do what we have to so those days can come again. Get some rest, people."

The Tuttle Twins and the Days of Darkness

There was no cheering, no *rah-rah* whipping up of the crowd. This was something they had to do, and Faraday was matter-of-fact about doing it.

Ethan and Emily went for a walk late that night. Neither of them had much to say. Finally, Ethan spoke the question that was on both of their minds. "Are we really going to kill people?"

Emily held up her hands as if she were looking for answers written on her palms. "I don't see that we have a choice now."

"We know what violence leads to," Ethan said, kicking at a pebble on the tarmac.

"But we also know that we're part of the group that stays here—the only people that are going to be in our crosshairs are people that are trying to kill *us*. It's basic self defense. I have a lot less of a problem with that."

"But still... not *no* problem."

"Yes. I have a problem with it. I don't want to do it. But Faraday is right—it's already bad. We're not choosing between a great option and a terrible option. We're choosing between competing terrible options. Kill or be killed." Emily stopped and looked up at the stars.

"This was a lot simpler when Mom and Dad just told us what to do," she said.

"Mom and Dad almost *never* told us what to do," Ethan said, putting his arm around her and joining her in examining the heavens. "But they always seemed to *know* what to do. I miss them. I wish we could pick up something on the radio about them. I know they'll be looking for ham radios to try to get in contact with us."

"It's fun to talk to Fred. I'm glad he's okay."

Fred was, in fact, one of their most consistent contacts. He'd gone to live with the mutual assistance group and seemed to be doing fine, though Emily suspected there were things happening there that he wasn't telling them. That went both ways—Emily hadn't told him about this upcoming skirmish, either.

"I wish we were at Grandma's right now," Ethan said.

"I wish we were back home with Mom and Dad and working refrigerators."

"And Wi-Fi."

Emily moaned. "Yes! And Wi-Fi!"

But there was nothing to be done, and none of that was going to happen, so the twins found themselves in the defense group as night came. It was D-day. Emily had volunteered along with two other teens, Hannah and Rubal, to take care of the kids—there were forty or so of them that were too young to be part of things—in the small Cessna hangar on the north edge of the field.

"There's no reason anyone would go there," Faraday had said, "and we're not going to call attention to it. If they come that way, they'll almost certainly just leave you alone."

Ethan, however, had been assigned lookout duty from the tower. He had a walkie-talkie and a pair of high-powered binoculars. Two other youths, about the same age, were assigned there with him, each responsible for scanning a third of the field.

Down below, the tarmac was wide open, with no trees or any cover of any kind. But there were lots of buildings, and even though they'd stowed most of the aircraft in those buildings to minimize obstructions, there were still far too many places to hide.

The worst duty of the night by far was the decoys. Faraday believed that if Mort and his men showed up at the field and saw the whole place dark, they'd suspect a trap and pull back, so he stationed ten or so of the Fielders to putter around in the lit portion of the field just behind the terminal, apparently doing odd jobs and just being—as Ethan saw them—targets.

One benefit to being in the tower was that they had a radio and could hear what was going on in the raid at the Gas Station. It would have driven him crazy not being in the loop, Ethan thought. Then he thought about Emily and felt a little guilty. But it wasn't his idea to volunteer for babysitting duty, and it wasn't his call to put him in the tower. Sometimes things just worked out for a guy.

The night dragged. It was after midnight when the radio crackled, and a muffled voice said, "Faraday here. We're in position."

"Field One to Faraday, copy that. Quiet at the field." That was Bill in his command post on top of the terminal.

"Say again, Field One."

"Field quiet. No activity."

There was a long pause.

"Then where *are* they? We have no presence at the gas station. Repeat, no presence."

"They have to be inside, Faraday Field. They have to be there. They wouldn't leave it unguarded."

Another pause. "Operation Sandblast, go. Repeat, all teams go." That was Captain Faraday, who apparently didn't want to wait around to see why there wasn't anyone apparently at the gas station.

Well, they'd find out in a minute or two, regardless.

Then there was a lot of chatter on the radio that didn't make any sense. Ethan swept his glasses over his third of the field, but there was nothing out there. He turned to the other lookouts with him in the tower. "You guys got anything?"

"Negative," Harper said.

"I got nothing. All clear," Junebug said.

The static on the radio resolved itself. "This is Captain Faraday to all Field posts. We have a serious problem at the station."

"Field One, we read you."

"It's empty, repeat, empty. No one is here. The place has been gutted. There's no gas in the reservoir, no supplies, nothing. It's been cleaned out."

Now the pause was longer. Ethan felt a bead of sweat trickle down his neck and between his shoulder blades. Mort was gone. But gone *where*?

"Wait, I got something," Junebug said. Ethan stayed at his post, but Harper stood and focused his glasses on Junebug's zone.

"Is that… "

"Not one of ours, that's for sure." Junebug grabbed the CB and punched the button. "Tower to Field One, we have movement in zone three. Multiple bogeys."

"Tower confirm," Bill said.

"This is Harper, Field One. I confirm. Multiple men in dark clothing just appeared around Building 14."

"Are they coming this way?"

"Negative. Or, it's hard to tell. View obstructed. But they appear to be taking up positions."

Bill growled. "Waiting for us to come to them. Which we have to do."

Junebug turned to Harper. "Why do we have to?"

The blood had run from Ethan's face, though his heart was hammering in his chest. "We have to," he said, his voice hoarse with strain, "because that's where the nursery is. And my sister."

"What I want to know," a tight-faced Faraday said, "is how the heck he did this." She saw Junebug flinch over against the window of the control tower, startled at her arrival in the tower. "No, Junebug, this isn't on you. He obviously knew what he was doing, and he planned very well. You couldn't have seen back there. It was the one place we were pretty sure he wouldn't come. That's why we put the children back there."

The radio crackled, and there was Mort's voice. Ethan would have known it anywhere. "Faraday, if you're smart, you won't drag this out much longer. I've got kids here that need to use the bathroom."

Faraday looked like someone trying to swallow a frog. Ethan was sure it was an expression she hadn't worn very often. "We've been over this, Mort. You can't have what you're asking for."

"But I can, or you can kiss this place goodbye."

Faraday ground her teeth and set the mic down on the windowsill. She stared out at Building 14, where the kids were under guard by Mort's gang. Not all of his gang—that was part of the problem. Maybe twenty of his men had come with him on this raid, but he had more, and nobody knew where they were. Not at the gas station, that was for sure. Faraday had miscalculated badly, and Mort was twisting the knife.

"I thought he'd come around to something reasonable," she said.

Bill tugged at his beard. "We have to give him what he wants. We can't risk the children. He's right about that."

"We can't. That's for sure. But we can't give up that much fuel, either, and I'll never let him have a plane, no matter what he thinks of his flying abilities."

There was no way out. Either of the options was unthinkable.

The Tuttle Twins and the Days of Darkness

Ethan stared out over the dark field, now completely shrouded in night, and tried to imagine how his sister must be feeling.

Furious. That was the name for it. Emily was white-faced and shaking, not from the terror of what the men around her might do, but for what her kids—and they were, for tonight, *her* kids—must be feeling being cut off from their parents.

Yes, most of them were sleeping. The quiet knock on the door had come after 1 a.m., by her watch, by which point the "sleepover" had settled down into actual sleep for almost all of the kids. Emily, Hannah, and Rubal had tucked them into their cots and laid them in their sleeping bags a couple of hours before, then told bedtime stories until their throats hurt. Only two of the kids, Ewan, who was six, and Abigail, who was ten, had been awake when Mort's raiders slipped through the door.

Oh, in retrospect, she should have known. They hadn't been completely incautious. At first, they'd only opened the door an inch or so. The man whispered—Dan, his name was—through the crack in the door that it was over and they could come out now, that he was there to take the next shift with the kids. And it had been Emily at the door, who knew very few of the people on the field, and he looked familiar enough and friendly, and it was dark.

And then he was inside and brandishing a weapon, and they had no choice. A couple more of the kids had awakened and cried out for their parents. Hannah shushed them and took them to the back of the large room with its gently snoring children and read them a book, showing extreme calm and courage. Rubal, however, broad-shouldered and simple-minded, they had locked in a bathroom. Emily they kept to tend the sleeping children, lest they should awaken and cause chaos.

Mort himself was there. Once the building was secured and a perimeter set up, Mort poked his head in, saw Emily, and gave a single bark of laughter. Now she could hear him through the door, talking on the radio to Faraday, she guessed, making demands about foodstuffs and airplanes and fuel. Always fuel.

And she couldn't do anything. At her back was Dan, twice her size, his pistol lazily held at his side. He picked his teeth and smelled like manure, but he was watchful. Spread out before her was a mass of thirty or so children, asleep but for six under the LED light a hundred feet away, gathered around Hannah. But they were frightened. She could see it in their faces. When they'd cried out for their parents, two or three of the big men from Mort's group had picked them up and hissed in their ears that they would be quiet or they'd take them outside.

It worked, though Emily thought they would cry instead. Fortunately, they followed Hannah's bravery. And now they were trapped, and Emily had never been so angry in her life. Not when they robbed her at the gas station. Not when they shot at her in the forest. No. This was far worse, and she boiled inside, helplessly trying to think of a way out.

Faraday couldn't give in. But the children—if Mort hurt even one of them, Faraday would have little choice but to capitulate, however horrible the cost.

Or... would she?

The layout of the hangar was simple—it was a giant box with tools along one wall and a couple of small offices along the other. Huge sliding doors made up the fore and aft walls, into which were set a couple of normal-sized doors like the one the men had come through. Emily and the thug, Dan, sat ten feet or so from one of those doors now—it was open, and the smells of the night wafted in on an uninterested breeze.

The hangar wasn't large, as hangars went, but it was pretty big for a bedroom, and the kids were clustered tightly together in one corner of the floor, the one closest to Emily and the door. The big hangar doors had motors to open and close them, but those motors were useless, and the doors could only be operated manually. It would take several men a few minutes to shove them open, so for Emily's purposes, they were just walls.

But the door was open.

Leverage, she thought. *It's all about leverage. Mort has it because he has the children. He has control. The situation is quiet, and the pieces on the board are orderly and calm.* Captain Faraday's people might have been surrounding them right now—Emily was sure they were—but they couldn't do anything because they couldn't risk the children's safety. Mort's raiders had the inner ring around the building. They were exposed, in one sense—in a firefight, they'd be reaped like barley—but they still had the upper hand because Faraday didn't know how many raiders there were or how many of them were inside, where their precious children lay sleeping.

Balance. Order. As long as those things remained, Mort had better cards to play.

Someone needed to upset that order.

Faraday couldn't do it. Too much unknown risk. Mort wouldn't do it—the current order benefited him. The only one that could do it was someone on the inside who knew what the full risks were and where there was room to change the odds.

Emily realized that she knew those things. It was up to her.

Start with the guards. Dan was fierce-looking and plenty big and smelly, but he wore a wedding ring. *Before,* he'd probably been a tradesman or a contractor of some kind. He'd have kids.

She'd only seen a few of Mort's people as they came in and out or passed by the door, but they were all pretty much the same—men, exclusively, most of them ordinary, regular people Emily wouldn't have given a second glance to if they were watching a ball game together. And that, she realized, was what they were. Not two months before, they'd been accountants and grocers and computer programmers who volunteered in the Boy Scouts and went to church on Sunday.

They were just the people of Accord Landing. They weren't paramilitary thugs. One or two of them, sure, young men with no kids to worry about, had probably gotten excited about playing army—those were the ones in the woods—but the rest? They were with Mort because they were afraid, and he offered them security. The age-old balance, right there—liberty versus security. Mort had tipped the balance to security, but how far?

Security for their *families* was the key. They wanted their kids to be safe in Accord, and the strongman was Mort, who could make that happen or take it away. But if push came to shove, would they be willing to hurt other families—other families' kids—to keep Mort in control?

Emily was willing to bet that they wouldn't. Their loyalty to him was based on fear, not real respect or friendship.

If one of the children got hurt, Faraday might have to stand down. But it would radically alter Mort's own forces' determination, too. And Emily thought that might be enough to bring the whole house of cards down on his head.

At first, it was just the glimmer of an idea, not even formed enough to call hope. It would depend on how good the night vision of her guard was. Dan didn't seem to be any too intelligent, but it doesn't take too much brain power to reach out and bonk her head hard enough to give her a concussion. If she moved, what would he do?

Only one way to find out.

Ten feet from her, a little girl named Emmeline slept on top of her covers. The night was warm, and her cream nightgown rode up on her spindly legs. Her blonde hair splayed on the pillow like the mane of a lion. She and Emily had been eating meals together the last week, so they knew one another, and Emma might not completely freak out if Emily's face was the first one she saw when she woke up.

Next to her, though, was Sol. He was six and terrified of the dark. He would do nicely. Emily counted to ten, tried to calm her heart, and wiped her hand on her jeans.

Then she bolted for Sol's cot.

"No, Sol, it's okay!" she said, rather louder than she had to. In the silence of the room, it was as good as a scream.

Sol didn't move. So Emily shook him, trying to make it look as if he was doing it himself. "Sol. Sol! No! Go back to sleep!" She was shouting now, and it was having an effect. Not enough, though.

"Hey! Stop that!" Dan called, moving toward her, reaching out.

Come on, Sol!

Then about ten things happened at once.

First, Sol woke up, wiped his face, saw the vague, shadowy form of Emily shaking and shouting at him, and did just what Emily hoped. He screamed at the top of his lungs.

Several children had already been disturbed by Emily's shouts, but they came bolt upright at Sol's scream and added their own terror to the mix.

Dan, distracted by small bodies rising all around him like specters from a graveyard, panicked and stumbled forward, crashing into Emmeline's cot and tumbling headlong into the mess. And that was all it took.

The room exploded. Children shrieked and jumped from their cots, crashing into each other in the darkness and screaming louder.

"Run!" she shouted, stepping very hard to her left, right on Dan's fingers.

He bellowed like an enraged bull. Emily put all her weight down and twisted her bootheel. The pitch of his madness rose a couple octaves.

The kids who had been with Hannah added their fright to the smoothie of chaos. At the door, two faces appeared shocked, mouths agape. In some kind of warpaint camouflage, no less, with long beards and white eyes, like every beast from scary movies since the dawn of time. They couldn't have been more perfect if Emily had cast them in those parts herself.

Kids tore through them like the hounds of Hades had been loosed behind them. Like stampeding cattle, once a few kids found direction—Emily made sure it was the right one—the rest followed in a herd, tiny voices crying out in terror as they bolted into the night, screaming for their mothers.

Emily saw the children greeted on the other end of the airfield by flashlights as the massed forces of Faraday's Army scooped them up in welcoming arms.

Only a couple children left. Emily windmilled her arm to Hannah, and together they herded the last few toward the open door. Dan fumbled for them, but Hannah kicked out and caught him in the chin with her pointed cowboy boots. He roared in pain, adding rocket fuel to the propellant as the last of them shot out the door, toward freedom, toward friends.

Then someone grabbed her arm.

"Stop them! Stop them all!" bellowed Mort, close enough to overwhelm her ears. Thugs came out from their hiding places, grabbing futilely at the loose clothing, the nightwear of a dozen howling children. Not one

of the children was captured. They turned about aimlessly, all order lost.

"You!" Mort said, spittle erupting from his mouth, "are more trouble than you're worth. I should have dumped you in the compost when we first met. " With a furious wrench, Emily tore her arm from Mort's grasp and bolted. Somewhere. Anywhere.

And Mort did what Emily thought he might if he were properly provoked if all his planning and guile and deception came apart.

He leveled his weapon and pulled the trigger.

Something struck Emily in the back, something hard, as if someone had taken a baseball bat and slugged her between the shoulders. She fell too fast for her arms to catch her, slamming her chin into gravel and dust. Then the pain arrived, a wave so overwhelming she couldn't scream it because she suddenly couldn't get breath, either. A roaring sounded in her ears like a vast ocean pounding down on her.

Just before she lost consciousness, she heard the crack of another shot.

Emily awoke to a jumble of impressions. Whispers above and behind her. She lay on her front, face off the end of… a table? It was dark and light and dark again. The whispers swirled and danced like fairies. She blacked out again.

The Tuttle Twins and the Days of Darkness

Overwhelming thirst. A raging, unslakable thirst that tore at her throat like claws. She tried to cry out but could not; her mouth filled with sawdust. A straw on her lips. She sucked greedily, and the liquid was the sweetest thing she'd ever tasted. Before her thirst was slaked, the straw withdrew, and she whimpered. A small part of her brain felt that to be a major achievement. Then she slept again.

This time she remembered the children and tried to cry out, but when she tried to breathe deeply enough to scream, someone stabbed her in the back with a branding iron.

"Small breaths," a voice said. A woman's voice. It was kindness itself.

"Em," said Ethan in her other ear.

"Ethan," she breathed. "Where am I?"

"Hospital. Or, you know, the airfield hospital."

"The kids!" she said, wriggling.

Ethan grabbed her arm. "Steady," he said. "All safe, thanks to you."

She tried to relax, but the muscles of her back spasmed and wouldn't let her until she felt the stroking of her forehead and the gentle voice in her ear. Then she let it go, little by little and went limp, but this time stayed conscious and tried to listen as Ethan told the story.

Her ploy had worked a bit too well. Children scattered all over the field, shrieking like furies, and found adults in chaos, the kind of chaos that only thirty or forty terrified children can create.

Faraday's forces had, as she suspected, come out in force and surrounded Building 14. They hadn't been able to do anything meaningful, however, against the shifting, amorphous mass of Mort's crew. Then the kids came out like bottle rockets, all of them in light-colored nightwear that shone like neon under the waxing gibbous moon.

Some of the kids—most of them, bolted for the tower, knowing that the tower and the terminal were neighbors. If they did that, they ran right into Faraday's legion. But others were disoriented and ran in circles, and some of those were recaptured by Mort's thugs, where their wailing just made things more chaotic.

"Then you came out," Ethan said. "I saw it… " He had, actually, from the tower, with his binoculars. He had seen her come out. Had seen Mort grab her, the flash of his snarl visible from a hundred yards away. Had seen her slip free and run.

Had seen Mort drop to a knee and shoot.

And Emily went down like a marionette with her strings cut.

And then, one of Mort's men, mouth agape, turned with rage in his eyes and shot Mort dead from point-blank range.

"He, um, was a father. Had a teenage daughter that was in New York on a school trip when the Event happened. He says she looks a lot like you. When Mort shot you, he lost his daughter all over again, and he just snapped."

Another voice took up the thread. Faraday's voice sounded far away and tired. "Without the head, the snake isn't particularly dangerous. This snake went limp the moment Mort's body hit the ground. Apparently, no one had really signed up for this sort of thing. Taking stuff from rich people, even helpless people, wasn't too bad, but children were beyond the pale. They gave up right away."

"Even helped us find those three that chased us into the forest. They were left cruising Accord on motorbikes, keeping watch on the families being held hostage in town." Ethan rubbed the back of her neck.

"So that's that," Emily said.

"That's that. Only one of our heroes got hurt, so we've still got work to do," Faraday said. She came over and knelt down on the floor, scooting so that her face looked up into Emily's. "You were shot in the back, in the upper left shoulder blade. It broke some important things and did some serious muscle damage. You won't be going anywhere for a while. But," she said and swallowed, and Emily thought she saw a glimmer of wet at the corner of one eye, "you are the hero of the hour and the day and the Event itself, and as soon as you're up to it, there are seventy-odd parents that would like to adopt you."

It was a week more before she could get up and another week before she was allowed to begin walking laps around the Field. Every child was her brother or sister, and every mother and father was her doting aunt and uncle. It made her rather sick, actually, except for the part that loved having done something that mattered.

When she was ready, she and Ethan were put into a small, single-engine prop plane and flown the impossibly short ten minutes to Gnarled Oaks, where they landed on Main Street to gawking as if an alien spacecraft had appeared in town.

Three minutes later, face red and tears streaming, their father sprinted across the grassy area in front of the library and wrapped them in a hug. It lasted long enough for Mother to get there, too.

THE END

"Nothing has changed for me," Emily said. "This is still home. If anything, we're more entrenched here than ever. We have the chickens now. I say we stay."

"But something *has* changed," Ethan said. "We're going to be attacked. The police weren't kidding around about that. We've seen the signs. They're out there, and they're going to come for us. We're the fat target after the Cunninghams."

"Before the Cunninghams," Fred said. They had never seen him look so tired. "They'll come for us first. If there were three, five, or six of them, we could set up a defensive fire zone and have a chance. But there are more of them, and we can't protect everything. It would be tough to get in here," he said, looking at the stout front door, "but they don't really have to, do they? They can burn us out."

"I've been thinking about that," Ethan said. "I don't think they'll do that. They need supplies. They'll have to come in and get them, and if they torch the place, they get nothing. That's not going to get them what they want."

"So you vote to stay, too," Emily said.

"I haven't made up my mind."

"Yes, you have," Fred said. "And so have I. If we go someplace where they put us in cages and only let us out for exercise, I'll die just as fast under that kind of regime than being murdered by red-blooded Americans. I'd rather fight, even if we lose."

"One more thing," Ethan said. His voice was very quiet. After a minute, he got up and opened the front door. He pointed down the block to the Chamberlains. "If we leave, those people are dead."

"They might be dead anyway," Emily said.

"But *might* is not *will*. If we run, who stops these gang people? We're better equipped to do it than anyone."

There it was—it was a hard enough situation if only they were involved, but they weren't. There were other people affected by their decisions, people whose lives would be changed by what they did.

"There's another thing," Fred said. "Defending ourselves means killing. Probably. It's no small thing to kill a man."

"It might not come to that," Emily said.

"I hope it does," Ethan said. "I'm ready."

Fred stared hard at Ethan for a long time. Then he shook his head like he was too tired to say what he had in mind. "More than one man has said that to me before. It's no shame to be reluctant to kill another human being."

"Even if they're trying to kill you?" Ethan said.

"Even then. There are worse things than dying."

Ethan scoffed. "I can't think of any."

"You haven't met people who could hardly bear to live with the things they'd done. I have." Fred said it very quietly, but it rang like a bell, and they all heard it strike.

After a moment, Emily said, "We could give them our food."

"And we starve to death?" Ethan said, disgusted.

"No, silly. Not all of it. Just… some of it. Put it out there on the curb and let them come and take it. They might decide to leave us alone."

"They might decide we're a fat target and kill us."

"*That* they can decide anyway. But sharing our food with them, that's got to change the math for them. Why kill people to take what they're already giving you?"

Ethan's normal pacing got more frenetic. "Because they know you didn't give them all of it. And why not take all of it if you can?"

Fred scratched at his face, wincing. "Emily has a point, though. They might be able to take all of it anyway. This at least gives them a chance to walk away from the conflict. It also gives *us* a chance to walk away, metaphorically. We choose peace."

"They'll just come back for more the next time!"

"We don't know that," Emily said. "And who knows what could happen in the meantime? We might find more food and have more to share. The gang might find another place to go. They might run into another rival gang and get wiped out. It's a thing we ought to try."

"Not me," Ethan said. "Line in the sand. This far and no farther."

He and Emily locked gazes, and neither backed down.

"Guess it's up to me, then," Fred said. "If we're voting. And we *are* in my house."

If you think the group should share food with the gang, go to page 91.

If you think the group should prepare to fight, go to page 197.

"No sense getting ourselves caught," Ethan said. "They'll see us the moment we come over this hill. And I'm tired. We'll use less water if we sleep through the middle of the day."

"Suits me," Emily said. "My feet are killing me. It's one thing to hike around Spoonerville with Mom and Dad, but this isn't fun like that."

Fifty yards or so back the way they'd come, under the cover of the rise, a boulder sat next to a huge elm tree, making a kind of hollow that was easily large enough for two people.

They dragged themselves over to it and crawled in, ignoring the dirt and dust and even a couple of spiders whose webs became seriously disarranged. The way the boulder sat, leaning on the tree, wind or water had worn away the soil underneath so that they could get almost all the way under, with just their feet sticking out. It wasn't cool inside the hollow, exactly, but it was out of the sun, and their fatigue was such that it didn't bother them for long. They fell asleep almost immediately.

Ethan awoke when someone kicked his foot.

He tried to sit up but found the ledge of rock above him didn't allow that. Crawling in had been easy, but crawling out would take some gymnastics. He was caught as surely as if he'd stuck himself into the trap and sprung it on purpose.

"Wha—" he started to say when he heard the unmistakable metallic click of a weapon being cocked.

"Don't get twitchy," a voice said from outside. Ethan couldn't see any more of her than a pair of well-worn cowboy boots and the first few inches of blue jeans. Had to be a *her*, though, by the voice.

"We're not armed," Ethan said. This woke Emily, who tried the same sitting-up trick Ethan had, with a similar lack of success.

"That may be," the voice said. "And may not be, too, so let's do this friendly-like. You two come out slow, easy, a little at a time, and I won't have to make bad decisions."

There wasn't, when it came to it, any other way to get out from under than slow, but easy it wasn't, what with having to brace their arms underneath themselves and scootch out on their behinds. But they managed this in the end and could see their captor.

Sort of. It took a moment for their eyes to adjust and for Ethan, at least, to wipe the dust from his nose. But when they did, they saw that the woman wasn't tall—not even as tall as Emily, it didn't look like—whip-thin and tanned so dark she might have been a wooden carving. Her hair was long and braided, the braid thrown forward over her shoulder and reaching almost to her waist. She was dressed like a stereotypical cowgirl—jeans, flannel shirt despite the heat, broad-brimmed hat, even a bandanna slung about her neck. And she carried

a shotgun, held lazily in one arm where cords of muscle said it had sat many a time and could stay there all day before the owner got tired of holding it.

"I don't know you," she said. "But you're on my land, and I'll thank you to depart."

"Right. We can depart right now," Ethan said, starting to scramble up.

"Ah ah ah," she said, the muzzle of the gun wandering slightly in his direction. "Slowly."

Emily, though, didn't move. She sat with her head down and shoulders slumped. "That's just it," she said. "We can't depart. We have no part to depart to. We were resting here because over that hill are a bunch of people who, at the least, would love to hurt us. Back that way—" She pointed down the road they'd walked that morning. "—are probably the same people who already robbed us at gunpoint this morning. All they left us was this pack. So without wishing to argue with you, ma'am, there's no departing for us. I guess you'll have to shoot us."

For a moment, Ethan thought the woman might just take her up on that, but then her face burst into a grin, and she laughed, low and smooth like a rich gravy. "Well, now. That's brassy. I admire brassy at times like these." The grin made her look years younger, and Ethan realized she was young. Early twenties. Unmarried? No rings on her fingers.

The Tuttle Twins and the Days of Darkness

The shotgun came down and to the side, and the woman reached out with her other hand to help Emily up. Despite her small frame, she hoisted Emily so hard she bounced a little on her feet from the momentum.

"You'll tell me who you are, though, and whence and whither, as my granny would say, before we're going to be friends."

Ethan just barely remembered that whence was where they came *from* and whither was where they were going *to*. "Uh, we're Ethan and Emily Tuttle. We're twins," he said unnecessarily, not really understanding why that was relevant but not much able to help himself. "We're from Spoonerville. Our parents are... well, missing, I guess, at this point... and we're headed to Gnarled Oaks to our grandmother's house."

"And I'm the big bad wolf. Better give me a banana." The woman said this as if it ought to make perfect sense. Ethan began to wonder if they'd done a kind of reverse Rip Van Winkle and slept backward to a time when people talked and acted like this woman.

Emily, however, did not seem fazed. "Your name isn't Keith, by any chance?"

The woman laughed. "It is not. But I see we have something in common." She took a moment to contemplate the sky. It was bright and cloudless. No breeze remained to stir the grass. "I don't know Spoonerville, but that means it isn't close. What brings you down my path?"

"Like my brother said, we're trying to get to Gnarled Oaks—"

"Another town I've not heard of, and which sounds, beg pardon of your grandmother, like something you made up."

"We didn't make it up. And my grandmother's house is bright pink—"

The woman's mouth dropped open. "Your grandmother lives in that little pink house on the Monongahela?"

Now it was Emily's turn to have her jaw drop. "Yeah. That's it! With a little—"

"—dock sticking out into the river," the woman finished. "I don't believe it. I thought that house was a mirage. Or built by fairies. I've seen it from the river many a time."

"Well, that house is in a town called Gnarled Oaks," Ethan said. "So that exists, too."

The woman held up a hand, the shotgun now pointing at the ground. "You convinced me a while ago. But that doesn't solve your problem or mine, and we ought to discuss how that's going to happen."

The twins exchanged a look. "We're not busy. Go ahead," Emily said.

"Not here," the woman said, with a glance at the sky and back toward Verl's Gas Station. "Too public, and I don't know what sort of trouble you're bringing down on my head. We'll talk at Defiance."

For a moment, that made no sense to either of the twins, but then Emily said, "Is Defiance something we ought to know about?"

"Sounds to me like you're already blessed with plenty of it," the woman said, "but in this context, it means the homestead yonder." She jerked her head back over her shoulder. Down the hill a ways lay a farmhouse shaded by a stand of oaks the size of the beanstalk Jack grew.

Ethan said, "What if we don't want to go to Defiance. What if we're, you know, *defiant* about it?"

"I thought you might be. Hence the accompaniment of Bernard here." She patted the shotgun. "He's quite convincing."

"You would shoot us to get us to come to your house for a chat." Emily was in disbelief.

The woman shrugged. "I've done sillier things. In this case, though, probably not. I'd just fire the gun up in the air and let the buzzards come get your sorry carcasses."

That did put a different light on things. Even with the racket they were making on the road, they'd hear a shotgun blast from there and come and investigate, sure as the sun rising in the east.

"It doesn't look like we have any choice," Ethan said, trying to sound glum, though the truth was he was fascinated by this woman and didn't mind the chance to see what made her tick.

"You always have choices," the woman said, using the gun to motion them forward along a dirt path that wound down the hill. "Just, in this case, almost all of them are bad."

Emily wouldn't have been surprised to find that the woman—who still hadn't given her name—lived by herself as a sort of mystical hermit and that the ranch house occupied a different plane of existence, sort of like the Brigadoon. Or maybe a modern version of the gingerbread house from Hansel and Gretel. She was half prepared to bolt at the first sign of a candy cane.

But it was just a house—albeit a larger one than it had appeared from the ridge above—and she did not live alone. Not even close.

First, there were the dogs. More than a half-dozen of them came boiling out when she reached the wood-rail fence at the edge of the property as if they were triggered by her entrance to the fields. They were a motley bunch—a couple of larger dogs, a retriever of some kind and another that might have been a German Shepherd, and a whole passel of smaller ones, including a couple of border collies and maybe a shorthair terrier (that was the best guess Emily could make).

They gamboled about their mistress, and she playfully cuffed them and ordered them about. Some came over to sniff Emily and Ethan in turn, making sure they were friend, not foe, but they clearly had no fear of them and weren't the barking, growling types. Mistress had brought them; therefore, they were approved and admitted. Case closed.

That made a roisterous bunch as they advanced on the low-slung ranch house. A single floor, it was built in a curious manner, a square with an empty courtyard in the center. The living space, Emily saw, was around the perimeter of the house, leaving a large open space in the middle. It seemed a waste. Why not put the house in the center and make the field outside larger.

Not, she supposed, that it really needed it. The ranch was huge. The woman said it reached the edge of the valley in all directions, and that was a lot of land. Cows grazed in one section, with horses chasing one another in an adjacent one. One-quarter of the land seemed occupied by orchards, fruit trees in long, graceful rows, and another chunk in corn and some other kind of crop; Emily didn't recognize its low, dark green stalks.

Nearer the house was a garden, comparatively small against the size of the rest but still in itself larger than the lot the Tuttles' house sat on. In the center of this plot of carrots, lettuce, beans, and tomatoes stood four large white hutches.

"Bees," Emily said.

"That's right," the woman said. "Acquainted with the ways of bees, are you?"

"Indeed," Ethan said, drawing a sharp glance from Emily. Now he was going to talk like her as well?

"We've kept bees awhile," he went on. "We know their, uh, well, we know a lot about them. We've had a lot of honey from them the last few years."

She nodded, taking in that information.

Right up against the house was another row of hutches, and inside them, small forms hopped about. Rabbits. A chicken coop occupied a corner of the yard, and a couple of dozen chickens bobbed about like corks on a pond.

Overspreading all of it was a ring of oak trees of a size Emily had only seen in places like Gnarled Oaks, named for a dense pocket of enormous, ancient trees in the town center. These were easily too big for Emily to wrap her arms around the trunk; she doubted that she and Ethan together could have reached. They towered fifty feet or more into the sky, and their canopy was so large Emily wondered if, when it rained, any drops at all hit the house and yard below. Their shade was deep and cool, and when they walked into it, the day went from oppressively hot to perfectly pleasant in a matter of a few feet.

It was a perfect farm, the kind that occupied storybooks. Yet it had the feel of something otherworldly, as if it were a farm in Hobbiton, not the Appalachians.

"Ahoy, Defiance!" the woman called when they reached the house.

"Ahoy, the traveler!" came an answering call, female and powerful enough to carry to the end of the valley.

"A child of the house and two passengers," she said, "Emissaries from the Little Pink House!"

A pause ensued. "What are they doing here?" a voice called.

"Hiding, I believe. Make a berth!"

Chickens scattered from the stoop, clucking and scolding. The woman let them in, and the sense of unreality only got stronger.

The inside of the house was immaculate, modern, almost space-age. Chrome, stainless steel, marble, and tile competed to outshine one another. The front room had couches, all in a cream suede that looked like nothing so much as a cloud for lying on. Emily's fatigue increased, and gravity dragged on her just looking at those couches.

From the kitchen, somewhere off to the left—the house seemed to go on forever in both directions—came the smell of roasting meat and the unmistakable whirr of an ice cream maker. Ethan reached out and grabbed hold of Emily's arm. He had heard it, too.

"Magdalen! Bring me your guests!" The voice was much louder here inside the house.

"Your name is Magdalen?" Emily said.

"It is indeed. But if you call me anything but Maggie, you'll be sleeping in the barn. Come with me." She started off, weaving through the couches and down a long hallway in hardwood with woven tapestries on either wall.

Shortly they came to a huge kitchen, and here they found another woman standing before two giant stone ovens, both of them roaring with flame, and over the flame roasted two haunches of meat, enough to feed ten people with a week of leftovers.

The woman herself was even thinner than Maggie, steel-haired, with a face lined like a topographical map, brown as new-plowed earth, but with eyes that danced, green and lovely. "Ah, the voyagers from lands afar. From what are you hiding?"

"We're not… at least, I guess we are," Emily said. "We were robbed at the gas station, and we're trying to walk east to Gnarled Oaks, where the Little Pink House is."

"You're trying to *walk* it? That's bold. And unlikely to work, times being what they are. Well, you've found a port in the storm, and that's certain. Dinner isn't for a bit yet. Magdalen will square you away. The Green Room, I think," she said to Maggie.

With that, she turned and resumed carving some sort of vegetable with a short paring knife, the slices landing in a wide pot that already had considerable contents.

Maggie said, gesturing to the older woman, "This is The Grand, and she is the queen of the household. Two hundred years old and still cooking for everyone every day."

"I'm not a day over a hundred and thirty, and you know it," The Grand said, whipping a wooden spoon around to smack Maggie's backside. "Now get along."

"This way," Maggie said, leading through the kitchen and out into the courtyard.

It was big, at least twenty yards wide and half again that long, mostly scraggly grass with some piles of play sand bedecked with yellow metal tractors—toys. Around the edges ran a walkway that allowed doors from the house to open onto roofed concrete, like balconies that didn't overlook anything because they were set at ground level. Clearly, children played in the center, and Emily began to see some wisdom in the design. There was plenty of running around room but all of it was enclosed, like a bull ring. Safe as houses. The kids could run wild, and nobody had to supervise them because to get outside, they had to go inside first.

At one end of the courtyard, the arrangement was different. The house rose up a second level, and below it on the main level was a large opening from the courtyard to the outside, but gating the path was an old-fashioned portcullis, just like in a castle, iron, black and sturdy.

"What kind of place is this?" Ethan wondered aloud.

"It's our place," Maggie said. "Come on. This way. No gawking."

She led directly across the courtyard to the opposite side and through a bright green door into a bedroom. Two beds flanked a nightstand, and a narrow door in the wall led to a private bathroom. It was the perfect little guest room. "This one's yours," she said.

"You just have this ready in case you capture a couple of vagabonds on the road?" Ethan said. He was joking, but she didn't seem to take it that way.

"Of course," she said, face registering incomprehension. "There are always travelers. They need a place to rest."

The Grand's voice hallooed from the kitchen across the courtyard. Maggie turned to go.

"You'll have a few minutes before dinner. Then we can talk." And she sauntered out. She had never put the shotgun down the whole time. She carried it like other people carried cell phones, casually, an extension of her person.

Emily sat on one bed—deep, comfortable, with a heavy quilt despite the summer—and Ethan sat on the other, facing her. They just stared at each other for a long while.

Then Ethan said, "No plugs."

"What?"

"There are no plugs in this room. Electrical outlets."

"There have to be. You can't build a house without electrical sockets."

"And yet there aren't. There's power—" He pointed upward to a ceiling fan. "—but not anything like you'd expect in a modern house."

Emily frowned. "I don't have the feeling this is a modern house. In fact, I don't feel like this house is part of the world at all."

"It does have that fairyland quality to it, I admit," Ethan said. "Right down to the witch in the kitchen with her big stone ovens."

"You thought of that too, did you?" Emily said. "Not that I don't like it. I do. It feels... restful. Even more than home did, there at the end."

Ethan got up to run a finger over the ancient wallpaper by the door. "Like nothing bad can come here. It's what it felt like when Mom and Dad were home."

And Emily was crying. Just right out of the blue, with no warning, she felt the tears well up and overflow and pour in a great cascade down her burned cheeks. She put her head in her hands. After a moment, she felt Ethan's arm around her shoulders.

"I know," he said. "As long as I was fighting to stay alive, I didn't have to feel anything."

But now, just for a moment, they had time to feel the disaster of things. Fred lost to them—who knew what would happen now—their parents, somewhere in the middle of an increasingly dis-United States, the truck lost, all their possessions sitting in an abandoned house, and now they were walking more than fifty miles to grandmother's house when they had no idea what they would find when they got there.

They were sitting in a stranger's house, and no matter how kind they were, it still wasn't home. Would there ever be a home again?

"Are we that terrifying?" Maggie's voice said from the door.

Emily hurriedly dried her tears. Ethan stood up, positioning himself between the two girls. "We're just… a little tired. That's all."

"You'll be far more tired yet, I shouldn't wonder. But if you're hungry, vittles is up. I hope you don't mind eating in the kitchen. We have a dining room, but we never use it unless the clan is assembled."

Emily thought she understood about a third of what Maggie was saying. But the smell of food was eloquent and easily understood, so she followed as the willowy girl led across the shadow-strewn courtyard and through the door opposite.

The Grand greeted them with courtesy and pointed them to a pair of seats on the bench of a picnic table, already set with plates and silverware and steaming with two deep, gleaming pots. "We'll wait just a moment, if you please, for the rest."

"The rest?" Emily said, sliding into her seat.

"They'll be along presently. It's a bit of a ride."

Alive with questions, Emily nevertheless spent a couple minutes examining the decor, including the intricate—though crude—carvings on the table itself. It seemed that whoever sat at the table could simply carve whatever he liked into it. The carvings overlapped each other, ran together and split, curled around and spilled over the edge of the table. She wanted to see if one particularly ornate… mermaid… continued on the underside, but she didn't think it would be polite to crawl under and look.

The Grand puttered about… no. She danced. Never did she move from pan to table to cutting board without a pirouette or a little hitch step, as if she were hearing music in the sighing of the wind and the bubbling of the pots.

Speaking of pots—she craned her neck to see into them and found one half full of mashed potatoes and the other at least that full of some kind of greens she didn't recognize.

On the edge of her awareness, there was some sort of humming. It was low and steady, like a fan of some kind, but of course, it couldn't be that. Then she realized that one, there was a refrigerator in the kitchen—an old, squat, rounded model that had to be at least fifty years old—and two, that the fridge was *running*.

She tapped Ethan on the arm without taking her eyes off the fridge for a second, for fear that if she did, she'd find that it wasn't there anymore when she looked back.

He shrugged her off. She grabbed him and lifted his arm to point at the appliance. The working, humming appliance. It was that machine that was making the noise she heard, and she hadn't heard it in so long it didn't register what it was.

"What… wait," Ethan said. He looked over at Maggie, who was churning a tub with ice—real ice—around a central core. Ice cream. "You have electricity?"

The Grand snorted. "As if we need it. But yes." She pointed to the ceiling. Or perhaps to the sky. "Sun power."

"And wind," Maggie said. "Defiance was never wired up to the grid when the first little bit of it was laid down. That's the bit on the west side," she said, jutting her chin in that direction while not breaking the beat of her churning. "The Great—that's The Grand's mother—didn't hold with the witchcraft of electric devices, and it's only been the last few years, since the Great moved on, that Omma and Oppa persuaded The Grand that having cooling might be a boon."

"But naught else!" said The Grand as if pronouncing the Will of the Queen. "You'll churn and like it, or there'll be no ice cream."

"Ah," said Maggie, with a wink at the twins, "but without the infernal device, there wouldn't be ice for the cream to freeze in, would there?"

The Grand scoffed, but Emily saw the affection there for her granddaughter. For her part, Maggie kept up a strong rhythm, whirling the crank around and around with little apparent effort.

"I'll take a turn," Ethan said, getting up.

"Not for guests," The Grand said, but Maggie pursed her lips and gazed steadily at Ethan for a moment.

"All right," she said. "Mind you don't spoil it by going too slow."

Ethan swore he would not and took over from Maggie with only a slight pause. Immediately he grunted with the effort, and his eyes went wide. Emily could see the strain in his arm as he cranked, but she knew he'd never admit it in front of Maggie, who had acquired a kind of mythic status already. She was pretty, Emily had to admit, in an elfin, otherworldly, but decidedly earthy sort of way, as if she were made of rods of sculpted iron.

"Ahoy, Defiance!" called someone from outside to the north, the way they'd come in.

Maggie moved to a small round window in the kitchen wall. "Ahoy, the riders!" she called back.

"Herd's in, and we're weary!"

"Vittles is up, and you're welcome," Maggie said. "I'll raise the portcullis."

Now Emily was glad she hadn't volunteered for the ice cream because she desperately wanted to see how the portcullis worked, and she wasn't shackled—as Ethan was—to the churning.

"May I come with?" Emily said.

Maggie turned those steely gray eyes on her. Emily felt as if her bones were being examined minutely for the signs of a flaw.

"Take her," The Grand said. "I've read the leaves. They've nothing of evil in them."

Maggie seemed to take this as permission and led Emily past the door they had come in, into a part of the house they had not seen. They walked through what looked like a living room—again, no television—and through a sitting room/library with a wrought-iron spiral staircase leading up.

They mounted this staircase, corkscrewing up through the ceiling and into a room that reminded Emily of the mechanical room for an elevator. A tapestry of wires and pulleys covered an entire wall. Set into the wall was a captain's wheel, like you would see on a ship. To the left, the wall had narrow reinforced slits set into it, like arrow slits in a castle wall, through which, if she squinted, Emily could see across the valley. Standing in front of what Emily guessed was the east wall of the house, two men sat on horseback, leaning on the pommels of their saddles, waiting for the portcullis to rise.

Emily couldn't imagine that even together, she and Maggie would be strong enough to raise the portcullis and open the south wall of the courtyard, so she was completely shocked when Maggie grasped the captain's wheel by herself and began to spin it without significant effort. From below, there was a periodic squeaking, metal on metal, and a clanking from inside the wall that spoke of something heavy being raised.

"How… " Emily said, coming over to peer into the guts of the wall.

"Physics," Maggie said. "Pulleys divide the weight of an object being raised. Get enough pulleys, and a five-year-old could raise the Titanic." There were certainly a plethora of pulleys set into the wall and no apparent strain in raising what must have been hundreds of pounds of iron.

Something thunked in the wall, and the horsemen disappeared from outside, only to reappear below them as they rode into the courtyard. They tied up their horses to a hitching post to the right of the guard-house—because that's what it was, Emily realized—and sauntered through the kitchen door.

"Randolph and Roborous," Maggie said. "My brothers."

"Older?"

Maggie nodded. She pulled a lever on the wall, and the wheel began to spin back in the opposite direction. She kept a hand on it, gently allowing the weight of the portcullis to do the work of falling back into place.

"If you don't mind my asking, how old *are* you?" Emily said.

Maggie's eyes twinkled for a moment before lapsing back into their customary unreadable state. "How old do you think I am?"

Trick question. But it was just the two of them, and a guess couldn't do any harm. "I'd say twenty-two."

Maggie nodded. "Pretty good. Most folks guess very high. I'm nineteen."

"*Nineteen?*" Emily said. "You seem so much… "

"Older?" This time Maggie laughed, a trilling, merry laugh that echoed off the stone walls. "Don't fret. I don't take offense."

"More capable than most nineteen-year-olds is what I was going to say."

"I wouldn't know much about that. I don't mix with the townies my age. Once or twice a year, I go to a dance or some other event, and I see if any of the kids there have grown up at all. They haven't so far. I'm far more comfortable with my own."

Emily got a faraway look in her eyes. This touched on her own situation pretty closely, and it brought the deep sadness a notch closer to the surface, where she could not allow it to be. She shoved it back down, but she was certain those piercing gray eyes saw her do it. "I know a little about what that's like. We're homeschooled, Ethan and me. We've done a lot more than most kids our age."

"Homeschooled all my life. I thought I recognized the attitude. And now you've wandered into Defiance on your way to the Little Pink House. It's a fairy tale for sure," Maggie said, setting the lever back into its original position. She wiped her hands on her jeans.

"Come along for vittles," she said.

"We don't have a lot of electric devices here because we never have and never needed them," Randolph said. He was a tall, muscular man in his mid-twenties, Emily guessed, with the hooked nose and dancing green eyes of his grandmother. "Seemed more of a distraction than anything else."

"Folk get to rely on that stuff, like crutches," Maggie said, heaping potatoes on her plate in such a mountain that Emily wondered if she were starving and only ate when company came. "Then the crutch is taken, and wham! Down they go."

That was a fair description of what was happening in town, in every town. It was even happening to them, and they thought they'd been prepared, better than most, to handle whatever came. Now look at them.

"Seems every time we talk about these things, the young lady gets a look in her eye like we've stepped on thin ice, and it's cracking, and if we busted through, there'd be no end to the water below." The Grand's eyes locked onto Emily's and held them. She couldn't look away. She didn't want to look away. She needed to tell someone, anyone. Maybe The Grand was right, and there was no bottom to their troubles, but Emily wanted to try draining the lake anyway.

So she did. A little at a time. Starting with the power going out and right through everything that came afterward. Emily was very hungry, but the roast sat on her plate with the potatoes and greens and gravy. She spilled out words upon words, what it felt like to hear her parents on the ham radio, what it felt like when they went dark, the decision to make a run for Gnarled Oaks, the robbery, all of it. Tears tracked down her cheeks and fell in the gravy, and she did nothing about them, hardly noticing they were there. It had to come out, like an infected tooth, all at once, no matter how difficult the operation.

And as she did it, she felt the burden get lighter. Her audience said nothing—they hardly even ate, just kept their soft gazes upon her and nodded here and there, soaking in every word. They heard her. They understood, to some extent.

A burden shared is a burden halved. This one was lightened a great deal more than that.

She did not so much finish the story as run down like a top, wobbling until it finally fell over, out of momentum. Somewhere in the middle of the telling, Ethan had reached over to take her hand, and he still held it, warm in his own, while Emily sat with a bowed head. This did bring her nose close enough to the meat and potatoes that she got a long, deep lungful of their fragrance.

In response, her stomach growled so loudly it could have been heard in Accord Landing.

So naturally, the whole room broke into laughter, Emily included. She picked up her fork and began to shovel food into her mouth as if she'd never eaten well before.

"That's quite a tale," The Grand said. "I believe that once a body has eaten at our table and told us her troubles, she's entitled by the ancient law of guesting to assistance in her plight. I so pronounce."

"So let it be written," Rouborous said.

"And it shall be done," Randolph said.

"But not until we get a little help ourselves," Maggie said.

Ethan sat up a bit straighter and removed his hand from Emily's, perhaps concerned that if he left it any longer, Emily would eat it. She had inhaled the plate of food and was in the process of dishing out some more.

"What troubles do you have?" Ethan said. "It looks to me like you have Camelot here."

Rouborous' eyebrows went up. "The boy invokes Arthur. I don't think we're quite as well set as he was."

"A lot fewer knights, for one thing," Randolph said.

"But more with them than without them," Maggie said. "I think they'll help us. I think they were meant to."

"And then, when they lend their strength to ours, we will send you to deliver them to their kin," The Grand said, nodding. She stabbed her knife into the table an inch deep. "That's a fair exchange."

"We're willing to help you," Ethan said, shifting his position so he could see everyone at once, "but I, for one, would like to know what it is we're helping you with."

The four of them exchanged looks in the way some people held whole conversations. Every glance seemed to be a whole book's worth of information. Finally, some decision was reached, and Rouborous began to speak.

"You'll have noticed we have a moit of cattle," he said. Emily wasn't sure what a "moit" was, but she got the idea anyway. "When we had Omma and Oppa with us, we were still stretched pretty thin to guard them all. Not that we needed to, most days. We were left alone right up to when the power went out. But then things got dicey." He looked to Randolph, who picked up the story, twirling his fork for emphasis.

"Here's the rub, as Hamlet would say. Centralized power is very efficient but also very fragile. Even before the power went out, all over creation areas went dark here and there pretty often. You have experience with this, I see from your faces. That's not a serious problem unless the grid gets extra loaded or loses cohesion somehow. Texas, during the ice storms a few years back. California, as soon as it gets above 70 degrees on the coast. Bad, widespread outages."

He took a bite of potatoes, chewed, and swallowed. "Now, attend. We don't hold with that centralized idea. Yes, our solar and wind are much less efficient than the wired grid, but they're more robust. You have to take out the sun or stop the air from moving to cut our power. This modern civilization is a tradeoff between collective efficient fragility and distributed inefficient robustitude. We opted for the latter, in schooling, in power, and in food production."

"Granted," The Grand said, tossing in her comment like a rock into a river, "we have land for it, and most don't. But the principle applies."

Rouborous retook the narrative. "We produce our own food, mostly, and that means that we need every head of cattle and every pig and every chicken. Right after the power went out, we began to lose cattle. Not many. One here, one there. Not every night, not from every part of the valley. But some. Enough that we are close to having the herd crash in numbers. We can't lose more. But we don't know how we're losing them or who is taking them."

Now it was Emily and Ethan exchanging a look. "Mort," Emily said.

"Has to be," Ethan said, nodding. To the rest, he said, "We met a fellow that works just like what you're describing. He's local. I'd bet money it's him."

"But I don't see how we can be terribly helpful," Emily said. "It's been a while since we rode horses, though we know how."

"And we're, uh, not skilled in fighting," Ethan said. His knife scratched at the table, his eyes down. "And usually it just makes bigger problems than the one you're trying to solve."

Emily expected that to change the mood on the other side of the table, but it didn't seem to. "Fine by us. We don't plan any killing, though there are always folks that deserve it," Rouborous said. "But to pull off our plan to secure the herd, we need a couple more hands."

"And here you are," Maggie said. "As if you fell from Heaven."

Emily would have contributed something, but her mouth was full of whatever the greens were. They were flavored with bacon and had a sour, savory taste she couldn't get enough of.

"Collard greens," Maggie said, a smile in her voice. "They'll grow on you. Metaphorically."

Randolph wiped his mouth and carefully set his napkin by his plate. "We've been planning for a couple of weeks now how to set up a trap to catch the thieves. Tonight is the night we spring it. We might be able to pull it off, the four of us, but I won't lie to those I like—we would look on your assistance as a mighty boon."

"We'd do it even if you hadn't promised to help us get to the Little Pink House. But you have. We'll take that as a mighty boon ourselves," Ethan said with a wry smile. "Whatever you need, we'll be happy to do."

One of the problems with working with authentic Appalachian hillbillies—like the people of

Defiance—was that when they hooted like an owl, it really sounded like an owl.

"How am I supposed to know when it's an alert or a real owl marking territory?" Ethan whispered as he and Emily lay hidden under low-hanging branches deep in the woods.

"I can tell the difference," she said.

Ethan scoffed but now wasn't the time for a discussion. Spread out before them was the panorama of the Defiance property. The moon was bigger than half, and there was plenty of light shining on the fields and pastures once your eyes got used to it. Dark smudges against the slightly lighter valley floor were cows. There were twenty or so of them, all that remained of the herd. Rouborous and Randolph had driven them down here to the lowest part of the vale—which also happened to be the part closest to town. The treeline, in fact, came right to the valley floor and to within fifty yards or so of some of the cows.

There was no guarantee anyone would take the bait tonight, no matter the preparations. Ethan's eyes began to strain, and imaginary things danced across his field of vision. He wished he had night-vision goggles to help him, but of course, Defiance didn't have any gear like that.

To the twins' right, halfway around the side of the valley, Maggie was concealed in her hiding place. Her job had not been explained to them. The two brothers were in the woods on the opposite side, directly across from the twins, maybe a half mile or a little more. Their job was simple—catch the rustlers.

It was the twins who were to make that possible.

Just behind them was a wooden wall, braced with logs to keep it upright against the pressure building behind it, where the brothers had dammed a substantial creek. A trickle of it still flowed, and in the moonlight, a twinkling ribbon of water wound its way across the valley floor like a strand of discarded Christmas lights.

It was very quiet. So quiet, in fact, that Ethan could hear his heart beating in his chest.

An owl hooted. Ethan put his hands to his mouth and got ready to respond. Emily hit him in the ribs with an elbow. "That was a real owl," she said.

Ethan had no idea how she could tell, but he kept his mouth shut and watched. For a long time, not much happened. And then there was a low-level hum, just barely in the range of hearing, and the snap of a twig, somewhere off to their right. A half-audible piece of conversation, just part of a word. Someone was out there.

Another hoot of an owl. It sounded just like the other one, but Ethan was pretty sure this time it was an alert, and sure enough, Emily got up from her crouch and went to the barrier. She picked up the heavy rubber mallet and got ready to execute her part of the plan.

Ethan unbent as well and moved over to his side, where there was another mallet about the same size. He kept his eyes pinned on the valley floor, though, hoping he'd be able to see what was going on. He'd promised to execute the plan regardless, but he wanted to know if it worked.

Something moved in the tree line.

The movement was right where Maggie had her post, so at first, Ethan thought it might be her and that the plan was off for the night. But then, a shape detached itself from the dark line of trees and slid out into the valley toward one of the cows. Another followed it, and a third.

Maggie began to sing.

It had to be her. The song was wild, plaintive, not even in English, as far as Ethan could tell, but it felt like lost love and longing, and it made the hair stand up on his arms.

Then he saw her.

Again, it had to be her, but even knowing that there was a plan to catch the thieves and that the thieves were in the valley in the middle of the heist and that the plan must therefore be in motion, Ethan stood transfixed by what he saw. A willowy figure, ethereal, white, glowing like a star fallen to earth, was gliding through the woods. Her hair streamed out behind her as if she were in a wind unfelt in the mortal world, and she sang her

spectral song quietly, serenely, but with a wild edge that filled the whole bowl and chilled the blood.

The shapes in the field froze and turned toward her.

An owl gave two hoots. The signal.

Emily and Ethan swung their mallets and released the flood of the creek.

With a mighty crash, the water tore through the falling logs and thundered down the hill into the valley.

Even with the doom of a tsunami falling on them from the hill above, the three men in the field obviously had to tear their gazes from Maggie's performance, wasting precious seconds trying to understand what was happening. And by then, it was far too late.

Emily had been worried that the torrent would be fatal, but she saw immediately the wisdom of the plan and its non-lethality. Rouborous had promised her it would not be dangerous—except to she and Ethan if they didn't get out of the way—because: "One, I don't hold with killing where there's any way to persuade, and two, don't forget, our cows lie peaceful and sleeping there in the valley. We don't want to hurt them, either."

Releasing the makeshift dam did send a huge wall of water down the hill, but by the time it had rumbled through the trees and the bracken and made its way to the field, it had lost most of its intensity. The leading edge was still a significant wave, but it was the kind the twins would have tried to body surf at the beach, not the kind that disaster movies were made of.

But it was still a substantial amount of water. The men in the field tried to evade it, but they were directly in its path. It washed passed them and rolled across the valley to the other side, where it ran out of momentum against the rising ground there.

"Oh," Ethan said. "I get it."

Explaining the plan earlier, Randolph had said that as quick as the Defiance crew was on horseback, all the thieves had to do was reach the woods, and the horses were at a major disadvantage. "Plus, they have motorized transportation up there. They pick out a cow, drive it into the woods, shoot it, load it onto a four-wheeler or a small pickup, and away they go. The key is, we have to keep them from making it to the tree line."

And this way, they could. The rustlers were drenched, heavy, and standing in three feet of water on top of what was now a marshy bog. They couldn't run. They couldn't really move at all.

From out of the trees on the opposite side rode Rouborous and Randolph slowly, letting the horses pick their way. Lassos whistled through the air and dropped neatly on nearly stationary forms.

The cows, for their part, seemed greatly annoyed and were moving their ponderous way to where the ground was firmer and wasn't so wet. They lowed and bellowed their discomfort, and one of them appeared to tread on one of the rustlers, who cried out in pain or alarm, the twins couldn't tell which.

Emily realized that Maggie had disappeared.

"How'd we do?" Maggie said, appearing between the two Tuttles as silently as a ghost. They jumped back, and Ethan fell over a loose log.

"Pretty good," Emily said, recovering. "Your brothers are just about to explain to the rustlers the error of their ways."

Maggie stepped forward to have a better look. Even right next to them, she still projected a weird, untamed aura. Not for the first time, they heard the echo of another plane of existence, as if she—more, even, than any of the others—was not entirely of this world.

Heated voices rolled up from the valley floor, followed by laughter—gales of it, surely from the throats of Rouborous and Randolph. A shrill whistle sounded, and Maggie jerked her head at the twins. "That's the all clear. The brothers want us."

Among the three trapped, roped, tied-up raiders was Mort himself. He didn't look nearly as scary in this situation, much more like a drowned rat. His frustration and anger were so hot the water steamed off his head.

"*You.*" He spat the word at Emily and Ethan, who responded with cheery smiles.

"Not sure why you're upset with us," Ethan said. "It wasn't the little backpacks you left us that got you into this."

"You did that on your own, with your greed." Emily thought for a moment. "But it *is* true that if you'd left us the truck and just sent us on our way, we wouldn't have had the pleasure of drowning you tonight. So maybe it is our fault after all."

Rouborous tipped back his cowboy hat and leaned on the pommel of his saddle. "They've promised to be real good from now on and not take those things that properly belong to others."

"We have *not*!" one of the rustlers said. Emily didn't recognize him.

"Well," Rouborous said, unfazed, "they were about to."

Mort swelled up as much as his bedraggled self would allow. "You caught us, yes, but there are a lot more of us than there are of you. We'll keep coming. You can't cover the whole valley. Your little band here isn't going to be able to keep your herd for yourselves. It's unfair. And we're going to even things up."

"Like you did this morning," Emily said dryly. He wasn't nearly as scary like this, and now she could see through his act. He was scared and acting tough.

"The way I see it," Randolph said, swinging a leg over his saddle and dropping to the ground, "you didn't prepare. You weren't ready. You and your folk were only too ready to laugh at us before. We were the hicks, the backward weirdos. Now we get to reap the rewards, and you don't. It's pretty simple."

"Whatever," Mort said. "You're still the weirdos, and there are still a lot more of us than there are of you."

The brothers looked at each other for a long moment, having one of those silent conversations.

"Tell you what," Rouborous said. "Why don't we keep you here for a week or so?"

Mort's spluttering was an eloquent response.

"I've heard a saying," Randolph drawled, "about what happens when you chop the head off a snake."

Emily got into the spirit of it. "I wonder how many other people's stuff is collected at the gas station."

Ethan nodded, rubbing his chin. "Quite a bit, I'd bet. And not all of it came from people cruising through town. Some of it will belong to people in the town."

Through all this, Maggie kept silent, her unsettling gaze pinned to one of the three, a smaller man who hadn't raised his head an inch throughout the whole exchange.

"You," she said, with that crackle in her voice. She raised her arm and pointed it at the man. "Why are you here?"

"Don't answer that," Mort said. He wriggled against his ropes, trying to reach the man.

Rouborous saw it and backed his horse a pace, cinching Mort's rope a bit tighter. He squawked and stopped struggling.

"Tell me," Maggie said, her arm still straight as the mast of a ship. "*Now.*"

"I'm... I'm sorry," the man said.

"For?" Maggie kept the pressure on.

"For stealing. For not being ready. For being… weak."

"You *are* weak," Mort said.

Rouborous backed his horse again, and Mort fell over into the mud. Face down. He twisted and jerked and blew bubbles but couldn't get himself free.

"He might drown like that," Randolph said as if he was observing the phases of the moon.

Rouborous sighed and tugged the rope, rolling Mort onto his side. He sucked in a huge breath and apparently decided he'd said all he had to say for a moment.

"You have to understand what it's like up there," the man said, pointing his chin up the hill. "Mort was always a bully. But now he's… he's taken over everything. He has his thugs, and we can't really fight him."

"Who are you?" Maggie said, with just a little less menace in her voice.

"Grant. Grant McAllen."

"*Mayor* McAllen?" Randolph said as if he found something funny.

The man just nodded.

All five of his captors—the twins included—exchanged fascinated glances. This time the twins had no trouble understanding the messages being sent.

"Perhaps," Rouborous said, "You should come to Defiance and tell us your story."

The Tuttle Twins and the Days of Darkness

They locked Mort and his henchman, Thayne, in one of the old outhouses. It looked rickety, but Randolph assured them it would hold just fine. Then they had the mayor inside for some stew and a wash and let him tell the story.

It didn't take long, and it was very familiar. The mayor hadn't been ready. He hadn't prepared. When the crisis came, he didn't lead out, didn't help give people a sense of confidence that they could get through it. Mort had money, Mort had muscle, and Mort took over effective control of the town.

"At first, it wasn't bad. He brought in some food and kept order. But it wasn't long before he started taking over everything—and taking whatever he wanted," the miserable mayor said.

The twins knew that story well from their history classes. It was predictable.

And the rest was predictable as well. One by one, Mort cut out anyone that could oppose him, mostly driving them off but severely beating some who wouldn't leave. Then the food ran out.

"The only place we could get it was here." He spread his hands, an apology. "I have kids. We're hungry, and he threatened to... do things... to us. He would, too."

"You were elected Mayor," The Grand said. "I even voted for you. You must have some spine somewhere in the jellyfish carcass."

McAllen winced.

"Question is, can you find it again?" The Grand leaned over the table and stared the man in the face. Her eyes searched. Searched. Finally, she gave a small shrug. "Maybe," she said. "Hard to see."

Silence reigned in the kitchen, broken only by the deep tick-tock of the grandfather clock in the corner.

"I want to try."

The Grand looked at him again. "What was that?"

His head came up, and his eyes were steadier, his face filling with color. "I want to try. I owe it to my town. And my kids." He ran a hand through his thinning hair. "I don't want this to be what they remember their father for."

It took a couple of days. That night, the Defiants—that was what Emily started calling them—returned the mayor to his home and rode through the town, ringing bells, like Paul Revere and William Dawes, calling out the town for a meeting.

Without Mort—who was fed bread and water in his little prison—the control of the gang wobbled and eventually fell completely apart. Mayor McAllen proved as good as his word. He did try. And when he saw that people wanted to follow him, he tried harder. He reasserted leadership in the town and began to make a plan for how to share resources, working together with trade, instead of pulling apart with force and lawless plunder.

"Don't know if it will work," The Grand said, helping to load a huge wagon with barrels of meal and flour from Defiance's stores. "But we'll sleep a moit better than we have been, that's certain."

And true to their word, as the situation in the town stabilized, the Defiants saw the twins delivered to Gnarled Oaks.

One morning, Maggie wakened them and said, "Time to go, Tuttles."

"Go where?" Emily said groggily, trying to wipe sleep from her eyes.

"The Little Pink House," Maggie said. "Come on. Your chariot awaits."

"Esmeralda! We can finish our road trip." The old truck was filled with fuel, water, and supplies, and even a weapon for protection. Emily's face broke into a big smile.

"I declare myself in your everlasting debt," Emily said, curtseying low to the whole family assembled in the courtyard.

"So you are, so you are," The Grand said. "Thus your payment is to return to Defiance annually to do your obeisance."

Ethan bounced around the truck and once more into the driver's seat. "Ma'am," he said. "You have yourself a deal."

The twins were welcomed to Gnarled Oaks by their Grandma, and their aunts, uncles, and cousins a bit more than an hour later. The whole Tuttle clan was there, except for their parents who would arrive eventually, a few weeks later. The town itself had rallied without needing to fight off a gang lord. Early on, town leaders organized a community militia, just like in colonial times, and an economic system of local trade. And with the river so close, they had most of the resources they needed. The community even thrived. When the power came back on a year later, many people there weren't entirely sure it was a good thing—although they changed their minds after becoming reacquainted with hot showers and air conditioning.

True to their word, the twins returned to Defiance every year until the death of The Grand nine years later.

THE END

If Grandma's house had been a little closer, say, a three-hour drive instead of nine or ten, they might have chosen that option. It was certainly a good one. If they couldn't stay home, there was no place they'd rather be than at the Little Pink House.

But staying home was no good, and being out on the road with no resources but themselves was daunting. Who knew the hazards out there? Right now, they weren't sure they'd want to drive through Malantown, let alone four states.

And... they couldn't leave Fred.

Emily kept glancing over at him while they talked through their options. He had never looked his age before. Deep lines ran like plow furrows across his forehead and down his hollowed cheeks. He had always been clean-shaven, too, and now he sported two days' grizzle on his cheeks and chin, all of it whiter than bleached linen. The mottling of the bruises on his head gave him an unnatural appearance, like one of those zombie shows. His eyes kept closing.

No, they wouldn't leave the man who, outside their own family, meant the most in the world to them. He'd been by their side through so many adventures; they could—they must—support him when he needed them most.

He had always been a good judge of character, and if he trusted this Amihan Legaspi, then they probably could, too. And they needed friends right now more than any other resource.

Funny—Emily had always thought that in an emergency, water, gold, or maybe ammunition was the most precious resource. She was wondering if the most necessary thing in a crisis might actually be community… *friends.*

The twins talked it over deep into the night. Ethan was reluctant to put his life into the hands of someone he didn't know, but he had to admit it was probably better than keeping it in his *own* hands since his hands were shaking and unsure.

Fred looked, Emily had to admit, somewhat relieved when they told him. He immediately went down the street to talk to Ms. Legaspi and get instructions for what they could and could not bring with them.

Fred sat at his kitchen table, sipping an apple juice from his food storage. "They didn't seem all that excited about you two coming with me, but I vouched for you. I know you're good workers and contributors to whatever community you're a part of. They'll be glad you're there."

"I'm not sure we want to be part of a community that has to be talked into taking us," Emily said.

"Don't take it personally. Most teenagers are not the sort that are terribly helpful in a crisis."

Ethan lounged against the wall. "So what did they want us to bring?"

Fred tugged a small notebook out of his pocket. "The truck. All the gasoline we have. The generators. The radio. First aid supplies. Weaponry and especially ammunition."

Emily waited for him to go on, but apparently, that was it. "No food storage?" She was shocked.

"No, they said they had a team that would come and take all that stuff up to the camp. We don't need to worry about it, although they'll probably want us to bring our inventory. Oh, yeah. Batteries, flashlights, knives, and any propane or white gas cylinders we have, whether empty or full. That's it." Fred looked up. "That shouldn't take us very long to get together."

It took less than half a day. When they had finished, they couldn't help taking a walk back through both the houses, looking carefully at everything, pausing, reaching out to touch things they weren't sure they'd ever be back to see again. But they would, wouldn't they? This was temporary, just until the power came back on. Right?

By mid-afternoon, it was obvious to all of them that they were just stalling. One by one, they filed out of Fred's house and climbed into the truck and drove away.

None of them looked back. All of them wanted to.

Fred had a map given to him by Ms. Legaspi showing the location of the Mutual Assistance Group, or

MAG, as she called it. It was north, some distance, a hundred miles or more. Was it really necessary for it to be so far away?

According to the map, the closest town to the group was not Spoonerville but Clingman, a town so small they'd never heard of it. The closest city of any size was Jellico, which Ethan thought sounded like something from *Cats*. They'd never been there. Even Fred hadn't.

The truck, fortunately, was full of gas and capable of handling even some modest off-roading if necessary. It didn't come to that, in the end—though the roads were one-lane, no-shoulder death traps. They were fairly well paved all the way into Auntarkin, the last dot on the map before the X marking the spot.

A few miles out of that one-stoplight town, the directions had them take a right onto what proved to be a dirt road leading into a forest. The trees grew so thickly around the road that they scraped the sides of the truck as it jounced along. There wasn't anything to tell that this road had been used recently, and Ethan began to wonder if this whole map thing was just a wild goose chase.

The road didn't get any worse, and in fact, after a mile, it got substantially better. Someone had laid gravel down fairly recently and carved back the encroaching foliage, resulting in a well-tended track that came to a dead end just over the lip of a long, gentle hill, in a parking lot. Ethan counted twelve vehicles there, mostly trucks, but a couple of cars and a pair of road-grade motorcycles, along with a motor scooter.

At first, Ethan thought no one was there, but as they rolled to a stop in an open stall, Ms. Legaspi stepped out of the trees. One moment she was effectively invisible, and the next, she was right there, a small smile on her face. She was dressed in olive drab—not camouflage, but not the sort of thing one would expect outside a military base, either. She had on an Atlanta Braves baseball cap, with her hair down to her shoulders. She raised a hand in greeting.

Fred jumped down from the cab, winced when he landed, but hauled himself upright, and the two of them shook hands.

"Glad you could make it," she said. Her voice was very deep, a smoky alto that jarred a bit coming from such a small woman.

"We're grateful for the invitation. The police were… aggressive… in suggesting we come with them."

She cocked her head to the side like a scientist examining something interesting. "That offer didn't appeal to you?"

"It did not. Nor to them," he said, jerking his head to indicate the twins.

Her smile was thin, a tight line. "You won't have to worry about any of that here. The police don't come out this way. It's not a smart thing for them to do."

Fred frowned. "What does this group do to them?"

She held up a hand and shook her head. "No, no. It's not us. But there are people in the woods—have been for centuries—who don't want anything to do with authority. That's why they live out here. They have secrets, some of them, and they're, uh, aggressive about keeping them."

Ethan whispered to Emily, "That's like when we learned about the Bootleggers during alcohol prohibition. Police went into the woods to try to arrest them, or at least to collect taxes from them, and things got ugly."

Emily whispered back, "Sounds like that's not just from 100 years ago."

Fred was saying, "We brought the stuff you asked for. Pardon me, but I don't see much of a settlement here for so many cars."

Legaspi's smile got just a little bigger. "Secrets. This isn't MAG HQ, naturally. It's just a car park. The real settlement is up the hill a bit. We prefer that people walk it, but you have gear that should probably be driven. Come with me a sec."

She marched Fred over behind a large camper. The twins jumped out of the truck and joined them. There, hidden from the road, was a single-lane dirt track that wound up through a thicket and presumably up the hillside. It wasn't obvious that there was enough room for the truck to make it up the "road." But Legaspi seemed confident, so Fred obediently put the truck in gear and plowed through the brush.

The bushes parted with reluctance, and once they had, the road improved immediately—wider and smoother than had appeared possible from the car park. Which, of course, was the point.

"They're pretty serious about their security here, aren't they?" Ethan said.

"And how," Fred said, leaning out the window and inhaling. "No way would we—or most anyone else, for that matter—be able to find this place without a map and a guide."

The air was fresh and piney, with here and there a whiff of woodsmoke. Someone nearby had a fire going. And it was humid—sticky, even, although the temperature was cool. Among so many trees so close together, there wasn't any room for the wind to move the air around.

HQ, as Legaspi called it, did not appear. And did not appear. And still, did not appear. The truck kept going, winding back and forth as it climbed a fairly substantial hill, but the road did not end.

Finally, after what seemed like ten minutes, the truck abruptly burst from the trees into a clearing that spanned an enormous distance—big enough, Ethan thought, to hold an entire baseball stadium. And here, at last, was the HQ.

People. Lots of people—probably sixty to a hundred, and that was just what they could see moving around in the open. A large, low building ran thirty or forty yards

directly in front of them. Set deep into the ground, not much more than a few feet of the building showed above the dirt, plus the metal roof on top. A building like that could hold a hundred people easily. Three hundred, even, and maybe more.

Nor was it the only building. Behind the longhouse—Ethan immediately thought of it that way, from his studies of the Norse—a flagpole occupied the center of a large square without a single leaf of vegetation in it. Around the square were arrayed a number of smallish cabins, each with a door facing into the square. At each corner stood a larger building, each one also abnormally low, with sod steps cut into the ground leading down. These would be storage buildings, Ethan guessed. Food, clothing, and maybe weaponry.

Solar panels decked the roof of each cabin, and behind the central square of cabins, an uncountable number of tents had also been erected. Just at first glance, it was obvious that HQ had been built to house a large number of people, far more than they had expected.

"So much for fifty backwoodsmen hiding out in the hills," Emily said, wonder in her voice.

"Yeah. There might be more people here than there are left living in the homes of Spoonerville," Ethan said.

A man appeared in front of them in hunting gear, a bright orange vest included. He waved the truck over to the left, where an area had been flattened for vehicle parking. Six to eight trucks, jeeps, and off-road vehicles sat here, along with a huge number of motorbikes; Ethan got to fifteen before he stopped counting.

Another man pointed them to the place he wanted them to stop. When they did, he came over to the driver's window. "Just back it up this way, okay? Save us some back labor." He seemed friendly enough.

Fred did as instructed. As soon as the truck shut off, people materialized as if from out of the ground, converged on the truck, and had everything unloaded from it in two minutes flat. All of it disappeared into one or another of the corner buildings.

The radio, however, remained. A woman leaned on the truck, peering in. She was blonde, with her hair back in a braid that terminated in what looked like a giant alligator clip.

"Is that a Kenwood?" she said.

"No," Emily said. "It's an ICOM."

The woman turned to her. She had dark eyes, and her skin was very white. "How many watts?"

"1500."

The woman's eyes got wide. "What's the farthest signal you've had on it?"

Emily thought for a second. "Kazakhstan, once."

The woman let out a low whistle. "And look at all the extras. Police band, BaoFeng handhelds… wow. This thing makes my setup look like a backyard toy. It'll draw a lot of power, though. Bern!" she yelled over her shoulder, "Come look at this!"

Another woman, short and muscular, with tight copper curls, jogged over from somewhere by the longhouse. She and the blonde immediately began examining the equipment, commenting on its quality and figuring out how to power it.

Fred approached them and stopped a few feet short, hand outstretched. "I'm Fred," he said. "This is Emily, and that's Ethan."

The ladies shook his hand. "Carol, but everyone here calls me Squawk. This is Bern. Don't ask what that's short for."

Fred obeyed and did not ask. They shook hands all around.

Amihan jogged up. "Looks like I'm too late to help. And you already found the radio heads in camp, so I don't even get the fun of introducing you to them. I think you'll have a lot to talk about." To the ladies, she said, "These are the kids that are missing their parents."

The women exchanged a look. "You'll have to tell us more about that. You talked to them once on the radio, right?"

The twins nodded, but Amihan said, "Time for that later. You need to come and meet Cap."

She led out toward the longhouse through a whirlwind of activity. Everyone seemed busy, going places, carrying gear, jogging, doing calisthenics, practicing martial arts, repairing and building, and studying. It was the busiest place the twins had ever seen.

Amihan took them down steps that were cut into the hard-packed dirt and paved with slate into the wide door at one end of the longhouse. They had thought it would be dark inside, but it wasn't—hatches in the roof had been removed to allow light in, and the effect was actually quite cheerful. Being up so high and having the ventilation of the open roof, plus the half-underground design of the structure, made it quite cool inside, even though it was toward the middle of the day.

The inside of the longhouse held rows of heavy plastic folding tables with their accompanying folding chairs, all laid out as if with a ruler. At the far end, three men occupied two tables set together, on which a map was mounted with a number of tokens placed on it. They couldn't tell what the map represented, even when they got up close. It was topographical, not political or highway, and they couldn't make it out.

"Cap, these are the three from Spoonerville I mentioned," Amihan said as soon as the man on the right looked up.

He was young. Very young, not that much older than the twins. Or—maybe his open, friendly face was a bit deceptive. There were lines at the corners of his eyes, and he held himself as someone used to commanding others.

He smiled at them. His teeth were very white.

"Fred Christensen, isn't that right?" he said. Fred seemed surprised by the young man's grip. "I'm Cap, or so everyone calls me. My parents named me Clarence Andrew Partridge. Cap. It stuck." He transferred his gaze to the twins. "And you must be Emily and Ethan Tuttle. Call me Cap, please."

His grip was firm, and his eyes never left theirs. He seemed immediately to be someone whom you could trust.

"Amihan tells me you're baseball players," Cap said.

"Yes, sir," Emily said.

"We haven't really had time for baseball yet, too much to do, but I bet the time for that will come. We're glad to have you. And you, Fred, I almost feel like I should call *you* sir, given your service."

Fred waved that away. "I'm just Fred. Thank you for offering us a place to be."

"Glad to. Things are getting pretty dicey down below, I hear."

"In places, yes. Ms. Legaspi's offer came at a particularly good time."

"Well, excellent. I'll have her get you settled in if you'll excuse us for just a moment." He beckoned to Amihan, and the two of them moved over to a corner and spoke with their heads together. The other two men at the table took the opportunity to shake hands as well. Both of them were older, not quite Fred's age, with close-cropped hair and loose, heavy clothing, the kind serious hikers wore. They gave their names as Conrad and Ed. Emily thought she'd have a hard time telling them apart the next time they met.

Amihan returned, a broad smile on her face that Ethan thought looked as if she'd just pasted it on. She took them out the near door—there were doors at each end of the longhouse—and into the sunshine.

They retrieved their personal packs from the cab of the truck and followed Amihan down the right side of the square. About halfway along, she took them between two of the cabins and back into the rows of tents. There were two of them, almost to the tree line, that hadn't been fully erected yet. "Home sweet home," she said.

"I'll take this one," Fred said, pointing to the one on the left.

They dumped their packs and examined the tents to see how to get them put up. Amihan helped tighten ropes and pound in stakes, and in a few minutes, both tents were squared away and tight enough to repel water.

"You've done this before," Fred said.

"I helped put up most of these," she said. "We have sixty now. Yours are the last two, completing the square."

They saw that their tents were, in fact, the only ones that hadn't been set up and that every row was now full, with tents lined up in a way that reminded Emily of a Roman legion camp.

Amihan, her dark eyes missing nothing, saw Emily's face and said, "Looks military, doesn't it? Well, it is, sort of. Cap never served, but his company supplied all sorts of tactical gear to military and ex-military personnel. He got to know a lot of those men and women and adopted plenty of their ideas in planning this place."

"Planning?" Emily said. "The power just went out a month ago."

Amihan nodded but pointed to the longhouse. "That, you can't build overnight. Cap bought the land here a long time ago and has spent years quietly building cabins, cutting trees, and setting up a retreat. He used it for company parties, sometimes. That's how I met him. I'm his Executive Officer. We've worked together for four years."

"You'll know all about him, then," Fred said, stowing his pack on one side of the tent and climbing in after it. He spoke out of the open flap. "What sort of man is he?"

Amihan considered this for a moment as if it were a question she'd never been asked before. "That's hard to answer. There isn't anything I can tell you that you won't see much better for yourself. But I'll say that if there's anyone to ride out the end of the world with, he'd be my first choice."

"High praise."

"He'll earn it. You'll see. You three are actually quite lucky. You're the last ones to camp."

Ethan stopped unpacking for a moment and stuck his head out of the tent. "Last ones?"

"We're not accepting any more people, no," Amihan said. She wiped her hands on her cargo pants. "Cap believes—and I agree with him—that there's such a thing as too many people to take care of. We chose the first group of people pretty carefully, then filled in the rest with people that had the kinds of skills that could help us."

"Fred, I understand," Ethan said, "but what about us? What were the skills you sold Cap that we're supposed to have?"

She smiled, and Emily wasn't entirely sure she liked what she saw there. "Willingness," she said.

The camp certainly used their willingness in the first several days they were there. From the moment the sun rose—pretty early in the summer—to the evening meeting in the Longhouse (they had started calling it that officially, between themselves), they were used to run someone's errands or another.

The stream of work was endless, it seemed. There was always a tree to be cut, or wood to be hauled, or plants to be tended—or eradicated, depending on the plant. The camp had another clearing on the other side of the hill, terraced into the mountainside and irrigated by a creek that flowed out of a cleft in the rock, fed by taller mountains to the south and east of them. The terrace grew all sorts of vegetables: squash, cucumbers, corn, pole beans climbing up to seven feet or more, shell peas, and potatoes in profusion, all in barrels lined up at the top of the field. The work to make those vegetables grow and keep them free from weeds was backbreaking.

They weren't the only ones doing it, of course. Among the 300+ people in the camp were a number of families with children, all of whom were put to work essentially the moment they could walk. Supervising those children, and keeping them from trampling what they were supposed to be weeding, was one of the worst of the jobs the twins were set to.

Fred also had jobs, but those were quite different. His military expertise sent him to the drilling ground in the central square, where he taught older teens and young couples basic military drills. Not marching in formation, but urban fighting—shooting from cover, working in teams, covering fire, and clearing broken ground. In the afternoons, he was sent on long hikes with small groups to teach them woodcraft and survival. He returned to their part of the camp late every night, so worn out he wasn't even in the mood for stories.

On Sundays, the work was much lighter. There was a church service in the morning—Bible verses and some preaching by a fellow that had done that work before—and leisure time in the afternoon when they finally had a minute to talk with one another about the camp.

Because it seemed perfectly normal. And also... not.

It wasn't that Cap was a dictator. He was definitely in charge, but it seemed that everyone was in charge of something, and Cap expected those people to do their jobs without a lot of management from him. Emily said that Cap had come out to the Farm but hadn't come to give orders.

"He said he heard that the beans were needing some extra weeding, so he came to lend a hand."

"And he just… weeded?"

She nodded. "He was pretty good at it, too, not that it's super hard or anything. But it was hot, and he was right in the sun. He didn't complain or whine about it, though he was sweating hard enough to water the whole tier. He just came out there, worked, and left."

"Did you talk to him at all?"

"I was weeding a different tier. But he came through, yeah, and said, 'Hey, Emily. You're doing great work. Make sure you drink a lot—it's super hot out here.' And then he went over and said something to Sarah, then Jacob, then Angelo. He knew all our names."

Ethan scratched his head. "Yeah—it was like that on wood detail, too, a couple days ago. The boss out there is Cammy and nobody better mess with her or she'll take your head off. But Cap came out and hauled wood with us, knew everyone's name, and didn't make a big deal out of any of it. Then he spent a minute with Cammy, just chatting and laughing, and that was it."

The Tuttle Twins and the Days of Darkness

Through this retelling, Fred kept silent, listening intently to the twins' reports. When they were finished, he still didn't say anything. Finally, Ethan said, "I mean, it's weird that it's so normal. I expected him to run the camp like a dictator, but he doesn't do that. So I think it's weird how totally not weird it is."

"There's a concept in the military called disciplined initiative." Fred sat on a stump, slowly whittling a piece of branch he'd found. Little curls of shavings danced down the shaft of the wood and drifted to his feet. The smell of woodsmoke was sharp against the woody dampness of the forest. "I have to be honest—most leaders in the military don't embrace it. Even fewer in the business world do. But the basic principle is simple and powerful."

He took the stick and drew a circle in the dirt. "This is the objective." He drew a line from the first circle to another one. "This is the unit. It could be an army or a platoon. It could even be a corporation. Now, it looks pretty simple, right? You go from here—" He pointed to the second circle. "—to here." He pointed to the first circle. "The problem is that it's never a straight line." He scribbled a series of wavy lines through the straight one. "Something always goes wrong."

"No plan survives contact with the enemy," Emily said. "I think a general said that."

"If he did, he was right," Fred said. "The enemy could be anything, too—weather, economic conditions, or even an actual enemy. Time. Entropy. Really *anything*. No plan ever works just the way you draw it up. And when it doesn't, the people on the front lines are the ones who know first. Then something in the plan has to change. But who changes it?" He looked up expectantly, and the twins knew right away they were back in class mode.

Emily said, "Well, whoever made the plan should change it. He's the one that knows what changes to make."

"Okay," Fred said. "So the information is obtained by the front lines, passed up the chain to the top, then back down the chain to the men in the field, right? But how long does that take?"

"Could be quite a while," Emily said. She saw right away what the problem was. "And in the meantime, things are changing again, and the people on the ground don't have any instructions."

Fred nodded. "Or worse, they keep trying to execute the original instructions even though the plan has moved on."

"Disaster."

"And yet that's the way most armies—and most companies—have been run for centuries. After World War II, with the non-standard, asymmetrical wars the US found itself in, the US decided to try something different." Fred paused for a moment as if he were waiting for one of them to take up the thread.

Ethan gave it a shot. "You still need a commander. Someone that sees the whole board. But then... you can give the next line of commanders some freedom to improvise. And the next line. And the next."

Fred's eyes twinkled. "What happens then?"

Ethan was thinking hard. "Well, some of it is pretty risky. A commander might make the wrong decision. He might put his men and the men of the units around him in more danger. But the risk is there anyway, and it's probably bigger if you try to micromanage him like a marionette puppet." Ethan took up a stick and began to draw circles.

"You break the army into small units. We already were doing that. But then you say, 'Fellows, we're going to take that hill over there. That's your objective. Do it however you have to.' Then when they hit the chaos in the middle, they have the freedom to respond as best they can, always keeping the main goal in mind."

All of his circles had squiggly lines drawn from them to the objective. "Then the chaos doesn't break the plan. It's flexible enough to allow individuals to take their own path."

Emily crouched down by the drawing. "If I were the objective, I'd be terrified of this. You have soldiers coming at you from all over and no way to tell how they're going to come after you. They could appear out of nowhere."

"That's precisely what happens," Fred said. "That's disciplined initiative. The army is a tool, a fine instrument—so good at what it does that it has to be used only for the most precise, most necessary objectives. Otherwise, you could create monstrous messes because make no mistake—if you order the army to take an objective, it will do it. But you might not like what happens afterward."

"How does this apply to the camp here?" Emily said, standing up and wiping her hands on her jeans.

"You tell me."

Ethan paced a little, inhaling the scent of burning wood. "First, people really like it when their bosses give them the freedom to make their own decisions. I know I do when Mom and Dad trust me enough to do that."

"Second," Emily said, "you can get things done a lot faster because the top leader doesn't have to be an expert at everything or control everything."

"Except—" Ethan said, "that's exactly the problem with where we are now. The power—I mean, the electricity—was concentrated, run by a central hub. It was easy to take down. We didn't use… whatever it was you called it… "

"Disciplined initiative," Fred supplied.

"Right. Disciplined initiative. We didn't let the individual power grids do their own thing. And here we are."

Cap's running of the camp made it a fairly pleasant place to be if you ignored that they were all sleeping in tents, had limited running water, rationed food, and had no individual communication with the outside world.

Although that was not precisely true. The radios ran almost all day and night. The two women—Squawk and Bern—kept a steady flow on the dials. The twins had been allowed to watch but not to take a turn on the set, not even on the one they brought.

For the first week or so, that didn't really bother them. They were new, after all, and needed to get integrated into the life of the camp. But their parents were still out there, and they wanted to do something to make it possible for Mom and Dad to find them or make it easier for them to get home. The only way to make that happen was to use the radio.

What were Bern and Squawk doing on the radio anyway?

When they got a chance to ask Amihan, she seemed quite willing to let them see.

"Why not? It's your radio, and you've clearly had experience with it. Honestly, I'm a little embarrassed I didn't ask for you to be in the rotation before now. You've done good work on the Farm and in the woods, so I think you've earned it."

That night after the general meeting—which they had to admit they had grown to like—Amihan pulled Cap close and whispered in his ear for a moment. The twins heard Cap say, "Okay by me. Do what you think is best."

Amihan smiled broadly at them and waved them toward the radio shack.

Sure enough, there were Squawk and Bern scrolling through channels, calling out to whoever was listening. Lit only by the soft glows of their radio sets, they sat back to back, each one with her own radio. Bern had a smaller set, maybe a Daimyo, something Emily didn't recognize. Squawk used the beautiful wood-paneled set of Fred's, a larger, obviously more powerful radio. They would call out, listen, sometimes say something back, sometimes not. Then they'd reach out, move the dial a notch or two, and do it again.

It became clear quite quickly that what they were doing was not random. There was some scanning, just listening, but when they dialed to specific bands, their calls were answered almost immediately. The twins couldn't hear what was being said because the two women had thick padded headphones on, but they could hear them broadcast—only what they said didn't sound much like English. Or, well, it *did*, but it didn't make any sense.

"Blue cows sixteen in the barn by nine o'clock." That was Bern on her radio.

"What sort of birds fly over your nest?" That was Squawk, squawking.

The twins looked at Amihan quizzically. She laughed quietly. "It's code, of course. There are people we talk to on a regular basis, other MAGs scattered around the region. We don't want to give anything away about us to someone else that might be listening. It's not like a phone call, after all. Anyone could hear."

"Ham radio transmissions are in the clear, I know that," Emily said. "But who would hear? And who would care?"

Amihan pointed to a map tacked to a sheet of plywood. The map at first looked as if someone had simply dropped a box of pins on it, but then Emily began to sort it out. Red pins, green pins, yellow pins, and some black pins—not very many of those—were all in a three-state radius. Out farther, in Minnesota, New Mexico, Utah, Nevada, and, she saw and swallowed hard, Oregon, there were other pins in blue.

"It's not very creative, I'll admit," Amihan said, bringing them over to look more closely at it. "Green, those are MAGs we know and have a relationship with. Yellow are the ones we believe to be friendly. Red are wild cards—we don't know what their true status is."

"And black?" Emily said.

"Ah. That's what I wanted to show you. The black ones are MAGs or other communities that have disappeared."

"Disappeared?" Ethan said, frowning. "How does a community disappear?"

Amihan shook her head. "You know the answer to that, Ethan. You lived in one. Your radio wasn't on this map—apparently, we were never on the same band at the same time—but if it had been, you'd be in black right now. People move. People run out of fuel for their generators and can't operate their radios. And… other things happen."

They just stared at her until she closed her eyes and came to a decision. "Okay. If you're going to be in this room, you should know. This one here," she pointed to a pin in eastern Pennsylvania, "was one of the MAGs we had a decent relationship with. Harv—you know, from the woods group—he had a brother there. We talked to them every night at the same time for two weeks. Things seemed quiet and peaceful—they're about 100 miles out from Philadelphia, and they thought they were safe."

"Safe from what?" Ethan said, his heart beating just a little bit faster.

Amihan's face hardened, but her eyes showed how painful it was to tell. "It was some sort of a gang. We don't know how many people, exactly, but quite a few. Hundreds, possibly. The MAG was located on a large farm. There were, oh, seventy-five to a hundred people there. Families. Kids. They were pretty well prepared, they thought. Well water, fuel storage, some wind power, lots of acreage for growing, and a good-sized herd of cattle. But they weren't careful. They transmitted stuff to us in the clear, told us what kinds of stores they had and what they needed. Ten or eleven days ago, their transmission was early, and the guy sounded nervous. Said some of their people were missing. Then we heard gunshots. The radioman must have kept his channel open right to the end. We heard a lot, and none of it was pleasant."

She looked off into the distance. Even though they were in the shed, she clearly was seeing something else. "I know about stuff like that. I saw it over in the Middle East. People going about their business and then bang. Gone. I saw us do it—not on purpose, but... panicked, sometimes. We never knew who was with us and who was trying to kill us. This, though, was some marauding gang. People get desperate, they do terrible things. And the eastern seaboard right now is pretty desperate."

"So, code," Ethan said very quietly.

"Code," Amihan said.

At about 11 p.m. there was a kind of break, and Bern put her headphones down, rubbed her eyes, and reached for her canteen. It was empty, not a slosh to be had. The air in the shed was close and stuffy, and she reached up and toggled two long slit vents open. Cool air drifted in, smelling of the forest. She sighed. Rotating in her chair, she said, "You guys are quite patient."

"We know how it works. You have to concentrate," Ethan said.

"I was studying your map," Emily said. "I noticed you have a couple of contacts in Oregon. That's where our parents are."

"Were," Ethan said.

"Were," Emily agreed, with a little shrug. "We don't precisely know where they are. But we know where they'll be listening for us if they can find a radio. We set up a time and a frequency for them to call. They have a code phrase, so we'll know it's them."

Bern stared at them with no discernible expression on her face. Emily had expected some reaction, but there was none or none that she could read.

Then Bern's arm snaked out and tapped Squawk on the shoulder, though her eyes never left the twins. Squawk shrugged it off. Bern tapped a little harder, then when that didn't get a reaction, she reached back, used a meaty palm to grab the blonde's head like a grapefruit, and turned it to the visitors.

Squawk ripped off her headphones and said, "What? I'm in the middle of something here."

Bern nodded at the twins. "These two tell me their parents are trying to work their way across the US, and they have a signal time and code so they can identify each other. That right?"

The twins nodded back.

"When were they supposed to call?"

Emily rubbed at her neck. It was very hot in there. "Nine thirty p.m."

"And what, exactly, would your code word be?"

"Um, it's a phrase. Li—"

"Wait." Squawk held up a hand. "Let me tell *you* what it is." She paused, and Emily noticed that her nails were very fine and pretty, even after a couple months of camping.

"It's Little Pink House, isn't it?" Squawk said.

The twins' mouths dropped open.

"I *knew* it!" Bern said.

"Hot dang," Squawk said. "You two are the key to our favorite mystery. I got a little carried away."

"Let me show you something," Bern said, getting up and coming over to the map. She pointed at the blue pins, like an exploded water balloon, across the country and into Canada and Mexico. "These are all the contacts we've made, or, well, most of them. All over the place. You asked about one in Oregon, and that got me thinking. Because we made a contact in Oregon five weeks ago that told us a story about a small group migrating east and asked us to keep a lookout for them. Unfortunately, we didn't get any details, and that contact went dark. That's this black pin here."

She moved her finger to another pin, an orange one, in northern Nevada. "Then, maybe a month later, at 9:30 p.m. we get a contact that refuses to identify itself but repeats 'Little Pink House' as its call sign. It does give a location but nothing else. We don't know that the location is legit, much less who it is. It was very cryptic. But we put a pin in the map anyway—orange, because… well, we had some orange pins and nothing to do with them."

She moved her finger again to Utah, but she didn't have to. By now, in the forest of blue, the twins could see a thread moving east, spaced out a couple hundred miles each time. If it hadn't been so dark, and the light mostly amber, they probably would have seen it before. Now, though, they couldn't miss it.

"Mom," Emily breathed.

"Dad," Ethan said just as quietly.

Then, as if they'd rehearsed it, they both turned and shouted, "What about tonight!? Anything?"

"Whoa, campers. No. In fact, we haven't heard from them in six days. Last contact was in Wyoming, outside of Cheyenne. But I can tell you your folks were alive and kicking six days ago on the Nebraska border."

The twins cheered and hugged each other, then hugged Amihan, who had watched the whole thing with wide smiling eyes, and then Bern and Squawk. They'd have hugged anyone if they'd shown up in the shack at that moment.

But six days. Anything could have happened in six days. And they were still one… two… three states away. Almost a thousand miles, or a little less. That was very, very far.

"We have to go get them," Emily said.

Amihan put a hand on her shoulder. "Whoa, camper. Not a good idea. They seem to be doing fine so far—that's a long distance they've covered, and they did it without you. You don't even know where they are at this point, only that they're somewhere in Nebraska, probably. As you can see on the map, Nebraska's a big place."

"But… they need help." Emily searched from face to face without finding the sympathy she was sure should be there.

"Don't we all," Amihan said.

Emily started to protest, but Amihan grabbed her by both shoulders and held her. "Hey. Look at me."

She didn't want to, but in the end, there was nowhere else to look.

"Your parents have made two-thirds of the journey already. They don't need more help than you do. Yeah, this place is fairly safe—fairly—but it may not stay that way, and every single person spends time trying to keep it together. That includes you, Emily. Everyone—*everyone*—is *this* close to the edge. You go out there after them, you're just adding one more body to the count of people who need saving."

Amihan scanned Emily's face, obviously trying to make sure she understood. "If your folks have made it that far, that means they know how to move and survive. Do you? You drove here in a truck, with two people you trust, to a place you could trust. It took, what, a couple hours? Do you know how to make it farther? What it's like out there?" She glanced at Bern. "You want to tell her?"

"I do not," Bern said.

"I want to know," Emily said.

"I seriously doubt that."

Amihan closed her eyes, and her face twisted. "Tell her anyway. Tell her as much as she can stand."

So Bern did.

There was no way to know precisely what had happened in many of the cities, but the ones they did know about all followed a similar pattern. The first few days were rough, as people's basic necessities ran out. Then things got extremely ugly. Fires. Riots. The power might have been out, but the guns worked just the same.

"Probably most people didn't go crazy. History says people help each other in crisis. They share and work together. But that didn't make food appear, or water. People died. A huge amount of people," Bern said. Her voice was pitched low, like a gentle murmur, which only made the horror of what she was saying that much worse.

"The big eastern cities—New York, Boston, Los Angeles, Chicago—they're gone. Probably ninety percent of the people there fled or are dead. 'Course, that means there are still a lot of people in the cities, doing whatever it is they do to survive. But the infrastructure and systems are gone. The medium-sized cities did better, some of them. Raleigh, I hear, is pretty good still. Charlotte burned. Atlanta had no real chance. Miami. But Orlando is still talking. Nashville. Some places will come back when the power comes on, if it ever does."

She bent over the map. Squawk's voice rolled out behind them as she went back to the radio, but the four others grouped together. It felt less horrible that way. Bern's fingers sketched out a route. "It looks like your folks have been loosely following the I-80. That runs from the east coast to the west. They picked it up somewhere in northern Nevada—Elko, maybe. Then they had a run of luck. Utah is intact, or at least that's what they tell us. Salt Lake had a couple days of rioting, but that settled, and they're making do. That's when the signal went from Nevada to Wyoming in no time at all."

Emily touched the pin in Wyoming, around Green River. Bern went on. "Wyoming wasn't all that dependent on electricity even before, and there are so many radios in that state it's like a springy metal forest. They were pretty regular through Wyoming. Nebraska, things will get tougher. Nebraska's huge. Corn's ripe, though, so they'll likely be eating. And there aren't any big cities in Nebraska until you get to Omaha, if that counts. Lots of beef cattle in Nebraska. Iowa, too, so I think they'll probably be okay through Iowa until Des Moines, which wasn't a place I ever wanted to be even when the power was *on*." Bern snickered.

"They won't come here," Emily said. "They'll go to the Little Pink House."

"Which is what?" Bern said.

"My grandmother's house on the Monongahela. Pennsylvania."

Bern made a thoughtful face. "How far from here?"

"Seven hundred miles. Maybe less."

She nodded. "Small town there?"

"The sprawling metropolis of Gnarled Oaks," Ethan said.

"Never heard of it."

"Exactly."

Bern blew out a long breath. "Well, that should be a good place, then. If they can get there. Point is, you can't help them. Leaving here is a terrible idea. You don't have resources to offer even if you knew where to find them. If by some miracle you did get together, you'd be another mouth to feed—or, probably two, since my guess is your brother would go with you."

Ethan didn't bother to answer. She could read his face well enough, even in this light.

"So. You two create a new problem when you get there. You can't take resources with you, not enough, anyway, so now your folks have two new mouths to feed and not a lot more help to figure out how to do it. *Think*, Emily. You're not stupid. If you were your parents, what would be your fondest wish for your kids right now?"

Emily struggled with that. The desire to be with her parents—to have *any* chance at all to be with them—was so strong it overwhelmed everything else for a moment. But Ethan put his hand on her shoulder, and Amihan put hers on the other, reassuring, not pushing.

She knew the answer. "To be safe. Cared for. Have enough to eat and nobody trying to kill them."

"And presto! Their wish is granted," Amihan said.

"I guess... I guess that's true."

"We still want to contact them, if we can. They'll give us a lot of information, but they're being cautious as well. If you don't have the countersign, they'll keep being mysterious," Ethan said.

"What's the countersign?" Amihan said.

Ethan started to tell her and then got a mischievous look in his eye. "I'll tell you. But they'll want to talk to us anyway, to make sure it's really on the level. So... if I tell you, can we get some radio duty? These two look like vampires being stuck inside all day."

Bern held up her arm. "Guilty," she said. "And I tan, too, so you know it's bad. We could use the help, Amihan, honestly."

Amihan considered for a moment, then nodded. "Okay. You two have proven yourselves reliable everywhere else. So, give. What's the countersign?"

Ethan smiled. "Big bad wolf."

The twins rotated into the radio shack every afternoon and evening after that. They heard from all kinds of places—Ft. Collins, Colorado, Portland, Maine (still doing pretty well, with access to the fish, though they had to do a lot more sailing than normal) Biloxi, Mississippi (hard times there, but they were used to it, they said)—but every 9:30 came and went with no response on the designated band.

They learned that Squawk had been a radio junkie since elementary school and had gone to college in communications only to find out that the kind of radio work she wanted to do, no college taught anymore. She dropped out and got work as a welder until the power went out.

Bern had been a college soccer star. She hadn't ever held a radio set until the power went out, but she had incredible stamina and could stay awake all night, sometimes more than one night in a row. And she got along well with Squawk, which not everyone did. Bern, it turned out, was the name her teammates had given her on the soccer pitch. What her actual name was, she did not volunteer, and when she was asked about it, she simply didn't hear the question.

Maybe it was because Ethan had spent so much time with his sister that he was accepted readily in what was essentially an all-female operation, but whatever the reason, he was the only male that ever operated the sets.

Emily and Ethan were never on the sets at the same time, but there was considerable overlap, and they saw each other at night and compared notes. Emily seemed happier, being able to at least try to find their folks, but Ethan never really believed she had totally bought into Bern's argument that their parents were perfectly capable of finding their own way.

A week went by. Two. Three. And finally, one night, Emily whispered, "Ethan, you awake?"

He hadn't been until she said something, but once she did, he was. "Uh, sure," he whispered back. Maybe this would be the chance to find out what was eating her. "What's... uh, what's wrong?"

"Everything. And, I mean, nothing. But also everything. Without Mom and Dad, everything's wrong."

"You're not still on about that, are you?" he said, though he knew she was. "You can't do anything—"

"I know what Bern said, and she's almost totally right, but I don't care."

"You... what? How can you not care?"

There was silence in the tent for a long while, then. Finally, Emily said, "I don't want to live here without Mom and Dad. I'd rather die trying to find them than stay here and be safe, and I know both of them would argue with me, but I also know they'd understand why I have to do this."

Ethan knew the tone of voice she used when her mind was made up. "What are you going to do?"

"I've already been hoarding some food. I don't have a lot, but I can fit probably three weeks' worth of dried stuff in my backpack. Water... it's too heavy. I'll have to trust to chance. We have those purifying tablets, anyway."

"This is stupid, Em. It's suicide."

"It's not. It's really not. I've done some prep work, too. With my time on the radio, I mean."

"*What!?*"

"Shhh. Keep your voice down. It's not like they'll let me keep working there if they know."

"You're cheating them on radio time?" Ethan was furious. His sister or not, a job was a job. You did it the best you could. You didn't cheat. That hurt everyone, yourself most of all.

"No. I'm not. I'm really not. I'm doing everything they assign and a little bit more. But I'm concentrating all my free bandwidth on towns between here and Cheyenne."

When he thought about it, that made sense. In fact, it was kind of ingenious. He was impressed. "Looking for Mom and Dad?"

"Well, yeah. Of course. But also looking for waystations. For, you know, for them, if we get them back on the radio. And… for me."

Ethan forced himself to count to ten before he said anything else. His heart was pounding. Was this thing possible? "You're building a trail."

"Yeah. At first, it was just a fantasy. Something to do to see if I could. But then I realized something. Bern was wrong about one thing. She said I couldn't do anything to help them. But I can. Now I can, anyway. I know how to get them home. I know where the safe places are."

Ethan heard the shuffling of a sleeping bag and the sound of crawling, then Emily was lying right next to him. "Ethan, *I can bring them in.*"

If you think Ethan should go with Emily, go to page 181.

If you think Emily is nuts and Ethan should stay at the MAG, go to page 70.

If you think Ethan should tell someone about Emily's plan, go to page 229.

"I don't want to starve. But I don't want to get shot or end up someone's slave or prisoner or whatever, either. I'm not feeling that bad. Just tired. I vote we keep going. We made some progress today. If we leave the river, who knows if we can ever get back?"

Ethan looked bleakly down the ribbon of road. Then he shrugged. "I can keep going," he said.

He was very nearly right.

But not quite.

And he might have been right altogether if, stumbling along in the dark, he hadn't put his foot right down on a ground-based hornet's nest.

At first, he couldn't understand what was happening to him. His leg burned right above the sock line. He scratched at it, and his skin *moved*.

Then there were things crawling up his arms, in his hair, buzzing in his ears. He swatted at them, but he might as well have been blowing on a thunderstorm to stop it from coming. In seconds, he had points of fire lit up all over his body. He cried out in pain and alarm and flailed about blindly, whacking and shouting and running… to nowhere. There was nowhere to run.

Emily first said, "Stop it, Ethan!" and then, "What is the *matter* with you?" and then, much more alarmed, "Ethan, *what*… Oh, no. Ethan, *run!*"

But the hornets knew where Ethan was and wouldn't quit harrying him. He ran smack into a tree

and wrenched his shoulder, but by now, his whole body was a welter of pain, and he staggered upright and crashed blindly through the forest, seeking some relief. Anything. But there was no relief.

Finally, in a panic, with nothing else to do, Emily tackled him into the river.

Frigid water hit him like a freight train. He screamed, but water filled his mouth, his ears, and ran down his throat. And the buzzing, the horrid, lethal buzzing, hardly let up at all. New lances of pain rippled through his body as the hornets, drowning, let all their fury go in one last assault on their tormentor.

Spluttering, gasping for air, Emily dragged Ethan to the surface, let him get a long breath, then pushed him back down. Her feet went out from underneath her, and she was under water herself, holding her brother beneath the surface lest the hornets find perch on his head and stay alive to continue their onslaught.

They were both being swept down the river. Ethan was dead weight in her arms. But then a new problem reared its ugly head—how could she get out of the water? How could she get *him* out? She was a strong swimmer, as Ethan was himself, but this was like nothing she'd ever attempted. The current was feral, a mad thing, dragging on her and on him while she tried, again and again, to force Ethan's head above water for him to breathe. She wasn't sure he was anymore.

With her other arm, she dragged at the night-dark water, trying to move them closer to shore. Her feet reached for the bottom but found nothing, nothing to push against, no help against the relentless flow.

Cold fingers gripped her arms and legs, robbing them of power. She pushed for the surface again, kicking out, lungs burning. She broke through, drew a ragged breath, and gagged as a wave broke over her face, choking her.

Then she lost her grip on Ethan.

One second he was there, a weight she struggled to support, and the next, he was torn from her numbing fingers, spinning off into the remorseless river.

"Ethan!" she cried out, reaching for him, for where she thought he was, but her fingers closed on nothing. It was all she could do to re-open them. Her eyes did her no good—less than no good—for the dark was total, above and below. She could see nothing, however desperately she searched.

With the last of her strength, choking, hacking up lungfuls of water, she kicked toward the shore, desperate to find some way to save her own life and then find her brother. He would float, surely. Would there be enough light to see him by? She could run along the bank, jump back in, and save him.

But it was useless. It took an eternity to reach a root, one of several jutting into the river from an enormous elm tree whose roots had been washed out by the ceaseless water. She clung to it with her arms, her hands uselessly claw-like, and vomited water back into the flow. "Ethan!" she called out again, but her voice did not carry five feet over the sound of the river. It was hopeless anyway. He could never hear her.

It was all she could do to pull herself to the bank and roll out of the tugging stream, utterly exhausted. River water mingled with tears as she lay there, lungs heaving, spitting muddy water, and coughing up what she'd breathed in. She should get up, run along, and search, but she could barely raise her head to look out over the black river.

She saw nothing but the rolling waves.

Then she saw nothing at all.

Emily never made it to Gnarled Oaks, nor did Ethan. Two years later, a group of backpacking scouts stumbled upon a skeleton propped against a tree. They reported it to the authorities, but they were unable to secure identification, and her case went into an enormous file of similar lost persons whose identities would never be known.

The scouts, though, had rummaged around the scene and found a note reading, "Find my brother Ethan. He's in the river."

That scout troop told the story over campfires until it became rather famous as a ghost story in the region. When the night is darkest, they say, if you listen to the river, you can hear the ragged coughing of a drowning boy and from the woods on the bank, the call of his sister, searching for him.

"Ethan! Ethan!"

THE END

"Thing is, we either find someone to help us, or we're going to lie down, go to sleep, and never get back up again," Emily said. "I hear starvation isn't a pleasant way to die."

The road offered no hints about which direction would be best to go. In both directions, the blacktop glittered in the moonlight, stretching away under a canopy of trees, and useless lampposts brooding over the road like long-forgotten statues.

"Okay, then," Ethan said. "We have to cross the river sometime; this is as good a time as any." Indeed, below them, streaming under the bridge, the river had been growing larger and wider for some time now, and it was no longer certain that they'd be able to wade across it at need.

But the far side of the bridge, the north, was the side Mort's thugs were on.

"I think we stay on this side and go south," Emily said. "I know the highway to Grandma's house is over there, but we don't have to get on it just yet. I'm much more comfortable heading away from where we've been."

"Evens and odds?" Ethan said.

"Sure."

The twins each put a hand behind their back, counted to three and then revealed their fingers to each other.

Ethan held out two fingers, Emily three. "Five. And you have the odd number. You win. South it is."

They lingered a moment at the bridge, listening to the water, then began to trudge down the road in Emily's chosen direction. By unspoken agreement, they chose to walk down the dotted line of the oncoming lane, side-by-side.

They said nothing. There was nothing to say.

But they were certainly making a lot better time than they had been in the woods, and that was comforting, though they didn't know where they were going. Nothing scratched at their shins or tugged at their clothing. In a few minutes, they'd left the river behind and were coming up a short rise to the top of a small hill.

At the top, they saw what looked like a town—a good-sized one—a mile or so down the road. It looked very much like the one Mort had been made king over. Only this one was profoundly dark, and there was no ice cream calling to them.

But that wasn't the most interesting thing. To the right, behind a chain-link fence with a barb-wire topper, was an airport.

There were no blinking lights or spotlights on the runway, no whirling radar dish on top of the traffic-control tower. But there was light. One of the hangars stood with open doors, and within it, a light shone, steady, yellow. Familiar but now also very strange. And rolling across the flat expanse of the airport was the unmistakable rumble of a generator.

It wasn't a big airport, much less a regional, two-runway hub where big jets could land; instead, it was a local airfield littered with prop planes and a few slightly larger aircraft, crowded like a rock concert with planes wing-to-wing from one end of the field to the other.

As they stood and contemplated this sight, something almost unimaginable happened—one of the planes began to roll. Slowly, but gaining speed swiftly, it rocked on its wheels, tried the air, bounced, and gained the breeze at last, roaring out over their heads, a great bird bound for... well, for who knew where?

"It's... open." Emily's voice was thick with wonder. It seemed a place of magic, of suddenly-animated relics of a bygone age, as if the Sphinx of Egypt had risen from the sand and gone wading in the Nile.

Hunger momentarily forgotten, the twins searched for a way in. The fence was well maintained and offered no gaps through which they might squeeze, so they followed the perimeter, wading through unmown grass until they came at last to a small concrete road that led to a gate. It was shut, chained, but there was a hut just behind the fence and a man sitting in it, a tiny light reflecting off something so that they could see his face. He was reading a book, another thing that seemed to belong to the distant past.

He hadn't seen them, but the shack door was open, and when Ethan called out, he looked up, set down the book, and came out. He was young, their age or a little older, in a rumpled beige uniform. Three-day scruff clung to his face like moss on a rock. He shined a light in their faces and said, "Who are you?"

"I'm Emily, and this is Ethan. We're from Spoonerville." What else was there to say? We were attacked in the woods by a bear because we were running away from the men that stole our truck that we were using to try to get to Grandma's in Gnarled Oaks because everywhere else there's nothing and no one, and we don't want to die?

They thought he wouldn't want to hear that as an introduction and also probably didn't need to. Whatever their story, it had to be spectacular for two teenagers to be standing outside a tiny airfield at whatever unholy hour of the morning it was.

"You can't come in," he said. "Flyers only."

"What about if I offered you a million dollars?" Ethan said.

They couldn't see his face because of the light shining at them, but the light wavered, and his voice gained humanity. "*Are* you offering me a million dollars?"

"No," Ethan said.

He clicked off the light and made to go back into the shack.

The Tuttle Twins and the Days of Darkness

"Listen, I'm sorry we're bothering you, but we were attacked by a bear, and we really need someplace to go," Emily said, taking a step forward and hooking her fingers through the fence.

With the light off, they could see a bit of his features in the moonlight. He looked skeptical, the best she could determine. "Is this another thing like the million dollars?"

"No, this is for real."

"A bear."

She nodded. What did she look like after two days in the wild? Stringy hair, dirty, surely he could smell her from twenty feet away. She should have dipped herself in the river, at least.

He was taller than she was, taller than Ethan. He had curly hair. He stood a moment in indecision, then clicked on the light again and shone it over them like radar. "Where's your gear? You just out for a stroll?"

"It's… a long story."

"I bet it is."

Other than begin blurting out everything that had happened to them since *Before*, there wasn't anything else she could think of to say. So Mom's training in manners kicked in. "Please," she said. "Please help us."

He told them later he hadn't been going to let them in until she said that. But he had a mother, too, and his training was just as hard to shake. They were teenagers. Kids like him. They had nothing but what they were wearing. He really wanted to hear more about the bear. And she had said the magic word. Also, she was pretty, not to mention.

So he reached for his belt, and they heard the jingle of keys. He clicked one into the padlock, unstrung the chain, and pulled on the gate. It rolled with a gentle squeak and made a gap. They walked through it and stood by the shack while he repeated the whole process in reverse.

Emily glanced into the hut. He had been reading *Speaker for the Dead* by Orson Scott Card. She knew that book. She liked that book. She thought that someone who was reading that book was a potential friend.

When he was finished, he stood uncertainly, looking at them as if he didn't quite know what to do.

Emily pointed to herself. "Emily Tuttle," she said. "This is my brother Ethan. We're from Spoonerville. We were robbed at Accord Landing and left with only our backpacks. The bear took the rest this afternoon. We've walked, um, a long way. We're very tired, and what you see is all we have." She paused for a moment. "We're *utlänning*."

His eyebrows went up, recognizing the strange word from the science fiction book he had been reading. It meant: *a humanoid from another land*. "You look like a *främling* for the moment." (A humanoid stranger from another planet.) Then a smile tugged at the corner of his mouth.

"I'm Alton Faraday," he said, removing his hat. "I'm from... right here. My mother runs the airfield. She's Rachel McKeen Faraday—" He paused for a second as if he was expecting recognition of this name. When he didn't get it, he went on. "And I guess that's where we ought to go right now."

His hand jerked as if he thought of offering it to them, but he didn't and instead walked past them and up the blacktop toward a long, low building with some lettering on the side that was probably quite visible in the daylight. They crossed a parking lot surprisingly full of cars and entered the structure through a set of glass doors that stood wide and, possibly permanently, open. They had been automatic—*Before*.

"*Utlänning?*" Ethan said.

"It's from the Ender's Saga. I told you those books were great."

They entered an airport terminal. Two counters stood to their left, dark, with the logos of airlines behind them, a couple of which the twins had never seen before. To the right was a waiting area with benches that had been pushed to the wall creating an open space in the middle. That open space was filled with cots. The cots were filled with bodies.

Small ones, big ones, female and male ones, all sorts and types. Each cot was ringed about with backpacks and, in some cases, even small bookshelves, like office cubicles with the walls removed. Here and there, a head popped up as they came across the once-shiny polished stone floor, but those flopped back down right away.

Alton turned and headed for the wall behind the airline counters. Two heavy doors there had been propped open, and he led them through into the guts of the terminal. Neither of the twins had seen this part of an airport before.

The first thing they noticed was that it was lit. The lighting was spotty but bright in the patches where LEDs had been rigged to hang over desks and tables, most of them cluttered with paper, most of them unattended. The odor of machine oil hung over everything. It was warmer here than it had been outside, and without air conditioning, the twins guessed it would be pretty hot in the daytime.

Toward the back of the sea of baggage conveyor belts and wiring was a brighter area where a few people sat around a table. A woman, tallish, muscled, with dirty-blond hair swept back into a bun, stood leaning over a map spread out before her. Her hands were stained with grease. As they approached, she looked up. Emily immediately thought this was the most tired person she'd ever seen in her life.

But then she spoke, and her voice was strong and steady. "Alton, who have we here?"

They threaded their way between a pile of luggage and a stack of plastic chairs and came into the lighted circle. "This is Ethan and, um, Emily Tuttle. They're from Spoonerville."

"Did they walk here?" Her voice was flat, and something about it said that it would be a good idea to get to the point quickly.

Alton apparently heard that as well. "No. Well, yes. Part of the way. They had a truck, but they were ambushed in Accord."

Faraday—Emily could not think of her as Rachel—turned that piercing gaze on them. Her eyes were very blue and showed no readable emotion. "Accord? You walked from Accord?"

"Along the river, yes," Ethan said.

She looked him up and down. "Fell in, did you?"

"No, ma'am," he said. She looked like she was used to being called ma'am. "I hid in the river from some people trying to kill us."

Alton's head jerked around at that. His mother didn't notice or didn't care. "Now you have people trying to kill you. For your belongings?"

"We, uh, don't have any. The bear took what we had left."

There was a kind of explosive sound from the four other people in the circle, and just for a second, Emily saw something flash through Faraday's eyes that might have been surprise and... interest?

But she said nothing for several heartbeats, and Emily wondered if she was going to throw them back out in the night as liars.

"If I put you in one of my very, very precious cots, and you are not asleep in two minutes, I will have you pitched from the roof of the control tower. If you move from those cots before the sun is up, I will have you pitched from the control tower. If you are found anywhere—*anywhere*—except those cots, on my airfield before I have given you express permission to move..." She did not have to finish the sentence.

"Ma'am, I think we can promise you'll have no trouble from us," Emily said. "As long as we can get a drink of water and one bite of something that isn't beef jerky before we lie down."

Faraday nodded slowly as if she were thinking hard about it all the way down and back up again.

Alton took that as a dismissal. "Come on," he said and led them back the way they had come. In the main area, there were a few cots in the corner of the grid that had no one sleeping on them. Alton pointed to two of them and said, "This is you. I'm still on shift, so I'm going back to work. I'll see you in the morning."

"Water?" Emily said.

"Oh, right! I'll be right back." He marched off toward a different part of the building and left the twins to figure things out—which wasn't difficult. Each cot was olive drab canvas, standard military issue, with a small pillow and a blanket of rough wool. Emily tested hers and found it sturdy, and very comfortable, but it didn't have to be. She could feel sleep sucking at her the moment she sat down on it. But she held out until Alton came hustling back with two bottles of water and two bowls of something that smelled like chili. It was thick and rich with beans and meat. Ethan's stomach growled so loudly he couldn't believe no one woke up nearby.

"Thanks," Emily said, with the best smile she could manage through her exhaustion.

"It's okay," Alton said. "Now I gotta get back." He trotted off toward the front doors again. Emily watched him go until he was out of sight. She turned back to find that Ethan had wolfed down his entire bowl of chili and bolted his liter of water. Her lips pursed.

"I was hungry, okay?" Ethan said, already lying down. "This will do. I wonder what time they get up around here."

"Doesn't matter," Emily said, "We were ordered not to leave. That's one order I intend to obey to the letter."

Neither of them could remember going to sleep— one minute, they were awake, and the next, they were dead to the world. And they stayed that way, too, despite a strange place, strange bed, and strange noises around them. They slept on, unmoving, right through the general awakening around them and into the morning.

When they finally *did* awaken, the skylights above them showed the sun well up into a blue sky with no clouds. Around them, the cot city was empty, not a soul in the place.

Ethan got up first, stretched, and took in the parts of the scene that were too dark the night before. The gates—there were only four—that embarked passengers were linked by a concourse now stuffed full of boxes. Most of them looked to be food boxes, judging from the labeling on the sides. All the walking room on the wide concourse was reduced to a tiny aisle between the boxes, narrow enough that he thought he might have to turn sideways to negotiate. The signboard on Gate A read, *Destination: Toronto.* Ethan wondered if that plane had ever taken off.

Behind him, Emily rolled over and sat up. Her hair was matted to her head, and her face was grooved by the pattern of the pillow. "What time is it?" she said.

He shrugged. "Mid-morning, maybe? I don't know."

"I would love some breakfast."

"If searching for it wouldn't get us thrown off the tower, I'd go get you some."

But neither of them doubted for a second that violating the terms of their acceptance would result in expulsion. Faraday had about her the air of the unquestioned commander, and they knew she would do precisely what she said.

They hadn't long to wait before finding out, either, because a few moments later, a different woman, but of a more advanced age, came across the cot-strewn floor to greet them. Though her hair was iron-gray and her face lined like the side of an ancient mountain, she was spry and moved like a cat.

"Welcome, Tuttles!" she said when about halfway across the floor. Her voice echoed in the space. "I bet you're hungry."

This was so different from the reception the night before that it took them a moment to process it. "Uh, yes. We are," Emily finally said.

She stopped a few paces away, a bright smile on her face. She was dressed simply, in canvas pants and an olive-drab top that did not bear military insignia or the bars for meritorious service, though it gave off the distinct impression that it might once have. A pair of leather gloves were tucked into her belt, and she wore sturdy boots, dusty with work.

"Get your shoes on and come with me, then," she said. While they complied, she said, "You've probably got a million questions—we do, too—but first off, my name's Emily, Emily Faraday, but everyone calls me Aunt Me. And before you ask, yes, Commander Faraday is my daughter."

"Commander?" Ethan said, lacing up his shoes.

"It's not just an honorary title—she used to be a wing commander in the Civil Air Patrol, though that was a while back. She retired to run this airfield, but things kind of got out of hand."

That brought up more questions than it answered, Ethan thought. But he supposed there would be answers supplied at some point. Right now, he wanted breakfast, and unless his nose deceived him, there was bacon frying somewhere close.

Aunt Me smiled even bigger. "Smell that, do ya? I suppose it's been a minute since you had bacon."

"Thousands of minutes," Emily said, standing. "Not since four or five days after…"

"After, huh? We call it the Event, although it's not really an event. More of a long series of events. But that's not my story to tell." She waved at them to follow her and went toward a set of doors in the rear wall, doors that had once been marked for authorized personnel only. "Don't worry," she said. "We're all authorized now."

When she reached them, she pushed the crash bar, and the light was blinding. They led straight out onto the tarmac.

There were airplanes there, yes, but there were also rows of plastic folding tables and bench seats pulled up to them. A few people were there eating, down at the far end by what looked like a barrel sawn in half to make a grill. One of the people there was Alton, dressed exactly as he had been the night before. He didn't wave at them, but he did watch them with more than a little curiosity. Ethan thought he watched Emily more closely than himself, but that might have been his imagination. Ethan was, after all, distracted by the bacon.

And eggs. And hash browns.

It was, indeed, a grill or, at the moment, a huge griddle. Behind it stood a tall, heavy man with a neatly trimmed beard and his sleeves rolled up, holding a spatula in each meaty hand. He wielded them like an artist wields a paintbrush. A mound of hash, all of the contents of the griddle mixed together, appeared at the side of the grill. He scooped half into one bowl and half into another and held them out to the twins.

"I'm Bobby," he said. "And this is the best food you've ever eaten."

Neither of the twins was in any mood to dispute that. Frankly, it could have been a bowl of gravel—if it was soft enough to eat, they'd have happily downed every bite. But it actually *was* the best. The hash was crispy and perfectly seasoned, the bacon was flavorful, and the eggs cooked just right.

They were finished in less than a minute.

Bobby laughed out loud, booming off the side of the airfield building and surrounding hangars. "Guess you were on the road a while. That's okay. Come get a little more."

The twins slowed down about halfway through the second batch, long enough to pay attention to the rest of the people at the table. Aunt Me, of course, and Alton, but there were two others as well—one they knew and one they didn't.

Commander Faraday sat at the end of the table, leaning back with a baseball cap over her face and calling absolutely no attention to herself. Across from her was a man with piercing green eyes and a face as thin as the blade of a hatchet. He was about their parents' age, sporting a shock of graying hair cut short on the sides. His shirt bore a nametag that read *Exeter*.

"Tuttles," the Commander said, "now that you've sampled our hospitality, I want you to meet Captain Exeter from the Pittsburgh airfield. He just happens to be in town, and since his wing is responsible for the Spoonerville and Malantown area, I hoped you could give him some intel."

"What do you want to know?" Emily said, scraping her bowl and licking her fingers. "Not that we know that much."

Exeter spoke with a voice like a road grader. "Situation. Spoonerville looks quiet, but we haven't done overflights in a while. Malantown... well, nothing would surprise me there."

"It's bad there, I think," Ethan said, shoving his empty bowl to the middle of the table. "We saw a lot of fires from the top of the hill. I think the refinery on the water is still intact, though."

"Spoonerville is fine if you like being locked up in government facilities," Emily said. "We were hoping to avoid that." She looked around at the people and the buildings and swallowed. "We have avoided that, right?"

Bobby boomed out another laugh, which earned him a look from Faraday. He put up his hands. "All right, all right. I'll get washed up."

"You *have* avoided that," Faraday said. "Though there are still things to be decided. For now, you are free to go at any time. As long as you're here, though, you'll work, so come back when you've helped Bobby with the washing up for breakfast."

That took a little while because the huge griddle had to be scoured and replaced, but water gushed from the taps and was collected in a huge tank, and the concept of running water was delightful. Bobby was good companionship—he was the chef at the cafe in the airfield terminal when the Event occurred—and he'd been with Faraday for years.

"All you need to know is that she's a woman of sense and integrity. But you'll see that right away."

Back at the table, Faraday took a deep breath and started. "First, I need to know your story. From the Event or a little before, and don't leave anything out. If it's not important, I'll stop you, and we can fast forward. Okay?"

The twins told her everything they remembered about their parents—Faraday's eyebrows went up when they told her about their ham radio—about being robbed on the road, chased to the river, attacked by the bear, all of it. She listened intently, and Ethan wouldn't have been surprised if she was able to repeat back to them every word.

When they were finished, she sat back in her chair and tapped her lips with a pencil. "Thank you for the thorough account. We had heard there was trouble in Accord Landing, but this makes that a no-go zone. If they're going to chase you, they're getting big for their britches. We might have to do something about that."

She tipped back forward and looked at each of the twins in turn. "Now, a little about us. I'm Rachel Faraday, and this is my airfield. We remain open and operational because I thought something like the Event might happen, and I've been preparing stocks of fuel and generators and other things for about ten years now. There's a network of like-minded operators at various airfields around the region—around the country, really—and we share resources. It keeps a little power on, and it keeps us in the know."

From behind her, a group of four teenagers in grubby overalls came around the edge of the building but stopped short when they saw the twins in conference with the boss. Faraday swiveled her head and saw them.

"Come on over, you four. You might as well meet our guests. Though they haven't said they'd stay."

The teens accepted the invitation and stood in a loose group around Faraday. "These are my garden workers, and they were hoping to add you to their numbers fairly soon. I'm going to have to disappoint them—" She saw their faces and smiled a little. "—though not too badly, I hope. These two," she said, indicating the twins, "have radio skills I can use. But they'll be yours half-time if they're willing. That do you?"

The teens said it would and waved as they moved off.

"What is the situation for the rest of the country?" Ethan said. "We don't know very much."

Faraday grimaced, a look that was echoed and amplified by Exeter and Alton. "It's bad, I won't lie to you. Pretty nearly everything in our world runs on electricity. We're gravity-fed here for plumbing, so we have facilities of a sort—no hot showers, sorry—and we have generators that can feed a lot of power if we need them. Of course, they suck fuel like the government sucks tax money, so we have to ration, even though we have quite a store of various kinds of fuels—enough to last...well, quite a while," she said, obviously not wanting to give too much away.

"The big cities are mostly a disaster area, and that goes for all of them. With no power to run their pumps, they went into meltdown weeks ago. None of those airports are usable. Most of the pilots who flew there bugged out for Canada or Mexico, or Europe, where they still have power. A good number of the rest headed for smaller fields like this one. We can't take a big jet—nothing larger than a 727—so we don't have them here, but we visit places that do."

"Our parents are out there," Ethan said, staring hard at the table so he didn't have to meet anyone's eyes. "They're trying to get back to us."

"On the roads?" Exeter said. He shook his head vigorously. "Not much chance of that. Nothing moves out there, at least nothing good. The roads themselves are mostly fine, but they're watched, and the people watching them are not the kind you want to mess with."

"We messed with them," Ethan said. "We know."

"We wanted to wait for our folks, but the alternative was for us to go to our grandma's place in Gnarled Oaks," Emily said. "That's what we were trying to do when we got bushwhacked in Accord."

"Yeah. Accord," Faraday said. "That's a topic for consideration a bit later today, I think. Given what these two have told me, we might need to act sooner than we thought."

Faraday stood up and stretched out her back. "For now, though, let's get you two situated for the day. I know we're going to have to have a longer chat about whether you're staying permanently or not, but I can't spare any more time, and you're in no condition to be out in the wild again. Spend a couple days here with us, and you'll have more reserves and a better idea of whether you want to move on."

She shaded her eyes and swept them over the airfield. "Let's split you two up. Emily, right? You'll go with Alton to the radio room. Ethan, you're with me."

Without another word, she marched off in the direction the teenagers had gone. It was as if she expected to be obeyed whenever she gave an order. And come to think of it, she probably was. Ethan wasn't going to be defiant, that was for sure.

When he looked back, Alton and Emily were headed for the control tower. Faraday led Ethan to a wide, flat dirt field where furrows had been dragged, and a gang of mostly young people were hard at work with various garden tools.

"I hope you know your way around a garden," Faraday said.

"I do, but I'm best with bees," Ethan said.

Faraday pursed her lips. "No bees at the moment. But I'll let you know if they come in. Meanwhile, present yourself to Rachel over there." She pointed to a short, black-haired girl who couldn't have been more than twelve. "She's the head honcho on this project."

She waved, and Rachel waved back, beckoning Ethan over.

Thus began four days of almost totally unrelenting work. At roughly sunup, the twins rose from their cots with the bulk of everyone else and went to whatever work was on offer that day. The "farm" was only one part of a massive operation that kept about three hundred people busy from morning until night.

Much more interesting was the radio work, which the twins took shifts at. The radios were all located in the control tower for maximum range, and they made good use of it. News came in from all over the east during the day and, via shortwave, everywhere else at night. They even checked in with Fred a couple of times. Adding to that, every day, two or three airplanes would come in, and some from Faraday Field—as everyone called it—would take off for various points of interest, carrying goods from Faraday and returning from Massachusetts, Virginia, Florida, Louisiana—anywhere that had a field that was part of the network.

The news was not good, not in any way at all. Because of the emergency, the federal government had declared martial law and suspended the Constitution—things Fred had predicted—but their ability to enforce their commands was so limited most people simply forgot they were there. State governments had essentially no authority—but some of them (Texas, South Dakota, Utah) had prepared better than others and had some limited structure in place to keep the worst of outcomes at bay. None of them were doing well. But some of them were so bad no one wanted to talk about it.

There hadn't been any reliable news from New York City since ten days after the Event.

Most towns were on their own and functioned more or less how they chose since transportation was at a standstill and communications were not much better. Fuel stocks were running out, as refineries were unable to ship product and could not receive new crude for refining. Whatever had been in the system was still there, but it couldn't move.

"We'll be fine this year," Faraday said. "We'll see what next year brings."

"This country was prepared for the wrong things," Ethan said one day, tearing off his headphones and rubbing his eyes. He was always tired these days. "We had food stored but no way to move it. We had emergency plans in place that all depended on electronic communications. We had alternative energy sources but no way to coordinate their distribution or hook them to the grid. If we had *tried* to make a system that would be totally useless when the grid failed, we couldn't have done any better than this!"

Faraday, who was almost never in the tower, carried over a cup of water and handed it to him. "Don't be too hard on us," she said. "We're only human. It's hard for us to imagine anything much out of the ordinary. Disasters always catch us by surprise even though we know they'll be coming."

"*You* weren't caught by surprise," Ethan said. He sipped at the water. It was metallic but cool and good.

"Actually, I was, kind of like everyone. I didn't know what to prepare for, so I tried to prepare for the worst possible thing, which I thought would be a coronal mass ejection from the sun. That would also have fried the grid, but it would have grounded almost all our airplanes, too. I spent a lot of money on a hardened hangar for a few planes to be protected from something like that. In retrospect, I should have used that money for another fuel storage tank." She shrugged. "You can't know."

Below them, a twin-engine Cessna rolled to a stop, and four people got out. They saluted and disappeared. Ethan heard the access door at the base of the tower squeak open and bang shut, and a minute or so later, two of the crew, a man and a woman Ethan knew as Ace and Deuce, reached the top of the stairs.

"Reporting, Cap'n," Deuce said. She was a hotshot pilot and looked the part right down to the jacket and aviator shades.

"Let's hear it."

"Not much doing in Accord. The gas station is still operating, but there isn't any traffic on the road. Mort is going to have to change up his tactics."

Faraday frowned. "That's not likely to be good for us."

"No, ma'am," Deuce said. "Also, there's no sign of their fleet of cars, though we know they have fuel. Nothing is moving. Maybe we should try tonight."

"No point to that," Faraday said, blowing out a breath. "They can hear us flying overhead, and know we can see them. They'll only move when they know we're not in the sky, and we can't afford to keep eyes up around the clock. Anything else?"

"We went as far as Grover's Corners," Ace said, leaning on the wall, "and there's a lot of smoke on the horizon in the neighborhood of Pittsburgh."

Ethan swiveled his chair. "Grover's Corners? Did you fly over Gnarled Oaks?"

"Negative," Ace said. "We came in from the east and crossed to the west, not down the river. Sorry. No news for you."

He swiveled back before he let his face show his disappointment.

Deuce cut in. "Thing is, ma'am, with nothing moving on the roads and no tractor or farm work getting done, Accord has no choice. They have to get supplies from somewhere."

"And we're that somewhere. Yeah. I get it." Faraday closed her eyes tightly and ran a hand over her tightly bound hair. "Well, we knew it would come to this. There are good people in Accord Landing. Not all of them will be with Mort. And if we wait any longer, we'll be fighting him on our ground, where we can't afford to lose an inch."

She turned to the lead radioman. "Hit the bell, Mac," she said. "Three bongs. Let's get the people together before it gets dark."

Everyone assembled just outside the doors that led to the Bedroom, as everyone called it. From a stack of crates, Faraday addressed the group, her words echoing off the concrete of the terminal. Maybe before, she'd have needed a microphone to speak to this many people. But not now.

"I won't insult you by pretending you don't know what this is about," she began. "I know how the grapevine works, and I know it's been buzzing, so let me just get to the heart of it—we're going to war. At least, I think we should, and I'm asking you to come with me."

This brought a murmur through the crowd, everyone commenting quietly to their neighbor. But no one seemed surprised. Faraday knew her people well.

"Accord Landing. Some of you are from there, and you're acquainted with a nasty piece of work by the name of Mort. Runs a gas station. He was quick on his feet when the Event happened, and he managed to take a lot of important resources for himself, especially the farm boys from the edge of town, who make up most of the region championship football team. He had weapons, and he had men, and he had fuel. That was enough for him to take over the town."

Silence. Most people knew this, Ethan thought, looking at the faces, but it was the way Faraday said it that commanded their attention.

"They could have made something work there by labor and trade, but they didn't decide to do that. Instead, they made their way by raiding. The last man standing was Buck Herdman on his ranch, but last night his place was afire."

This brought some shouts of "No!" from the group, and Faraday held up a hand. "Before you ask, we don't know what happened to Buck or Belle or any of the hands. We couldn't land there. Maybe they got out and fired the house themselves—that's a thing Buck might do. But what we do know is that all the easy pickings are gone now, and Mort isn't the kind to start begging. He'll be looking for richer targets now. And the one on his doorstep is Faraday Field. There's not much left in Crockton—nearly everyone that isn't here has gone to the state camp at Roxbury Point. And he'll never attack that. So it's us or starve, and he'll never starve without a fight."

Murmuring, but not much. Again, the rumor mill had already worked this out.

"We have a choice. We can let him come, hoping we can figure out how to guard almost six miles of fence line, maybe keeping eyes in the sky and burning through our fuel reserves. But we don't know when he'll come, only that he will. Or we can go get him. We know where he is, as sure as he knows where we are. Our fighting forces and his are probably a close match-up. Whichever side gets in the first blow will probably win the fight."

Alarm bells went off in Ethan's head. He turned to see if he could find Emily, but her blonde head wasn't anywhere he could see it. Then there was a tap on his shoulder, and there she was behind him. She kept her eyes locked on Faraday but whispered in his ear. "Sound familiar?"

"Very," Ethan said.

And it did. History was filled with leaders that thought the way to secure their people was to make sure they killed their enemies first. The thing was, it made sense. They'd met Mort themselves. They were certain he wouldn't hesitate to kill them if he got the chance—his thugs had taken shots at them, even. Given their limited but memorable interaction with him, they could easily imagine him attacking this place, and Faraday was right—if he did, the damage could be catastrophic. They were "doing fine" here at the moment, but it was all built on the frailest of structures. Take out any of them—the water line, the fuel reserve, even the rows of corn on the farm that would be made into precious new fuel in the late summer—take any of that away, and this place would collapse.

Not for the first time—or the last—Ethan marveled that such a solid-seeming thing as civilization rested on such flimsy foundations. Power—something you couldn't even *see* when you looked, ran everything that held it up. Satellites cruised by overhead, ready to send signals, but they couldn't. Water ran in rivers, ready to be pumped, but the pumps were silent. Communication. Travel. Supply. Production. *Everything*.

And now, with the power out, all but the most basic of necessities were simply gone. Those necessities rested on an even more tenuous platform. Take away anything else, and what then?

So protecting it was critical.

But—history also showed that defenders had a huge advantage. They knew the terrain, they had positions set up, and they were fighting for their own territory, homes, and families. No matter how complete the surprise, an attack needed miracles to be successful without massive casualties. And that, also, Faraday Field could not afford. They barely had enough hands to work the place right now.

Faraday spoke for another few minutes. Emily had to admit, she was good. She didn't whip them into a frenzy. She didn't preach hatred. This was simply something they had to do, and she expected everyone to do their part.

One thing was certain—Faraday Field was with its commander. Faces gazed actively on the Captain, resolute and firm. When she ordered them to go, they would go.

But would the twins?

When Faraday finished, she sent everyone back to their jobs but promised they'd have a communal meal that night, a party before the battle planning began.

"We'll talk then," Emily said and disappeared back to the farm.

That night, Ethan found Emily as they were queueing up for Bobby's excellent chow. He jerked his head at her, and she nodded. They made their way to the cornfield. The corn wasn't tall enough to hide them, but there was something comforting about the gentle rustling of the green leaves and the sense of growing things.

They stood together without speaking for a minute or two. Sunshine baked down on them, but it felt good, and the breeze was strong. They didn't even notice the smell of jet fuel anymore, or maybe the fragrance of the plants on the farm was strong enough to mask it. At any rate, it smelled like wholesome goodness and summer. Ethan took the blade of a cornstalk in his fingers and ran them over the ridges.

"We can't stay," Emily said. "We'd have to fight."

"We can't go," Ethan said. "We'd have to run like cowards."

They smiled at one another, a tired, rueful smile.

"Glad that's decided."

If you think the twins should stay at Faraday, go to page 269.

If you think the twins should leave, go to page 213.

What was there to choose, after all? Grandma's was the obvious choice. The biggest threat to their well-being? Lack of water. Secondarily, bad people trying to do bad things to them. Neither of those things would be a problem in Gnarled Oaks. People in that town would band together—the twins had seen it before. Grandma would be only too glad to see them, and she could use the help. The river would make travel a lot easier. Fishing provided protein, the Monongahela provided water, and the whole family provided protection.

Could they make it, though? Yes, they'd driven quite a bit with Mom and Dad, learning and practicing until both of them were pretty sure there wasn't a lot they couldn't handle behind the wheel of a car. But they never *had* handled it. On their own, who knew what troubles they'd face in the 700-plus miles to the Little Pink House?

Fred saw that their decision was made. He didn't try to stop them. In fact, he said, "You'll want to take the truck. It belongs to your dad anyway."

"No way, Fred!" Ethan said. "We can't take that! You need it."

Fred shook his head. "Not very much. I have my little car, and your minivan can handle any bigger loads I might need. You take your dad's truck. Esmerelda... she's old, but that means she's built tough and more easily repaired by hand." He put on a wan smile.

"The truck *would* be more practical," Emily said. "If we have to off-road and stuff. You know Esmerelda can do it."

"We've never driven Dad's truck, though," Ethan said. He got up and went to the stairs as if he were impatient to be gone. "That will make it weird."

"Everything's weird now," Fred said, getting up to join him. "Let's get you packed. You won't want to drive at night if you can avoid it. Your headlights would be the only light on the landscape, alerting every bandit in the midwest to your location. Too easy for someone to… set up a trap or something. We'll have to get map photos for you. Or even better, paper maps."

"We know the way pretty well," Ethan said.

"But you'll almost certainly have to find alternate routes. Maybe the freeway is open all the way to Gnarled Oaks, but I wouldn't count on it. If you need to detour, you need a map. We'll have to go back to Ezzy's. She'll have good maps."

Now that the decision was made, the twins couldn't wait to get their gear together and get on the road. It was getting late, so they planned to pack all that night and head out on the road the next morning very early.

"Bad guys don't like mornings," Fred said. "4 a.m. to 6 a.m. is about the safest time there is."

They packed water in big five-gallon jugs, two of them. Extra fuel was siphoned out of Fred's big tank and into a pair of red, three-gallon plastic containers. They filled the tank, too, of course. Then food—they took almost all the snacks that remained. "We're teenagers. We can live on snacks," Ethan said. "For a day, anyway. It's not that long a trip."

Some beef jerky from Fred's storehouse went into the cab, along with a change of clothes. They packed suitcases, taking along everything they thought they couldn't live without since there was no guarantee they'd ever come back here.

And Fred loaded a shotgun and two pistols, laying them on the seat of the cab. "You won't have to use these, but I know you each know how, just in case."

Before it got too late, they took the truck down to Ezzy's. There was no line this time, just a makeshift sign that read *We got no gas. Keep driving.*

They pounded on the door for a few minutes. Then Fred went around the back, hands in the air, walking slowly—Ezzy looked like the type that spooked fairly easily—and after a few minutes, a shadow passed behind one of the frosted windows, and there was Ezzy, looking seriously displeased. When she heard what they wanted, she got even more disgruntled, but in the end, Fred slid her $50, and she said, "Five minutes. That's all you get. Every second someone else is in here, I'm compromised."

How she would be compromised, she did not immediately say.

Once inside, both Emily and Ethan snapped pictures on every page of Ezzy's book of maps that could be even remotely useful.

"We wouldn't want to compromise you." Fred seemed unsure how to engage her in conversation.

"Just having your truck outside is bad."

"Bad how?"

Ezzy blew out a breath while she appeared to decide if she was going to answer. Finally, she said, "There are people out there that aren't just looking to take pictures of some maps."

Emily couldn't help glancing over at the posters, articles, and other bits of colorful scrapbooking stuck to the windows.

Ezzy saw it and began to laugh quietly.

"Oh yes, Missy, you see that stuff, and you assume paranoia. Well, first off, just because you're paranoid doesn't mean no one is actually out to get you. But second, that stuff doesn't matter now. A conspiracy to take over the world only matters if no one is trying to take over your town. And a coup in your town is only important when there's no one at your door with a shotgun. A smart man once told me all politics is local, and he didn't know how right he was. The more local it gets, the more politics matters."

"Politics?"

"Everything is politics. Politics is how people interact over who makes the rules and decisions. A fella with a gun breaking into my store is politics."

She strode over to the posters and ran a hand over them, smoothing them down. "International conspiracies. Ha. Well, maybe they are, and maybe not. Although lemme point out that you're at my place getting help and not me at yours. Keep that in mind. But Kennedy and aliens and the Illuminati… what do I do about that? This is a hobby, and it gets me a rep. You know? People think, 'There goes Ezzy, the nutcase.'"

Since that was exactly what Emily thought, she kept very quiet and concentrated on her maps.

"That reputation is camouflage. It's good camo, too. I get no respect, but I also get no hassle. No one is up in my business. Until now. People know I got resources. I made plans. Most people didn't. So now they want to take my plan and make it *their* plan. It leads to differences of opinion."

Fred leaned on the counter. "So having us here tells people—"

"That Ezzy still has the goods, yeah. Or something."

"Who is going to see that we're here?" Ethan said. They'd finished capturing images of anything even possibly useful.

"That guy holed up in the Freezy Speezy across the street," Ezzy said.

Ethan looked through the smidgen of window not covered by newspaper. The Speezy was a little burger joint, not much bigger than a garage. It was dark. Of course, it was dark, duh. He saw no one.

"And now you're thinking, 'There goes Ezzy again.' That's the thing tho. I don't wanna go nowhere. I wanna stay right here. I got stuff. I'm good. When it gets rough out there—and it's gonna get plenty rough—I'm snug like a bug. Unless the rats find a way into the restaurant."

Emily and Ethan exchanged a glance. "Is that a *Ratatouille* reference?" Emily blurted out, incredulous.

"Sure it is. You think I don't see the movies? I get out once in a while, you know. Or, used to," Ezzy said. "Besides, that movie's a conspiracy flick right to the core. Think about it."

They handed her back her book of maps. She grunted at them, which Emily chose to interpret as wishing them good luck, and out they went into the twilight. Two steps from the door, she looked back. There was no sign they'd ever been there. The place looked abandoned.

She hoped, for Ezzy, that everyone would assume it was.

When they got home, there didn't seem to be much to do all of a sudden. They stood around awkwardly in the garage, pulling on straps and not knowing what to say. Emily took deep breaths of the familiar air with the scents of gasoline, oil, grass clippings, and old rags. She thought of it as the smell of Fred, always there, but never noticed until she thought she might never smell it again.

"Thank you… " Emily started and had to stop. How could she condense ten years' worth of lessons, conversation, barbecues, charades—work, play, friendship—into a sentence? Into a paragraph? An hour-long monologue? There just weren't any words for it, no matter the length or the language. She kicked at the floor.

"You're welcome," Fred said and smiled. A simple, no-frills, genuine Fred smile, the kind they hadn't really seen since the... well, *since*.

"You could come with us," Ethan said.

"I couldn't." Fred shook his head and patted Esmerelda's bed wall. "This isn't my path."

"What will you do?" Emily said. She kept looking around the garage to see if there was anything else to take, but she'd done it seven times already, and there wasn't anything. What would they do with fifty pounds of grass seed?

Fred rubbed at his cheek. "Probably find Miss Legaspi's group. We couldn't really have made it just the three of us, but alone? No chance. The neighborhood is already emptying out. I'll probably go with it."

"Grandpa had a radio, just like yours. It'll be at the Little Pink House. We'll try to let you know what's going on," Ethan said.

Fred waved that away. "That's for tomorrow and the next day. For now, you need to get some sleep. You'll need it. And morning comes early."

But there wasn't any sleeping that night, not for Emily, and she thought Ethan was pretending a little too hard for it to be real. Thoughts kept running through her head—what would it be like on the road? The twins had never driven so far and had never done it without Dad's guiding voice and Mom's steady presence in the passenger seat. They'd never driven a truck. How different would it be?

And what would they find on the road? Even here in Spoonerville, there were odd things, people behaving strangely. They had seen the smoke and heard the reports out of Malantown—it looked like things were very bad there. They wouldn't have to go through Malantown, thank goodness—the highway ran by about a mile from the city limits—but would that matter? What if people from Malantown had gone out to the freeway to pick off likely targets, trucks carrying food, luxury cars, teenagers driving pickup trucks with goods piled into them...

The freeway ran most of the way there, but what if they missed a turnoff? And she got car sick. Terribly, overwhelmingly carsick. She wouldn't be any help to Ethan if he turned out to need it. And he surely would, somehow, somewhere. Could they even get into Gnarled Oaks? What if things there were as bad as they were in other places?

That one, at least, she wasn't too worried about. The Mayor of Gnarled Oaks was not their biggest fan, that was true, and the feeling was mutual. But the town itself rallied to save the Little Pink House when it was in danger. They'd come together this time, too. Wouldn't they?

Thinking these thoughts, she was never going to get to sleep. Except for one moment, she was staring at the ceiling, uncomfortable and exhausted but wide awake, and the next minute she heard the rattling ring of Fred's wind-up alarm clock, and he was shaking her awake.

"Time to get up, Emily. You'll want to be on the road here soon."

She rolled over, stiff and sore, but pushed herself up and got out of bed. One thing about not having water or power—it made getting ready for the day a lot simpler. She brushed her teeth without water and swished with a little mouthful at the end. Wiping a damp cloth over her face, hands, and neck made her feel clean, or as clean as any of them ever got these days. She scratched herself idly—everything itched—and slipped on her sandals.

Ethan was already up and in the kitchen. He had a bowl of cereal, though, of course, there was no milk. For a moment, Emily imagined the creamy goodness in her mouth, and then it went away. Who knew if she'd ever have milk again?

But wait… Ethan's spoon dripped.

She stared, shocked.

He saw it and laughed. If he could laugh, maybe things weren't quite so dire. "Fred broke out the powdered milk for a send-off. How's that for a good friend?"

It was good, was what it was. Before… well, *before*… Emily had said that she would rather pour water on her cereal than have to eat it with powdered milk; now, as she felt the first drop touch her tongue, she thought it was one of the sweetest, most delicious things she'd ever tasted. True, that was probably at least as much the

Frosted Flakes talking, but still. For a moment, it was possible to pretend that things were at least almost normal.

Fred sat at his usual place at the head of the table, and Emily tried not to notice how shockingly thin he'd become in only a few weeks. His eyes were bright, though, and he spoke to them of old times—the past winter, really—when their biggest concerns were the reconciliation of the Bill of Rights with the 14th Amendment. How blessed they had been to have a true friend and teacher, for which Emily thought she had been adequately grateful.

Not nearly grateful enough, she understood now. Just one small thing, the flow of electrons through a wire, had vanished from their lives. And with it, the luxury of theorizing about political history. Those discussions all seemed trivial now compared to... just surviving!

"Time to go," Fred said. "You can get a long way before the sun comes up if you hurry."

Neither of the twins trusted themselves to speak. There was too much fright there, too many memories.

"We will see you again," Ethan managed from somewhere inside the biggest hug he could remember.

"I'll count on that," Fred said with a chuckle. "Remember what I taught you."

Emily laughed a little. "Yeah, I'm sure the Fourth Amendment will be a major help to us on the road."

"We'll hang a sign out the window that tells all the bad guys we're versed in the principles of the Bill of Rights," Ethan said.

But Fred wasn't laughing. "Listen to me one more time, you two. There was a time before we had electricity in our houses. There was a time before cars, radios, and cell phones. That was the time those principles were laid down, and they mattered every bit as much then as they do now. You didn't stop being citizens of this country because the grid went down. The government is bound every bit as much by the Constitution today as it was three weeks ago. Don't forget that."

Both of the twins found their hearts aching to go back to three weeks ago and sitting at Fred's kitchen table eating cookies and talking about Constitutional law.

Fred had more, though. "It wasn't just government we talked about. Remember the stories. Remember the courage those women and men had. Remember that society of any kind depends on goodness and trust. Don't just be worthy of trust. Extend it, too. All our community depends on it. Yes, trusting someone who doesn't deserve it can be risky, even dangerous. But without that trust, there is no humanity, and without humanity, we're all doomed."

"I wish you were going with us!" Emily said before she could stop herself. "There's no one we trust more!"

Fred smiled, big and happy, just like before. "Now get. And Godspeed to you both."

Fred hoisted the garage door. It was so dark outside that they couldn't see even to the end of the driveway until Fred pointed his flashlight down the way. Clear. The night was quiet, only the crickets singing sleepily.

Emily's phone—charged with some precious generator juice—showed 4:07 a.m.

The twins realized that they hadn't discussed who would drive first.

"You're a better driver," Ethan said.

"If you do say so yourself," Emily said. "Okay. I'll drive. I know the roads out of town pretty well. And maybe I won't be so motion sick if I'm driving."

She took a second to familiarize herself with where everything was. Full gas, automatic with the shift on the steering column. Radio—not that she expected it would work. CB radio under the dash—when she asked Fred if he wanted them to leave it, he just shook his head—and cords for charging sticking out like antennae from the power port. They plugged their phones in. She started the truck. Fred waved them out of the garage, and they were going down the street with Ethan looking back as their house and their friend vanished behind them.

Emily drove carefully down mostly empty streets, her headlights sweeping across empty stretches of blacktop. Cars stood silent and empty in their slots at the side of the road. Ethan rolled his window down, wanting to hear the night sounds—and potentially anything else that might strike his ears. There was nothing but the rolling of the tires and the hum of the engine. No other cars traveled the roads, not at this time of the morning.

The blacked-out town looked, in the wrapped-up dark of the earliest morning, completely dead. Again, and still, the lack of lights made ribbons of chill run up their spines. They knew in their heads that there wouldn't be any lights, that the town would show nothing but reflections of starlight, but to know it was one thing and to see it another altogether.

"It doesn't look real," Ethan said very quietly. It was a scene that demanded quiet.

"Like something from a movie. Not a happy one."

The smell of smoke wafted in the window. Not woodsmoke, either, but something more acrid. Not strong. Not close to them. But out there, somewhere, something foul was burning.

Even blowing in at twenty-five miles an hour, the air was close and hung like old washing on a line. Emily negotiated the streets of their subdivision and came

out to a major road. She stopped at the stoplight, nose poking out onto the street. *Was it still a stoplight if there was no light for the stop?* Ethan wondered.

"Habit," Emily said, glancing over. "Stopping, I mean."

Ethan nodded, eyes forward, scanning. "Feels like we should."

But there was, again, nothing to stop for. No other cars traveled that road. It was clear in both directions as far as they could see, which would have been pretty far, had there been other traffic. Headlights would be visible literally for miles in such blackness.

To turn right would be to go down to Ezzy's and the center of the old town of Spoonerville. To turn left would be toward the new town, the part that had grown up near the freeway exit when it had cut across the state, bypassing the old Highway 27 that used to carry travelers through Spoonerville and on to Malantown and St. Bart in one direction and Pohick and Archerton in the other.

Both of them felt it—this was the moment they were really leaving home behind.

Emily blew out a breath and put on her blinker.

Ethan snorted. They glanced at each other, small smiles breaking through the weight of what they were doing.

"Habit," Emily said. And she pulled the car onto the high road.

Two blocks on was the crest of the hill their subdivision sat on, and they had a decent view down into the center of town.

Here, there were lights. Not many, certainly, and none that they could see from the private houses, but in the center, by the high school, the landscape was not entirely dark. Dim lights ringed a wide area—three or four blocks—making a kind of perimeter. Inside there were lights as well, brighter ones, though nothing like what had been before.

"That must be the compound where all the refugees are," Ethan said.

"Refugees? Don't you have to be taking refuge from something?"

"Refuge from… the dark, maybe? From having no water?"

"From what happens when the power goes out. Yeah."

Their line of travel would take them right along the northernmost edge of the perimeter. Emily rolled down the hill, keeping her speed low, well under the old speed limit, both of them listening and watching, senses reaching out to their maximum. If they were going to have trouble, this was one place where it would happen.

Emily was acutely conscious of the fact that she was driving without a license. She was breaking the law. And she was about to drive right past the biggest nest of police for miles. What if they stopped her? They could, couldn't they? And what would they make of the shotgun and the pistol on the floor of the cab?

Nothing good, that was for sure. She tried to slide them back with her foot, under the seat.

Ethan saw it. "Good idea," he said, reaching down. "That makes them concealed weapons now, doesn't it? Another law broken. We're on a roll."

"Haha."

On the corner of Main and Alexander, a new post had been cemented in, and long stretches of chain link fence ran east and north from it, shiny in their headlights. The fencing separated Spoonerville City Hall from the streets around it. Behind it, the red brick colonnaded building was the central city complex—community theater, library, police station—and the gleaming new high school that had only been completed a couple of years ago. If the Tuttles had not been homeschooled, they'd have gone there and been Swordsmen like most of their friends.

Many an evening, they'd been in the stands for football games or walked back to their bikes after seeing a play or a concert. All those things were done now, for a while at least.

But that didn't mean the fields were empty—on the contrary. In the pale light of the banks of LED lamps set up around the high school track, they could see row on row of tents set up on the football and soccer fields. A few people, even at this hour, walked around the track.

"This is... *horrible*," Ethan said, his voice husky with shock.

"Water and food," Emily said.

"And nothing else. Unless you want to walk around the track at 4 a.m."

It looked, no more and no less, like a prison. Even without the razor wire strung in coils on top of the fencing, it would have been powerfully like every movie of a concentration camp they'd ever seen.

Without really thinking about it, Emily put her foot down a little harder on the accelerator. She didn't want to be anywhere near this place.

Nose out to the street, several police cars were parked in a row along Main. They reminded Ethan of fangs set into the jaw of the compound. But they were dark, unmanned. A threat visible more than actual. The truck rumbled by them. Roads were clear, no traffic, and no cars strewn across the pavement, as they had been worried there might be.

They reached the corner of the compound, and Ethan relaxed a bit. "That's out of the way, anyhow."

That was when the police lights came on, and the siren pulsed directly behind them.

"What the... " Emily said.

"What did you do?" Ethan said, turning around to look out the back window.

"I didn't do anything! What do you mean, what did I do?! You were right here in the car with me!"

She had to pull over and put the gearshift into park. The police car rolled to a stop just behind them, canted at an angle. The light came on inside the cruiser, and Ethan saw the officer on the radio. On a whim, he reached over and clicked on the CB. He tuned to channel 9, which was as good a guess as any.

"...truck on Main. Two passengers. Need an ID on the license plate," said the officer, and read it off to the dispatcher, or whoever he was talking to.

The policeman sat there in his car, engine running, lights spinning, and waited for a response to his query. When he got it, he was going to come and ask them for licenses and registration information. They only had learning permits, and Ethan couldn't figure out where his dad stashed the vehicle's paperwork.

The officer would arrest them, and they'd end up somewhere in the compound. Fred would never know what happened to them, and they'd never get out until the power came on, if it ever did.

Emily put her head on the steering wheel like it was a headman's block, and she was waiting for the axe to fall.

Two shots rang out.

She jerked her head up just as Ethan grabbed her and shoved her to the floor. "Get down! Do you want to get shot!"

Behind them, glass splintered, and a third shot pinged off the car somewhere.

"Shots fired! Shots fired! Officer under attack Main and 4th North!" blared out of the CB.

From across the street, they heard the revving of a car engine and the squeal of tires. A car roared out of a parking lot, racing across the street. There was a rending of metal and a squeal of tires as the noise receded. The twins kept their hands over their heads and themselves in a fetal position. Then they noticed that the lights weren't flashing any more.

Emily risked a look out the window.

They were alone.

The street was empty of cars—moving ones, anyway, or those with angry flashing lights.

"Go." Ethan pointed down the road, at the end of which was the freeway entrance. "Like, *now*. Go right now!"

And Emily went. Maybe there would be another patrol car out there, but if there was, it would stop them anyway, so what the heck. She stomped on the accelerator, and the old truck bucked like a fractious mule and tore down the street, engine roaring.

Nothing stopped them.

The bulk of the first half of the trip to Gnarled Oaks was on the interstate, a big, wide six-lane road, which did wind around a bit, but not enough to bother Emily's stomach. She kept the accelerator down for the first hour, adrenaline pumping through her, eyes drifting to the rear-view mirror every few seconds as if she expected the Spoonerville PD to follow them. She didn't relax even a little until they hit the Ohio state line. Maybe it was irrational. Probably. But she couldn't help it.

Once they crossed into Ohio, she pulled over for a minute into a view area to refuel the truck and let Ethan take over. Stepping out of the car, she felt herself shaking. There was sunlight on the eastern horizon, though the land below was still profoundly dark.

Ethan's trip began just as Emily's had ended—a smooth, clear road ahead of them with only an occasional car. Any cars at all were a little bit surprising—and welcome. It made them feel a bit less alone.

But such good fortune couldn't last.

A few hours into Ethan's shift, the map told them to take a junction south which was an old, single-lane highway that the interstate had essentially murdered. It passed through a sliver of West Virginia's northern panhandle before hitting Pennsylvania, and farther down the road, it swerved back and forth like whoever had paved it was getting paid by the foot.

This was the devil's highway, as far as Emily was concerned. She'd never negotiated it without throwing up at least once, sometimes even two or three times.

Ethan clicked on the blinker and drifted to the left lane, preparing for the exit ramp. The interstate, for the last twenty minutes, had been completely empty, and the ramp into the trees felt to be a descent into the underworld.

"Finally, off the interstate," Ethan said. "You ready?"

"I guess," Emily said. "We're almost there, and that's good. We could be at Grandma's in a couple hours."

They coasted down the ramp. The concrete strip was particularly dusty, with trash-strewn along the edges. Apparently, this exit didn't get a lot of use anymore.

There were miles and miles of trees and fields, broken up by occasional spattering of structures on the roadside—buildings so few that these places couldn't even be considered towns. At one such place, the Tuttles used to stop to get really good peach ice cream shakes. Ethan licked his lips. But there wasn't going to be any stopping this time.

Except.

The gas station where the shakes got made was open. As in, it had lights. Power. The twins gaped at it like the Pearly Gates. From a quarter mile away, they could see the glow of the rotating *Verl's* sign—just as if everything was normal.

Nothing else appeared to have power, although at this time of late-morning, there wouldn't have been a lot of bright lights anyway. No street lamps. No house lights. But a gas station with power.

"If they have shakes... " Ethan said.

"They can't. They can't be running freezers."

"They're running the *sign*, Em. How... "

"I don't know how. It's like a dream."

The truck gauge showed they had just under a quarter tank of gas, but they knew the rest of the trip would burn that... and all the fuel containers in their truck bed were empty. Them having to walk the last ten miles to Gnarled Oaks was a real, and dangerous, possibility. But if this place had gas, and they could fill up, that changed everything. They could make it all the way instead with more to spare.

"You have to stop," Emily said.

"I do not," Ethan said, but he licked his lips again.

If you think the twins should stop at the gas station, go to page 122.

If you think the twins should keep on going, go to page 440.

"It could be a trap," Ethan said.

"But it might not," Emily said, "and it could take us the rest of the way to Grandma's."

Ethan braked right in the middle of the road. Just sat there, staring at the gas station, with the truck in park.

"What are you doing?" Emily said. She slapped his arm. "Come on! I'm thirsty! We're wasting gas."

Ethan shook his head. "I don't like it. Do you see solar panels on the roof? I don't. Do you see a windmill or some other source of power? I don't."

"It's a gas station. They have gas. They're running generators."

Ethan cocked an eyebrow. "To keep ice cream frozen? That's a lot of juice. And why aren't they out? Does no one in this town need gas? If they did, why didn't they get it? If they didn't, what's wrong with this town? You saw how fast the gas ran out in Spoonerville. But these people have some?"

Emily gazed steadily out the windshield. Then she rubbed her chin. "You're right," she said. "Something's off."

"Not stopping," Ethan said as he pressed on the accelerator. "We should remember that we're *going* to run out of gas unless a miracle happens. We knew we didn't have enough to make it all the way, even if we drove carefully and didn't gun the engine."

The Tuttle Twins and the Days of Darkness

Emily was very quiet as they passed the small sign that read: *Accord Landing - Come Back Again!*

And almost immediately, the road changed. Not so much that it ran like a roller coaster laid down by a drunk cobra—although it did—but that there were people on it. Not many, but a few, some every two or three hundred yards.

Not driving. Walking.

The twins glanced uncertainly at each other, and Ethan slowed almost by reflex. For the most part, the people walked on the shoulder, but some walked in the lanes, facing with traffic—had there been any. Other than the twins, there wasn't.

"What on earth... " Emily said, too intrigued by the pedestrians to remember to be sick to her stomach. Or maybe it was that Ethan didn't get the truck up above forty for fear that on the winding road, someone would be in the way as he came around a curve, and he wouldn't be able to stop.

It only took a couple of miles before one of the pedestrians heard them coming, turned to face them, and stuck out his thumb.

He was older, the age of their parents, with a huge hiking pack on his back to which was attached an array of pots and pans and other things. He gave them a broad smile.

Ethan slowed down.

"Ethan, no!" Emily said. "We can't!"

"We can. We should. What would we want someone to do if it was us on the side of the road. Look at this guy. He's fifty years old. He's got a huge pack. I'm sure he wasn't walking down the road thinking, hey, I'll get some kids to stop and take their truck."

Emily stared at him. "That's *exactly* what he's thinking."

But the truck had stopped just past the man. Emily had her window rolled up before he could jounce up to the bed of the truck and toss his pack in. The man climbed in after it, with some difficulty, Ethan thought.

He saw Ethan looking through the rearview mirror at him and smiled again. Ethan reached back and tugged the back window open.

"*Ethan!*" Emily hissed.

"Where you going?" Ethan said.

"Name's Steve. Steve Stockdale. I'm walking to Girondale. That's up here about thirty miles."

"Why are you going there?" Ethan said.

"Because it's not Accord Landing."

That was too much for Emily, despite her discomfort with the situation. "What's the problem with Accord?"

The man seemed to think carefully about his next words. "If you start driving, I'll tell you."

Something was deeply rotten in Accord, it appeared. The details were sketchy, but the city government had more or less lost control of the place, and a strongman had taken over, using the town for his own gain and pleasure. Ethan began to be glad he'd decided not to stop.

Steve said, "I'm hoping if I go to Girondale, I can find some people to help set things right."

Ethan thought that sounded like a significant long shot, but he didn't say so.

"Thanks for giving me a ride. Most people wouldn't, you know."

Emily had to yell through the window. "I told him not to."

"Smart. But this time, you got lucky."

Ethan did watch the road but gave almost the same intensity to his examination of each minute movement of the gas gauge. When they rolled into Girondale a little more than half an hour later, the streets were crowded with people. A few vehicles moved, too. It looked like a festival day.

Turned out it was.

Steve asked Ethan to pull over in front of a small yellow-brick building with a sign that read *City Hall*. The lawn there had fifty people on it, sharing some kind of drink from a huge cooler.

"Thanks," Steve said. "I hope you make it to Gnarled Tree or whatever that town was."

"Gnarled Oaks," Emily said. This time she had her window down. "Hey, Steve! Ask them if there's fuel in town."

Steve shouldered his massive pack and nodded, wading into the crowd. He came back a minute later and said, "No fuel. Sorry. The vehicles are all running on battery power. Apparently someone has a solar array that can charge those things. It's Peach Days here. Big festival, they tell me. Hundreds of people got up to run a race if you can believe it. Wanna stay?"

But the twins did not. It took a few more minutes to navigate the crowds, but then they were out of the town and running north again.

The truck didn't make it to Gnarled Oaks. At about 2 p.m., the machine sputtered and threatened to die. The twins poured the last few drops from each gas can and set out again, but they didn't make it to the turnoff before the truck gave up altogether. Ethan coasted it to a stop on the shoulder.

"We can't just leave it," Emily said, standing next to the bed with one hand on the side as if she were comforting it.

"You want to put Esmerelda in your backpack, be my guest," Ethan said. He pulled his straps tight. "I think we're about 20 miles away from Grandma's. Not as good as I thought we would."

"Shouldn't we, you know, maybe push the truck? Leaving it here seems… "

"Push it?" Ethan goggled at her. "You're nuts. Just walking by ourselves will be tough enough." He started off without looking back to see if she was following.

But of course, she was.

Three miles an hour was a hot pace for a hot day, and in the end, they couldn't keep it up. Tiny towns strung along the highway like pearls on a necklace. Carbonite. Lilimack. St. Jerome. They looked more or less deserted, though the twins did not dilly dally as they crossed through their centers. They had to make camp as it got dark. They knew they were close, but they didn't want to go blundering about in the dark and getting lost or attacked. They lay down under a canopy of trees and tried to get their worn-out bodies to relax.

It only partly worked. They slept poorly, tormented by mosquitoes, thirsty, and increasingly hungry, as their stomachs craved more than beef jerky and dried fruit. But there was nothing else to be had.

Then there were the people. Not as many as they saw fleeing Accord, but some all the same—and not all of them used the road. Every hour or two, someone crashed through the brush a few—or a few dozen—yards away. The twins would huddle and lie very still, hoping to remain unseen. In the pitch black of night, it really felt exactly like they were living in a zombie movie. There was no telling what those people would do if they found them.

They felt very alone.

But the next day found them safe and reasonably well, though sore and tired. By their best reckoning, they still had ten miles left to cover.

Seven miles later, the sign informed them that Gnarled Oaks was the next exit. By now, they had the road mostly to themselves. They'd seen one other person coming in the opposite direction. Ethan had wanted to stop them and ask them questions, but the other pedestrian, a woman, young, fit, and moving fast, kept her head down and paid the twins no attention. She never gave them a chance to say so much as "Hello."

Just off the highway, on the two-lane road into Gnarled Oaks, they stopped and had the last of their rations. "Just imagine how bad it would be if we had to walk the whole way. Or even half of it," Ethan said. "We'd be out of food before we got started, practically."

"Ethan, what will we find when we get to Gnarled Oaks?" Emily said. Her voice was a little raspy, whether from lack of water or from fear, Ethan couldn't tell.

Ethan sniffed, taking a moment before answering. There was a heavy scent of rotting leaves, and something else, something like... grilled meat.

But that was the question, wasn't it? What would they find? A gang-infested town, like Malantown? Government control of everything, like Spoonerville? A strongman running everything, like Accord Landing?

Or... something else.

"Grandma," Ethan finally said. "We're going to find Grandma."

In the end, it wasn't hard to do.

Instead of coming down the exit road into the town, passing Thusnelda's Malt Shoppe, they wearily took to the woods to the south of town, heading for the river.

If there was something wrong in the town—more than just the power being out—going this way would avoid it. Probably.

It was also excruciating. Not just because the forest there was a matted tank trap of brambles and poison ivy but also because this town was almost as familiar and safe as their own. They'd been coming here as long as they'd been alive. They knew most of the people here, and of course, there was Grandma's Little Pink House, the most famous house in a hundred miles.

And they were exhausted. Most of the way, they'd had the road to walk on and made good time, and here within a quarter mile of their destination, they had to take the long way, the hard way, the painful way.

It took more than an hour. They jumped at every sound as if they were being stalked. Their throats were raw, and their lips cracking from lack of water—which they could hear but not reach.

When they stumbled onto the path that led along the river to the Little Pink House, Emily fell to her knees and struggled to rise, her left knee cut and bleeding. Ethan reached down and tried to lift her but found that his strength was gone.

And then Uncle Brock said, "Ethan? Emily? What are you *doing* here?"

"I go out for a hike every afternoon," Uncle Brock said, spooning some soup into Emily's mouth. "Good thing, too. You two were toast."

"Still feel that way," Emily said, struggling to sit up in bed. Her bed. At least, the one she always slept in at Grandma's. It was possible, for just a moment, to believe that everything was going to be okay.

Grandma herself kept vigil at the side of the bedroom door, knitting something and getting up every few minutes to check on things elsewhere. The house was crowded. All the cousins, all the aunts and uncles, everyone had come to the Little Pink House, and it was called the *Little* Pink House for a reason.

The backyard had been colonized by tents, and a lot of the kids slept out there when they weren't sleeping under the stars. The Monongahela bred mosquitoes the way a garden bred weeds, so tents were better, but some nights they just couldn't help themselves.

In fact, things were almost perfect. Almost.

"Have we heard anything from Mom and Dad?" Ethan said, slurping soup off his spoon.

"Manners," Brock said. But he shook his head and shrugged. "No news. But how could there be?"

"You guys don't have a ham radio here?"

"We don't. Grandma wasn't going to get a license, and I never had any interest, either. Besides, what would we power it with? But there's a radio in town. When you're feeling up to it, we can go talk to Janine and see if we can make contact out there. It's a long shot, though. A major, almost impossible long shot."

"We know," Ethan said. "But we did get them once." And he told the story, everything he knew about where his parents were and what they were trying to do.

"This was how long ago?" Brock said, frowning. He passed a sleeve of saltine crackers to Ethan.

"Not quite a month, now," Emily said. Somehow, her entire bowl of soup was gone.

"They're pretty tough, I admit. But things are not good out there," Brock said.

The twins smothered a groan. Ethan said, "We know. We were out in it."

Grandma came back in, carrying the soup pot. "Here," she said, stirring with a ladle, "have some more. You two look like sticks."

Earlier, when they'd been dragged out of the woods, slung over Brock's bike like sacks of grain, they'd been forced to sleep for four hours before Grandma would allow them to tell their story, but the moment that four hours expired everyone in the family crammed into the room to hear it.

What they hadn't done yet was recover. And they didn't know anything about what was going on in Gnarled Oaks, except that nobody seemed stressed or particularly wary of danger.

"What has happened here?" Emily said. She leaned her head back against the headboard, still weaker than a newborn kitten. She felt silly, but when she reached for her customary strength, nothing was there.

"Here… where?" Uncle Brock said. "Here in the House, or here in Gnarled Oaks?"

"Both, I guess."

Brock scratched his ear. "That's some story, as I'm sure you can imagine. I'll try to do it justice. And keep it short. Grandma will have my head mounted on the wall if I don't let you get some more rest."

He settled back on a stool and leaned against the wall. "The House, well, things here have been pretty normal. The stove is gas, so we can still cook food, which is the most important thing to my mother. The fridge stopped along with everyone else's, but there's a surprising amount of cool that can be had in the river. We have coolers chained to the bank, strung out for about fifty yards on either side. We can use the motorboat because I had a 50-gallon drum of fuel all the way filled when the lights went out. That thing sips gas."

"When did the family start to arrive?" Ethan said.

"Within a week. Ben came down with their kids and said they didn't want to be anywhere else when the trouble started, but I think their main motivation was to keep Mom safe. Anyway, they set up a rotation to watch for trouble, which made us feel a bit safer, but it wasn't necessary, at least not so far. Jody came two weeks after that, driving all the way with extra fuel jugs packed in the back of their van. And then you two."

He didn't say anything about the twins' mother and father, but he didn't need to. Their absence was like a throbbing tooth—you could forget about it for a minute or two, but the pain was never completely gone.

Emily shifted her legs under the blanket. It was too heavy. Without AC, the house was uncomfortably warm already. "What about the town?"

"Ah!" Brock said. "That's where the news is really good. As you know—as well as anyone—the city council got a few new faces this year, and that's changed things a bit. The leadership was really good. A couple of days after the lights went out, the council got the whole town together in the park. They had to split everyone up because they didn't have an amp for their microphones, but it kinda worked, moving people from one to the other where they could ask questions and get answers.

"Bottom line," he said, "the town made a plan to share their resources, not by force and thuggary, but by a system of honest money and trade. They'd hold people's extra goods—food, tools, anything of real value—in the empty warehouse on Main. The Central, they're calling it. And anyone that made that donation received coupons that could be redeemed for… whatever. Wait. Here, let me show you."

He got up and went into the kitchen, coming back a moment later with a couple of gold-colored papers stamped in red in the center. He handed one to Emily and one to Ethan and sat back as they looked them over.

Emily's was just a piece of cardstock, not fancy—in fact, it looked kind of like Monopoly money. The slip

The Tuttle Twins and the Days of Darkness

read *GO Bucks* and had a sort of Celtic tree motif in the middle—for the tree in the central park. Then there were blocks on the sides into which things could be stamped or written. This one had *10* stamped in the left block and a date a few days before stamped in the right block.

"What's this?" she said, waving it.

"It's money," Brock said. He shrugged. "I don't really get it, but it's money. Some kind of money, anyway."

"Money is money," Aunt Jody said, sweeping into the room. "Brock, you're wanted on the dock. I'm to clean up the dishes and put these two back to sleep."

Brock smiled and waved and went out without a word. Aunt Jody saw the Bucks in the twins' hands. "I'll take those, and you two need to sleep."

"Wait! No, you have to tell us how this works," Ethan said, holding his above his head and out of easy reach.

"That's not... all right, but only for a few minutes," Jody said, seeing on their faces that they were not going to cooperate until she gave in a little.

"Here's how it works. We took some bags of flour to The Center a week or so ago. When we got there, the intake fellow—you met him, I think, one year when you were here. Carl Thomas. Anyway, he valued the contribution at ten GO Bucks per bag—"

"What does ten mean?" Emily asked, leaning forward.

"Ten is... there's a sheet with values on them. The more valuable stuff you give, the more it's worth and the bigger number on your stamp. See?" She pointed to the block on the paper. "Then the value of the goods you deposit goes down over time because of storage costs and suchlike. Every week there's a one buck loss on all contributions. So this buck is only worth nine right now."

Ethan scrunched up his face, trying to figure out how it worked. "That's terrible," he concluded. "Your flour is just as good today as it was a week ago."

"Maybe," Aunt Jody said. "And maybe not. Mice could have gotten at it. It could have got wet. And flour doesn't keep forever. So it makes some sense. The best part, though, is that the whole town has started using GO Bucks as money. Everyone knows they're backed by something real—goods in the storehouse—so people take them for everything. You can earn some yourself by working around town or for The Center. Then, when you want to go shopping, you take your bucks to The Center—or anywhere that will accept them—and spend them."

"Just like money," Ethan said.

"But that's the thing," Aunt Jody said, slipping close and taking the GO Bucks from his hand. "It *is* money. Money is just a store of value. You could use anything at all for it. Shells, rocks, trees, or, yeah, slips of paper. As long as it can't be counterfeited, and with the power out, that game is pretty hard, it will work. It's been a miracle for the town, I'll say that."

"How?" Emily said, but Aunt Jody was pushing her forehead back and dropping her flat on the bed.

"You'll see. No more right now. Go to sleep."

Neither of the twins was the least bit sleepy—yet they were snoring softly in two minutes.

By the next day, they were so sick of being in bed that they pushed their way past their mothering guards and went out into the sunshine. The cousins flocked around them and demanded that they tell all their adventures two or three times until they were sick of that, too.

Their bikes were right where they had left them, in the shed in the back, and by 10 a.m. they were on the road, riding through streets that were as familiar as the ones on their own block.

But they weren't the same. And the town had changed, too. More, it was completely different from any other town they'd seen since the power went out.

First, the town was clean. Aggressively clean. It had never been dirty, never like Malantown or some other gritty cities they'd visited. But now, it was spotless. Not a wrapper. Not a loose paper. The gutters and sidewalks looked as if they'd been scoured with steel wool.

"You could eat off these," Ethan said, pedaling past yet another house in pristine condition.

It wasn't just the sidewalks and gutters. The houses themselves were washed. Clean windows. New paint everywhere. Baskets of flowers.

"It looks like a postcard town," Emily said. She pulled up in front of Mrs. Abernathy's house, two blocks away from Grandma's. There were new planter boxes in front, and a man was repairing and painting the rickety fence that had stood there since the town was founded, they guessed.

In fact, there were people everywhere. Busy, working, cleaning, repairing, just as if everything were normal again.

Emily watched the man for a while. There was something familiar about him, his thin brown hair, the set of his narrow shoulders. He knew his way around a saw. "Mr. Yellich?" she said.

The Tuttle Twins and the Days of Darkness

The man stopped sawing and looked over his shoulder. "Yes. Wait… you're one of Patricia's grandchildren. You're the twins, right?" He smiled broadly and tugged off his leather gloves to shake hands. "You just get in town? That must be a story."

Ethan shook his hand. "I thought you were an accountant. Is this a neighborly thing?"

Mr. Yellich laughed. "Not on your life. I've got kids to feed. I take work whenever I can get it, doing whatever I can. I used to do carpentry jobs when I was a teenager, so I have a few skills. Everyone does what he can."

Ethan flicked a glance to Emily, who looked as puzzled as he was. "But… " she said. Right then, Mrs. Abernathy came out, stooped and gray but with a swing in her step and a twinkle in her blue eyes.

"It's starting to look much better, Hank," she said. "I'm glad to have it done, finally." She handed Mr. Yellich a sheaf of the gold papers, the GO Bucks. "Will this cover it?"

He shuffled through them like a deck of cards. "Absolutely. It's a little much, even. I'm not finished with the job yet."

"Check the dates," Mrs. Abernathy said. "They roll down today."

"I noticed that. I better find somewhere to spend them."

She nodded. "That's one reason I wanted to pay you now, so you'd have time to use them before they rolled down a notch. If you want to go now, I know you'll come back and finish."

Mr. Yellich gave her a brief hug. "Thank you, Maude. That's so kind of you. I'll be right back." And he hopped on his bicycle and rode off toward the center of town. Mrs. Abernathy sketched the twins a wave and went back inside."

"What did we just see?" Emily said. "She paid him before he was finished? He's an accountant, but he's doing carpentry? He's going shopping instead of completing the job? What on earth is going on here?"

"I have no idea. They acted like the money was radioactive, like if they didn't get rid of it in the next five minutes, it was going to combust."

It was the same everywhere. The town was buzzing. Unlike everywhere else, where people stayed in their houses or had left, this place had busy streets—bicycles, and pedestrians, of course, but there was also the odd motor scooter still puttering around—and many businesses were open, with customers passing in and out—sometimes even more than there would have been before.

Clearly, something interesting was going on in Gnarled Oaks.

"They've discovered cold fusion. That has to be it," Emily said. But the lights were off. Stoplights neither stopped nor lighted. Gnarled Oaks' prosperity did not depend on some source of power other towns did not have access to.

What was the secret, then?

Then they saw a couple people that could help them. Their friends they met last summer, protecting the Little Pink House!

"Xavier!" Emily said, with excitement in her voice.

Almost at the same moment, Ethan cried out, "Shannon!" And if his voice didn't have quite the same level of excitement, still, he was definitely glad to see her. "Now I bet we can get some answers," he said to Emily.

Xavier and Shannon came over hand in hand. Emily's face lost the excitement that had been in her voice. The last time they'd been here, these two hadn't been a couple. Things had apparently changed.

"Hey, if it isn't the gallivanting Tuttles!" Xavier said. He glanced over at Shannon and wiggled his hand, but she kept hold of it.

"Didn't know you two were in town," Shannon said.

"Got in a couple days ago, under, um, interesting circumstances," Ethan said. Shannon looked good. Better than he remembered, and he had a good memory.

"So what's with the buzz in the town?" Emily said, just a bit testily. "We've been all over the country—" It was only a small exaggeration. "—and everything is just... dead. And then we come here and the place is jumping. You guys find the fountain of youth or something?"

Xavier—pronounced Ex-ay-vier, Ethan remembered—got a sly smile on his face. "There's something the Tuttles don't know," he said to Shannon. "Again, the gods have blessed us."

"It's a good thing I've been exercising, or my heart might give out on me." Now she dropped Xavier's hand, but only to extend it to Emily. "It *is* actually good to see you again."

"Now the League of the Little Pink House can reconvene and… do great deeds… and also small ones, when it gets tired." Xavier's face was a little red, extending his hand to Emily. She ignored it and wrapped him in a hug.

Preliminaries observed, Emily pressed the issue. "You have to tell us. What we're seeing here, it's not just weird. It's, like, unique. Other places, it's mob rule and violence or police everywhere. And Gnarled Oaks is just the same as it was."

"Nope," Xavier said. "It's better. I mean it. And you know how deeply and thoroughly I love this town and everyone in it." He did not look at Shannon.

"Don't tell me it has to do with the GO Bucks," Ethan said.

Shannon looked at him. Ethan knew that look. "Okay, it doesn't have anything to do with the GO Bucks," she said.

"It doesn't?"

"Of course it does. But I like to humor you when you tell me to do something."

Ethan scowled. "Since when?"

And then they were all laughing, and Xavier asked if they wanted shakes, and the twins said they'd never wanted anything so much in their entire lives and what a shame there weren't any.

"But there are," he said, drawing his hand across his face mysteriously. "Come and seeeeeeee."

Thusnelda's was open. Fully, completely, and gloriously open.

It wasn't quite the same. Orders were taken at tables outside in the shade of Thusnelda's own giant elm tree, and the menu was slightly different—no Diablo Burger, for instance, which instantly made Ethan much happier—but for the most part, it was Thusnelda's, right down to the strawberry shakes that people came from miles around for.

They got four, and Xavier, who was still an employee of Thusnelda's, made them in a blender powered by a solar array mounted to the top of the restaurant.

"That wasn't here last time," Ethan said.

"Wasn't here until about two weeks ago," Shannon said. "But the economic contagion got to Thusnelda's just like everything else."

"Okay. That's just... how can this possibly be here?" Emily said, spreading her hands. "What difference does the kind of money make?"

"At last, a brilliant question," Xavier said, scooping precious ice cream from a bucket that he had removed from the freezer. The working freezer.

Miracles.

"First, allow Professor X to provide some background on money. Money can be—"

"Anything, right. We got that," Emily said.

"--ah, but if it's going to work well, it needs to be portable, exchangeable, and hard to counterfeit. Paper, coins, those things. Professor! Professor! I can hear you asking—'But we had money. Paper money. Everyone took it, everyone had it. Why not just use that?' Excellent question, class."

He handed a shake to Shannon. She didn't waste any time digging in. Xavier went on. "Because that green paper money doesn't represent anything of value now. It's totally disconnected with the needs of our localized economy in Gnarled Oaks. We can't get any more from the bank because *they* can't get any more from the central supplier. Not to mention that they didn't have much on hand anyway... it had turned mostly digital. What we were really using for money was electrons. That money is still there in cyberspace." He waved his hands around, windmilling. "But we can't read it anymore."

"GO Bucks, though—" Ethan began.

Xavier held up a hand. "I'm getting to that." He handed a shake to Emily. "With money supply nonexistent, and supply of other things cut off as well, the financial system ground to a halt. But we *need* it. It's almost as important as power. Might even be more important."

"More, I think," Emily said, between sips of shake—had it really only been a couple of months since she could have one whenever she wanted? "Economics is just another word for people trading with each other. No trade means pretty much everyone starves. Trade is wealth. Trade is… "

"Trade means civilization," Ethan said, handing the scoop to Xavier for the next shake. "Which I gotta say looks a lot like what's happening out there."

"Precisely, class," Xavier said. He dumped ice cream and fresh strawberries into the cup and hit frappé. "And trade depends on money. Sure, you can barter, but barter is super inefficient and hard to make work for more than a few people. A town this size—and I know it's not much—needs money, or the economy dies. And then the people do. Thus, GO Bucks."

Xavier cut the blender and pulled off the cup. Ethan held his glass out, and Xavier filled it. Then he said, "Fortunately, there was a guy here that understood that. Someone's crazy uncle—one of the city council. He came up with the idea for a currency based on something real. And how to make it work. For once, City Hall listened to a person with knowledge. And voila! Shakes!"

Which were, even by normal standards, fantastic. Xavier did have plenty of skill in this area; the twins had met him when they stopped at Thusnelda's last year, and he'd lost none of his touch.

"You still working at the library, Shannon?" Emily asked, because she knew Ethan wouldn't but would be dying to know.

She nodded through a spoonful of shake. "It's much busier than it ever was before. It's as if the whole town suddenly discovered a love of reading."

Ethan snorted. It looked painful.

"Back to the GO Bucks," Emily said, ignoring her brother's distress. "I still don't understand how the date stamps work. Or why they're necessary."

"I'm not the guy to explain the inner machinery of the human shopping impulse," Xavier said, leading them back out through the store and into the sunshine. "But I can take you to the fellow that is."

The Creator of the Gnarled Oaks Miracle sat in the gym of the elementary school on an old but well-greased rolling chair surrounded by long folding tables holding stacks of paper. Emily thought he was the most unremarkable man she'd ever seen—at first sight. Average build, mouse-brown hair, and about fifty years old, wearing a white shirt and a tie loosened just a bit around his neck. He looked like a banker from a wild west film, right down to the green visor on his head.

His setup, though, was impressive. It took up half the gym floor. They watched from the doors as paper-runners came in one door, left sheaves of paper—most of it obviously GO Bucks—picked up new sheets, and went out the opposite way. In the middle was the conductor of this train, rolling on his chair from table to table, moving paper.

"His name's Bernie," Shannon said. She waved. He saw her and waved back.

They walked over, staying out of the way of the runners.

"Got a minute?" Shannon said, stepping up to a gap in the tables.

"Maybe," Bernie said, not stopping his dance. "What about?"

"Couple of newbies here want to know how the GO Bucks work."

Ethan was sure he'd be annoyed at the interruption, but instead, his face lit up like Christmas morning. "Wonderful!" he said. "Come on in. You'll have to excuse me, things are pretty busy."

They stepped inside the square. Bernie took a moment to stand and shake hands. "I'm Bernard Reateil. But everyone calls me Bernie."

The twins introduced themselves.

Bernie rolled over to a far table, grabbed some bucks, and rolled back to another. He fixed Shannon with a surprisingly intense gaze. "You already tell them about how money works?"

"They already knew, but yeah," Shannon said.

He nodded, satisfied. "Then we can skip straight to the GO Bucks system. Now, don't get the wrong impression here—it's not my idea. I got it from a dozen different historical sources, not least the Bible and the archaeology of Egypt. This is my own attempt at it. It's based entirely on a different principle than the system that existed until a month ago—a system that relied on debt, lies, and power.

"Borrowers, including the U.S. government, would request loans from the Federal Reserve Bank, which would then extend that debt to be repaid with interest. Sneaky thing is, that so-called-bank didn't use real wealth to loan out in the first place—they would just invent new paper currency... an illusion of wealth. But you can bet they expected those borrowers to work, create true wealth, and pay them back... plus interest. It was really a system meant to enrich the banking class, and create debt slaves of us all. And also to manipulate the power of the government by paying off politicians to pass favorable legislation for their interests. The Bible calls this *usury* and the people of Israel were forbidden to charge it to those in their community and to the poor."

Xavier cut in. "The Qu'ran also says it's forbidden, just FYI."

His three friends stared at him. He shrugged. "I read widely."

Bernie laughed. "Okay, so here we are in a situation where everyone is poor, *and* at a time when we need a strong community, more than ever. I figured it was the perfect time to try out a system that honored that sentiment. Quiz time: what's the best way for people to increase their wealth?"

"Trade," Ethan and Emily said, exactly together.

Bernie looked stunned. He said to Shannon, "Are these two for real? Do they have degrees in economics?"

"They're annoyingly smart," Shannon said.

"You have no idea, really," Xavier said.

"Well, congratulations. You say trade, and you're correct," Bernie said. He rolled over to a stack of bucks and rolled back to the kids. "Look here. At the date."

They were one-buck notes, and the date was one week ago.

"These have expired," he said. "They are worth nothing. We're pulling them out of circulation because they have no value. But look closer."

Ethan plucked one from the stack and held it up. It was mauled like it had gone through the wash. Smudged, dirty, with a corner torn off and a huge crease down the middle. "It's pretty battered," he said.

"What causes money to get like that?" Bernie said, eyes twinkling.

Ethan thought fast. He liked getting the answers right. "Well, age. But... no. Just getting old won't do it.

This has to change hands. And the more times it does, the more beat up it's likely to get."

"A gold star for the whiz kid!" Bernie crowed. "These have been exchanged in a business transaction many times, even though they were only issued a week ago. Next question: what makes people trade?"

Emily was pretty sure that wasn't a hard question. "They want things. Someone else has something, they want it, so they trade for it."

"Good. But that's not the whole story. Party A," he said, holding up some GO Bucks, "must have the means to make the exchange with Party B, which has the goods." He held up an apple. "The motivation comes from the fear of loss. Party A has the money, and in the regular system, the longer he holds the money, the better it is for him. After all, the goods get less valuable over time, right?" He took a bite of the apple.

"But what would happen if the *money* were losing value faster than the goods? Every seventh day, a GO Buck loses part of its value. Everyone knows this. So what do they do with the money?"

"Spend it," Ethan said. "As fast as they can. It's like a game of hot potato."

"Hard luck for the one that gets stuck with the buck on the cut-down day, though," Emily said.

"Is it?" Bernie said. "They made a trade, or they couldn't have acquired the bucks. So they became richer with the trade. They knew before they made it that the bucks were going to lose value, but they made the trade anyway. So the trade made them richer."

"Unless the bucks go to zero."

"Ah, but remember, the bucks were generated by a donation to The Center. The goods are still there but even though that stuff is locked up tight, the community has still benefited from it. That's because wealth is created when trade is possible and incentivised. And those bucks that go to zero can always be redeemed for most of their original value from the storehouse. There's no force. No fraud. But there is powerful incentive to trade. And more trade means—"

"More wealth. Yes," Emily said. There was wonder in her voice. "But… these GO Bucks losing value over time sounds like the inflationary Federal Reserve money. How is this different? How do people save money?"

"They don't," Shannon said, walking across to one of the tables and stacking a pile of GO Bucks a bit more neatly. "Paper is not real wealth. It's good to be reminded of that."

Bernie continued. "Instead of storing up value in paper money, people can store it up in land, fields, livestock, raw materials, buildings, fruit, even ice cream… everything *but* money. Here we are in a crisis, and there are probably millions of those old dollars in bank vaults in this tiny town. What good does it do them? None. None whatsoever. The store of value ceases to be a store, just like that." He snapped his fingers.

"GO Bucks, on the other hand, are based in reality," he added. "Stores of wheat, rice, beans, cans of food, MREs, dehydrated milk. Sure, okay, if The Center burns down, that's a problem. That's a downside of physical goods that virtual goods don't have. But even more than the stores of food is the work of the people. One GO Buck loosely translates to a pound of rice or wheat. Unless the whole community goes on a low carb diet at the same time—that's kind of unlikely while food is scarce—the money here will always have value."

Ethan and Emily marveled at the simplicity of it. A few lazy flies buzzed about the room, and runners kept on coming.

They thanked Bernie for his time and strolled slowly out the exit door and into the sunshine.

"I still have my doubts. Like it's too simple. Surely someone would have figured it out sooner if it works this well." Emily shook her head, looking about at the center of the town, which was as busy as she'd ever seen it, even on holidays.

"But people *did* figure it out," Shannon said, taking Xavier's arm maybe a shade more aggressively than strictly necessary. "Bernie said there were historical examples. I looked up a few, although there isn't much in our library, as you can probably imagine."

"So why didn't people keep it up if it works so well?" Ethan said.

"I'm not sure. But Bernie says it has to do with the powerful people wanting to control the creation of money for their own advantage, without really contributing. This," she said, sweeping her arm across a half-circle taking in most of the town, "isn't controllable by anyone. It's everyone together. Everyone works. Everyone wins. But nobody is in charge, not even Bernie. All he really cares about is keeping the system working, and uncorrupted."

They walked through the grassy area framed by City Hall, the police station, and the library. People streamed in and out of the library almost without a pause.

"I bet your library is emptied of books," Ethan said. He didn't look over at her and Xavier.

Xavier laughed, his full, good-natured laugh that was almost impossible to resist. "Nope. There's more books than ever. People got into the spirit of this sharing thing and started bringing in stuff from their libraries by the boxful. Shannon hasn't had a day off in three weeks, trying to get them all cataloged and labeled."

"Our Brandon Sanderson section has never been more robust," she said with a large smile.

Ethan shoved his hands in his pockets. The town was perfect. The library was better than ever. Shannon had a boyfriend that wasn't him. Everything was *great*.

Well, no sense stewing about it.

"How do I get my hands on some GO Bucks?" he said.

Xavier's goofy grin lit up the already bright square. "Brother, that's the easiest bit. You have two hands, you have two feet, and you have—if you don't mind my saying so—a formidable mind. You can find a job just about anywhere."

"Naw," Ethan said, kicking a rock down the sidewalk. "I tried going around town and asking for jobs to do last summer. It didn't work. Nobody wanted to hire me."

Emily punched him in the arm. "Haven't you been listening? That was then when people had an incentive to hang on to their money. Now all the incentives are the other way—people need to get rid of their money and transfer that value into hard goods—clean walks, painted houses, repaired fences, security, books—holy *wow*! I just started to see what a big deal this is."

"You got it," Xavier said. "This GO Buck thing has flipped the whole job thing on its head. It used to be at Thusnelda's that we wanted to hire the fewest people possible, so we could maximize money. Now we're trying to hire people left and right. We get so much money coming in that we have to be pretty aggressive about getting rid of it."

"Where's your meat coming from?" Emily said.

"Ah! That one is one of the great secrets of Thusnelda's."

It really was good to be back in town.

Ethan found a job working security. Easiest job ever, as long as he was guarding The Center or doing rounds in town. Nobody wanted to break in when it was much easier to get the food legally.

Guarding the town from the outside world, though, was a little more challenging. Gnarled Oaks had decided as a town that everyone who was willing to work—no matter what work they could do—was welcome. But nobody was welcome to come and start trouble.

Some people tried. There was a truckload of hard-looking men that came roaring down the exit and through the vestigial roadblock set up there for traffic control. But it didn't get very far. Two U-Haul trucks, functioning as a steel gate, blocked the road around the corner from Thusnelda's, parked into place by the second-line guards. While the invading truck tried to figure out how to maneuver around the roadblock, a gang of ten-year-old boys scattered caltrops—wicked, oversized jacks made of horseshoe nails—behind them. The truck couldn't go forward and couldn't go back without blowing all of its tires.

The men piled out, wielding crowbars and baseball bats, yelling and glowering. They probably would have been a scary group, but by the time their feet hit the pavement, there were fifty townspeople standing in a circle around them, and many more on the way. The guard had rung the town bell in alarm the moment the truck passed the outer ring, and instead of staying in bed and hoping someone else would handle it, the whole town responded like New England minutemen.

Even these hardened, desperate men were reluctant to take on so many people, and when Grandma Tuttle herself explained to them that they were being covered by riflemen on the top of every surrounding building, they decided a discussion would be better than a fight.

Within a few months, seventeen local towns had joined the Gnarled Oaks system, and if there was a more prosperous, happier place in the whole US than Western Pennsylvania, nobody ever heard about it. The GO Bucks were a miracle in a time of desperation and great scarcity, but it turned out it wasn't a perfect system for the long term. Once everyone's needs were met, and there began to be an excess of real wealth, the incentive to spend GO Bucks quickly changed to an incentive to save for bigger, more time-intensive projects in the future. There was a rush to The Center to withdraw the donated goods.

Another town meeting was called where Bernie had to admit that, even in a system that had honorable intentions and practices, devaluing the GO Bucks over time in order to incentivize a rush to spend made them inflexible for the ebb and flow of a complex economy made up of individuals with different priorities. The answer was to allow competing storage centers to open—also functioning by honest means, of course. This created a competition between money, to see who could meet the demand for both spending and for saving individual demands.

"The same short-sighted folly was made by John Maynard Keynes a hundred years ago," Grandma Tuttle said. "Keynes never admitted his mistake. Honest people like Bernie, however, aren't afraid to learn and innovate."

During this time of regional peace and opportunity, Emily organized a group of what she called the Outriders—teenagers with vehicles that went out on the roads looking for refugees and helping them find places to go. Yes, the twins safely retrieved their old truck, Esmerelda.

This organization paid off big three weeks later when a group of Outriders, not far into Ohio territory, came across a band of twenty migrants trying to make their way east, struggling and hungry. The leaders of the group came forward, and the teens knew them immediately because they had been told to look for them.

It was Mr. and Mrs. Tuttle.

THE END

The Author

Connor Boyack is founder and president of Libertas Institute, a free market think tank in Utah. In that capacity, he has changed dozens of laws in favor of personal freedom and free markets and has launched a variety of educational projects, including The Tuttle Twins children's book series. Connor is the author of over forty books.

A California native and Brigham Young University graduate, Connor currently resides in Lehi, Utah, with his wife and two children.

The Illustrator

Elijah Stanfield is owner of Red House Motion Imaging, a media production company in Washington.

A longtime student of Austrian economics, history, and the classical liberal philosophy, Elijah has dedicated much of his time and energy to promoting the ideas of free markets and individual liberty. Some of his more notable works include producing eight videos in support of Ron Paul's 2012 presidential candidacy. He currently resides in Tennessee, with his wife April and their six children.